NEW Cornerstone 4

STUDENT EDITION
with Digital Resources

Pearson

New Cornerstone 4

Copyright © 2019 by Pearson Education, Inc.
All rights reserved. No part of this publication may be reproduced, stored in a retrieval system, or transmitted in any form or by any means, electronic, mechanical, photocopying, recording, or otherwise, without the prior permission of the publisher.

Pearson, 221 River Street, Hoboken, NJ 07030

Cover credit: Haye Kesteloo/Shutterstock

Library of Congress Cataloging-in-Publication Data
A catalog record for the print edition is available from the Library of Congress.

The publishers would like to recognize the contributions of our original Series Consultants, Anna Uhl Chamot, Jim Cummins, and Sharroky Hollie. This edition is published in memory of Dr. Chamot, an extraordinary educator, writer, and scholar.

Printed in the United States of America
ISBN-10: 0-13-523272-4 (with Digital Resources)
ISBN-13: 978-0-13-523272-9 (with Digital Resources)

www.english.com/cornerstone

Consultants and Reviewers

Carlos Eduardo Aguilar Cortés
Universidad de La Salle
Bogotá, Colombia

Rebecca Anselmo
Sunrise Acres Elementary School
Las Vegas, NV, USA

Ana Applegate
Redlands School District
Redlands, CA, USA

Terri Armstrong
Houston ISD
Houston, TX, USA

José Augusto Lugo
Cerros
Bogotá, Colombia

Jacqueline Avritt
Riverside County Office of Ed.
Hemet, CA, USA

Mitchell Bobrick
Palm Beach County School
West Palm Beach, FL, USA

Victoria Brioso-Saldala
Broward County Schools
Fort Lauderdale, FL, USA

Brenda Carbarga Schubert
Creekside Elementary School
Salinas, CA, USA

Gabriela Cecilia Díaz
Grilli Canning College
Buenos Aires, Argentina

Joshua Ezekiel
Bardin Elementary School
Salinas, CA, USA

Valeria Goluza
Grilli Canning College
Buenos Aires, Argentina

Veneshia Gonzalez
Seminole Elementary School
Okeechobee, FL, USA

Carolyn Grigsby
San Francisco Unified School District
San Francisco, CA, USA

Julie Grubbe
Plainfield Consolidated Schools
Chicago, IL, USA

Yasmin Hernandez-Manno
Newark Public Schools
Newark, NJ, USA

Do Thi Thanh Hien
The Asian International School
Ho Chi Minh City, Vietnam

Janina Kusielewicz
Clifton Public Schools/Bilingual Ed.
& Basic Skills Instruction Dept.
Clifton, NJ, USA

Mary Helen Lechuga
El Paso ISD
El Paso, TX, USA

Gayle P. Malloy
Randolph School District
Randolph, MA, USA

Le Tue Minh
Wellspring International Bilingual School
Hanoi, Vietnam

Minh Phuong Nguyen
CIEM-Education
Hanoi, Vietnam

Patricia Parroquiano
Gimnasio Campestre Reino Británico
Bogotá, Colombia

Adriano De Paula Souza
Liceu Jardim
Santo André, Brazil

Randy Payne
Patterson/Taft Elementaries
Mesa, AZ, USA

María Eugenia Pérez de Castro
Escuela Primaria Puerta Abierta
Buenos Aires, Argentina

Carolina Pérez Martínez
Thomas Jefferson School
Xalapa, Mexico

Lucy Reyes
Colegio Axis
Mexicali, B.C., Mexico

Sergio Rivera
Liceo Hermano Miguel La Salle
Bogotá, Colombia

Marcie L. Schnegelberger
Alisal Union SD
Salinas, CA, USA

Delphine Sichler
Keystone International Education
Córdoba, Mexico

Lorraine Smith
Collier County Schools
Naples, FL, USA

Shawna Stoltenborg
Glendale Elementary School
Glen Burnie, MD, USA

Kampanart Thammaphati
Wattana Wittaya Academy
Thailand

Hoang Dieu Thu
Edison Schools
Vietnam

Denise Tiffany
West High School
Iowa City, IA, USA

Classroom Language

Teacher

Come in.
Sit down.
Sit in a circle.
Stand up.
Listen carefully.
Please be quiet.
Please open your book to page … .
Turn to page 12.
Look at the board.
Work in pairs. / Works in groups.
Repeat after me.
Put your books / things away.
Close the door, please.

Student

I don't understand.
I don't know.
Please could you help me?
Please can you repeat that?
What page are we on?
How do you spell … ?
How do you pronounce … ?
How do you say … in English?
Is this correct?
I have finished.
May I go to the restroom?
Please may I open the window?
I'm sorry I'm late.

Welcome to **New Cornerstone**!

We wrote **New Cornerstone** to help you succeed in all your school studies. This program will help you learn the English language you need to study language arts, social studies, math, and science. You will learn how to speak to family members, classmates, and teachers in English.

New Cornerstone includes a mix of many subjects. Each unit has three different readings that include some fiction (made-up) and nonfiction (true) articles, stories, songs, and poems. The readings will give you some of the tools you need to do well in all your subjects in school.

As you use this program, you will build on what you already know, learn new words and information, and take part in creative activities.

Learning a language takes time, but just like learning to skateboard or learning to swim, it is fun!

We hope you enjoy **New Cornerstone**, and we wish you success on every step of your learning journey.

Unit 1

Contents

Animals, People, and Caring

Unit Preview

Unit Opener	**The Big Question: : How do animals and people show they care?**	page 2
Build Unit Vocabulary	What do you know about animals?	page 4
Build Unit Background	Kids' Stories from around the World	page 6

Reading 1: Informational Text / Science

Prepare to Read	**Key Words:** *young, protect, secure, communicates*	page 8
	Academic Words: *challenge, goal, involve*	page 10
	Phonics: Short Vowels	page 11
Reading Selection	*Taking Care of the Young*	page 12
	More About the Big Question **Reading Strategy:** Use Prior Knowledge	page 12
Learning Strategies	Reread for Details	page 22
Grammar	**Simple Present:** *Be* and Regular Verbs	page 24
Writing	Describe an Animal	page 26

Reading 2: Literature / Fable

Prepare to Read	**Key Words:** *shimmer, frisky, glowed, warm, breath, companion*	page 28
	Academic Words: *bond, encounter, occur*	page 30
	Word Study: Endings: -s, -es, -ed	page 31
Reading Selection	*The Star Llama* by Jan Mike	page 32
	More About the Big Question **Reading Strategy:** Identify Fantasy and Reality	page 32
Learning Strategies	Fantasy and Reality	page 38
Grammar	**Simple Past:** *Be* Verbs	page 40
Writing	Describe Yourself	page 42

Reading 3: Informational Text / Science

Prepare to Read	**Key Words:** volunteers, rainforest, captured, adopt, banned	page 44
	Academic Words: establish, recover, strategy	page 46
	Phonics: Long Vowels with Silent e	page 47
Reading Selection	*Merazonia: Saving Wild Animals*	page 48
	More About the Big Question **Reading Strategy:** Preview	page 48
Learning Strategies	Preview	page 52
Grammar	**Simple Past:** Regular Verbs	page 54
Writing	Describe a Place You Visit	page 56

Put It All Together

Apply and Extend	Animals	page 58
Listening and Speaking Workshop	Play a Description Guessing Game	page 60
Writing Workshop	Write a Descriptive Essay	page 62
Fluency		page 65
Test Preparation	Taking Tests	page 66

Unit 2

Contents

Powerful Forces of Nature

Unit Preview

Unit Opener	**The Big Question:** How do people protect themselves from powerful forces of nature?	page 68
Build Unit Vocabulary	What do you know about weather?	page 70
Build Unit Background	Kids' Stories from around the World	page 72

Reading 1: Informational Text / Literary Nonfiction

Prepare to Read	**Key Words:** volcano, lava, crater, erupts, ash	page 74
	Academic Words: consist of, evidence, similar	page 76
	Word Study: Pronunciation of Ending -ed	page 77
Reading Selection	*Lava Boat Tour!*	page 78
	More About the Big Question **Reading Strategy:** Predict	page 78
Learning Strategies	Sequence of Events	page 84
Grammar	**Simple Past:** Irregular Verbs	page 86
Writing	Organize Ideas by Cause and Effect	page 88

Reading 2: Informational Text / Internet Article

Prepare to Read	**Key Words:** lighting, thunder, electricity, temperature, evaporate	page 90
	Academic Words: appropriate, demonstrate, feature	page 92
	Word Study: Compound Words	page 93
Reading Selection	*Thunder and Lightning*	page 94
	More About the Big Question **Reading Strategy:** Identify Genre	page 94
Learning Strategies	Compare Genres	page 98
Grammar	Imperatives and Time-Order Transitions	page 100
Writing	Explain How to Do Something	page 102

Reading 3: Literature / Short Story

Prepare to Read	**Key Words:** breeze, hurricane, shelter, bolt	**page 104**
	Academic Words: assistance, impact, major	**page 106**
	Phonics: Digraphs: ch, sh, th	**page 107**
Reading Selection	*Hurricane!* by Tracey Baptiste	**page 108**
	More About the Big Question **Reading Strategy:** Visualize Setting	**page 108**
Learning Strategies	Clues to Setting	**page 114**
Grammar	Adjectives	**page 116**
Writing	Explain a Process	**page 118**

Put It All Together

Apply and Extend	Weather	**page 120**
Listening and Speaking Workshop	Give a How-to Presentation	**page 122**
Writing Workshop	Write a How-to Essay	**page 124**
Fluency		**page 127**
Test Preparation	Taking Tests	**page 128**

Unit 3

Contents

Telling Tales

Unit Preview

Unit Opener	**The Big Question: What do the characters in tales have in common?**	page 130
Build Unit Vocabulary	What do you know about reading?	page 132
Build Unit Background	Kids' Stories from around the World	page 134

Reading 1: Literature / Pourquoi Tale

Prepare to Read	**Key Words:** tidbit, mischief, nonsense, duty, satisfied, council	page 136
	Academic Words: emerge, react, respond	page 138
	Phonics: Long Vowel Pairs	page 139
Reading Selection	***Why Mosquitoes Buzz in People's Ears*** by Pam Walker	page 140
	More About the Big Question **Reading Strategy:** Identify Events in a Plot	page 140
Learning Strategies	Sequence of Events	page 146
Grammar	Singular and Plural Nouns	page 148
Writing	Retell a Familiar Story	page 150

Reading 2: Literature / Play

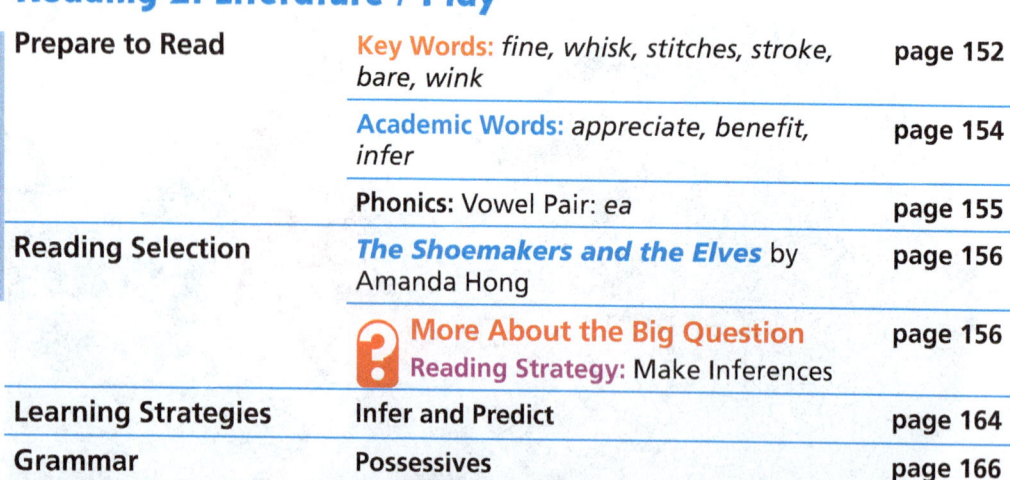

Prepare to Read	**Key Words:** fine, whisk, stitches, stroke, bare, wink	page 152
	Academic Words: appreciate, benefit, infer	page 154
	Phonics: Vowel Pair: ea	page 155
Reading Selection	***The Shoemakers and the Elves*** by Amanda Hong	page 156
	More About the Big Question **Reading Strategy:** Make Inferences	page 156
Learning Strategies	Infer and Predict	page 164
Grammar	Possessives	page 166
Writing	Write a Friendly Letter	page 168

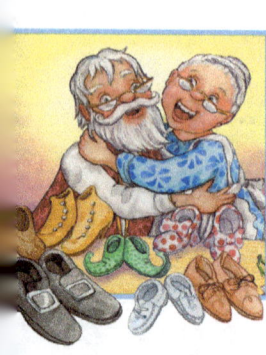

Reading 3: Literature / Tall Tale

Prepare to Read	**Key Words:** mighty, sledgehammer, machine, boasted, sputter	page 170
	Academic Words: anticipate, display, scenario	page 172
	Word Study: Synonyms and Antonyms	page 173
Reading Selection	*John Henry and the Machine* by Michael Dunn Moriarty	page 174
	More About the Big Question **Reading Strategy:** Identify Characters	page 174
Learning Strategies	Identify Character	page 180
Grammar	Quotations	page 182
Writing	Write a Dialogue Between Two Characters	page 184

Put It All Together

Apply and Extend	Tales	page 186
Listening and Speaking Workshop	Perform a Play	page 188
Writing Workshop	Write a Story	page 190
Fluency		page 193
Test Preparation	Taking Tests	page 194

Unit 4

Contents

Problem Solvers

Unit Preview

Unit Opener	**The Big Question: How do we solve problems?**	page 196
Build Unit Vocabulary	What do you know about problem solvers?	page 198
Build Unit Background	Kids' Stories from around the World	page 200

Reading 1: Informational Text / Photo Essay

Prepare to Read	**Key Words:** vine, bean, celebration, gardener, roots	page 202
	Academic Words: affect, eliminate, outcome	page 204
	Phonics: Soft and Hard *c*	page 205
Reading Selection	***The Trouble with Kudzu*** by Laura Sewell	page 206
	More About the Big Question **Reading Strategy:** Identify Main Idea and Details	page 206
Learning Strategies	Main Idea and Details	page 210
Grammar	Comparative Adjectives	page 212
Writing	Write a Persuasive Business Letter	page 214

Reading 2: Literature / Fables

Prepare to Read	**Key Words:** flatter, praise, advice, guzzled, scampered	page 216
	Academic Words: evaluate, resourceful, scheme	page 218
	Word Study: Thesaurus	page 219
Reading Selection	***The Fox and the Crow*** and ***The Fox and the Goat*** retold by Lee Martin	page 220
	More About the Big Question **Reading Strategy:** Compare and Contrast	page 220
Learning Strategies	Compare and Contrast	page 224
Grammar	Superlatives	page 226
Writing	Write an Advertisement	page 228

Reading 3: Informational Text / Social Studies

Prepare to Read	**Key Words:** solve, communities, purpose, concerned, waste	page 230
	Academic Words: creative, restore, objective	page 232
	Phonics: Diagraph: *ow*	page 233
Reading Selection	*Creative Problem Solving*	page 234
	More About the Big Question **Reading Strategy:** Identify Cause and Effect	page 234
Learning Strategies	Cause and Effect	page 238
Grammar	Adverbs of Frequency and Intensity	page 240
Writing	Write a Persuasive Brochure	page 242

Put It All Together

Apply and Extend	Problem Solvers	page 244
Listening and Speaking Workshop	Give a Speech	page 246
Writing Workshop	Write a Review	page 248
Fluency		page 251
Test Preparation	Taking Tests	page 252

Unit 5

Contents

Where We Live

Unit Preview

Unit Opener	**The Big Question:** What is it like to live in an unusual home?	page 254
Build Unit Vocabulary	What do you know about places to live?	page 256
Build Unit Background	Kids' Stories from around the World	page 258

Reading 1: Informational Text / Magazine Article

Prepare to Read	**Key Words:** native, extreme, architecture, underground, mining, efficient	page 260
	Academic Words: adapt, environment, located	page 262
	Word Study: Homophones	page 263
Reading Selection	*The Underground City* by Claudio Ponti	page 264
	More About the Big Question **Reading Strategy:** Identify Fact and Opinion	page 264
Learning Strategies	Fact and Opinion	page 268
Grammar	Capitalizing Proper Nouns	page 270
Writing	Write to Classify	page 272

Reading 2: Literature / Letters

Prepare to Read	**Key Words:** prairie, sod, climate, harsh, record	page 274
	Academic Words: correspond, previously, reside	page 276
	Phonics: Y as a Vowel	page 277
Reading Selection	*A House of Grass* by Kathy Furgang	page 278
	More About the Big Question **Reading Strategy:** Identify Author's Purpose	page 278
Learning Strategies	Author's Purpose	page 284
Grammar	Prepositions and Prepositional Phrases	page 286
Writing	Organize Ideas by Problem and Solution	page 288

Reading 3: Informational Text / Social Studies

Prepare to Read	**Key Words:** reindeer, seal, shelter, igloo, sled	**page 290**
	Academic Words: considerable, labor, undertake	**page 292**
	Phonics: R-Controlled Vowels: ar, or, ore	**page 293**
Reading Selection	**A Cold Autumn Morning**	**page 294**
	More About the Big Question **Reading Strategy:** Visualize	**page 294**
Learning Strategies	Visualize	**page 298**
Grammar	Present Perfect	**page 300**
Writing	Write to Compare and Contrast	**page 302**

Put It All Together

Apply and Extend	Places to Live	**page 304**
Listening and Speaking Workshop	Present a TV Talk Show	**page 306**
Writing Workshop	Write a Magazine or Newspaper Article	**page 308**
Fluency		**page 311**
Test Preparation	Taking Tests	**page 312**

xv

Unit 6

Contents

Links to Our Past

Unit Preview

Unit Opener	The Big Question: What was life like in the past and why should we learn about it?	page 314
Build Unit Vocabulary	What do you know about the past?	page 316
Build Unit Background	Kids' Stories from around the World	page 318

Reading 1: Literature / Short Story

Prepare to Read	Key Words: signatures, mission, astronaut, plaque, explorer, surrounded	page 320
	Academic Words: achieve, community, unique	page 322
	Phonics: Diphthongs: ow, ou	page 323
Reading Selection	*The Moon Tree* by Dan Ahearn	page 324
	More About the Big Question Reading Strategy: Identify Problem and Solution	page 324
Learning Strategies	Problem and Solution	page 332
Grammar	Compound Sentences: and, but, or	page 334
Writing	Plan a Research Report	page 336

Reading 2: Literature / Short Story

Prepare to Read	Key Words: thrive, hiking, trails, thrilling, valley, ledge	page 338
	Academic Words: equipped, motivated, route	page 340
	Phonics: Variant Vowel: oo	page 341
Reading Selection	*Following Grandpa's Footsteps*	page 342
	More About the Big Question Reading Strategy: Identify Plot and Setting	page 342
Learning Strategies	Plot and Setting	page 350
Grammar	Past Progressive	page 352
Writing	Paraphrasing a Source	page 354

Reading 3: Informational Text / Social Studies

Prepare to Read	**Key Words:** worth, trade, bartered, currency, rulers	page 356
	Academic Words: cooperate, initial, tradition	page 358
	Word Study: Greek and Latin Roots	page 359
Reading Selection	*The History of Money* by Mbeke Tsango	page 360
	More About the Big Question **Reading Strategy:** Summarize	page 360
Learning Strategies	Summarize	page 364
Grammar	**Complex Sentences:** *because, so, so that*	page 366
Writing	Quoting a Source	page 368

Put It All Together

Apply and Extend	The Past	page 370
Listening and Speaking Workshop	Give an Oral Report	page 372
Writing Workshop	Write a Research Report	page 374
Fluency		page 379
Test Preparation	Taking Tests	page 380

Unit 1
Animals, People, and Caring

Animals are fun to be around. Some keep us company. Other animals help us. It is important to take care of our animal friends.

Reading 1
Science

Taking Care of the Young

Reading 2
Fable

The Star Llama

Reading 3
Social Studies

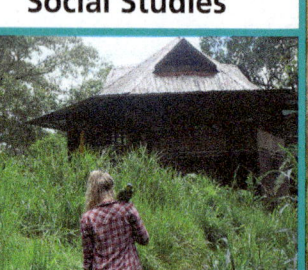

Merazonia: Saving Wild Animals

THE BIG QUESTION

How do animals and people show they care?

Listening and Speaking

You will discuss how animals and people show they care. In the Listening and Speaking Workshop, you will play a description guessing game.

Writing

You will practice descriptive writing. In the Writing Workshop, you will write a descriptive essay.

Quick Write

Why do you think people like animals? Write your answer in your notebook.

View and Respond

Talk about the poster for this unit. Then watch and listen to the video and answer the questions at Pearson English Portal.

Build Unit Vocabulary

What do you know about animals?

Words to Know

Listen and repeat. Use these words to talk about animals.

alligator

raccoon

elephant

parrot

skunk

giraffe

Practice

Work with a partner. Look up these words in a dictionary. Then ask and answer questions using these words and the words above.

| a bird | a mammal | a reptile |

Example: A: What kind of animal is an <u>alligator</u>?
B: An <u>alligator</u> is <u>a</u> <u>reptile</u>.

Write

Read the question. Write your response in your notebook.

What other birds, mammals, and reptiles do you know?

Make Connections

Complete the sentences with the following words.

a swamp

a rainforest

the woodlands

the grasslands

1. _____ is often warm and rainy. Parrots and monkeys live here.

2. There are plenty of trees in _____ . Raccoons and skunks are often found here.

3. _____ do not have a lot of trees, but they do have plenty of grass. Elephants and zebras live here.

4. _____ is a wetland. There is a lot of water, and alligators and frogs live here.

What about you?

Talk with a partner. Talk about your favorite wild animals. Where do they live?

Build Unit Background

Kids' Stories from around the World 🎧

Fez, Morocco

Hassan

I live in Fez, Morocco. Camels are very important here. They help us cross the desert. A group of camels is called a caravan. Camels can live for days without water.

Cassandra

I live on Santorini. It is an island in Greece. The streets are very steep. Our donkeys carry people and packages. I brush my donkey to keep him clean.

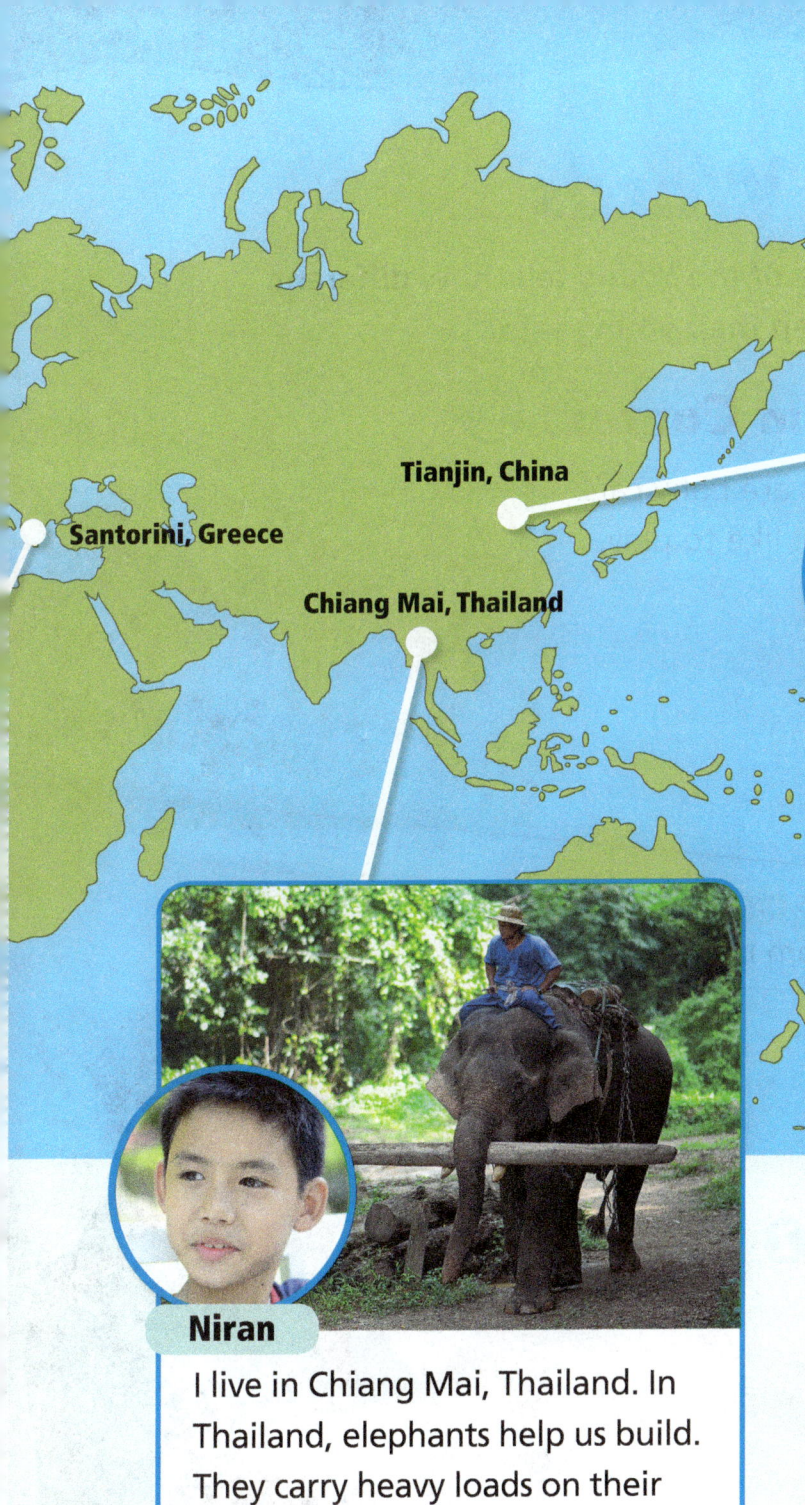

Santorini, Greece

Tianjin, China

Chiang Mai, Thailand

Lin

I live in Tianjin, China. Many people here love cats. They bring us good luck. You can see cats in many shops and homes in the city. I pet my cat every day to keep her happy.

Niran

I live in Chiang Mai, Thailand. In Thailand, elephants help us build. They carry heavy loads on their backs. They can lift things with their strong trunks. They can also drag heavy loads. I feed my elephants grass and leaves. This food keeps them strong and healthy.

What about you?

1. Which animal do you think helps people the most? Why?
2. Do you know a story about animals? Share your story.

UNIT 1

Reading 1
Prepare to Read

What You Will Learn

Reading
- Vocabulary building: *Context, phonics*
- Reading strategy: *Use prior knowledge*
- Text type: *Informational text (science)*

Grammar
Simple present

Writing
Describe an animal

These words will help you understand the reading.

Key Words

young
protect
secure
communicates

Key Words

Taking Care of the Young tells how different animals keep their young safe.

Words in Context

❶ Kittens are baby cats. The **young** like to play.

❷ Parents **protect** their children from harm.

8 UNIT 1

3 Animals try to keep their young **secure**.

4 Dolphins **communicate** by whistling and by making clicking sounds.

Practice

Make flashcards to help you memorize the words.
- Write a key word on the front.
- On the back, write the meaning.

Make Connections

Sometimes, animals need our help. Have you ever heard about an animal that needed help? Use some of the key words as you speak.

Speaking Skills

When you are not sure what word or phrase to use, you can use gestures to express your ideas.

READING 1

Reading 1

These words will help you talk about the reading.

Academic Words

challenge
something that is hard to do

goal
something you want to achieve

involve
include, or be part of

Academic Words

Words in Context

A penguin father has the **challenge** of keeping the chicks warm in freezing temperatures.

Emily's **goal** was to run five miles.

The science fair will **involve** everyone in the class.

Practice

Choose an academic word to complete each sentence.

1. The math test was a real _____.

2. The care of a community garden can _____ many people.

3. The _____ of the food drive is to collect food for hungry people.

Apply

Write the answers in your notebook. Use the academic words. Then ask and answer with a partner.

1. What school subjects **involve** using the internet?

2. What **goals** do you have for this school year?

3. Will reaching those goals be a **challenge**?

Phonics

Short Vowels

In this book, you will study words with the pattern **C**onsonant, **V**owel, **C**onsonant, or **CVC**. Consonants make sounds like *ch, k, v, b, r, t, sh,* and *g*. Vowels make sounds like *a, e, i, o, u*. Each word in the chart has one vowel. Listen. Then read each word aloud.

a	e	i	o	u
can	get	big	fox	cub
bag	den	his	not	pup

Rule

A word is likely to have a short vowel sound when:

- it has a single vowel.
- the vowel has a single consonant before and after it.

c a n   g e t   p u p
C V C   C V C   C V C

Practice

Work with a partner. Copy the chart in your notebook.

- Find the CVC word or words in each sentence.
- List each CVC word in the correct column.
- Read each word aloud.

1. I fed my cat today.
2. Horses like to rub noses.
3. A chicken can be a family pet.
4. A group of whales is a pod.
5. The big horses are not friendly.

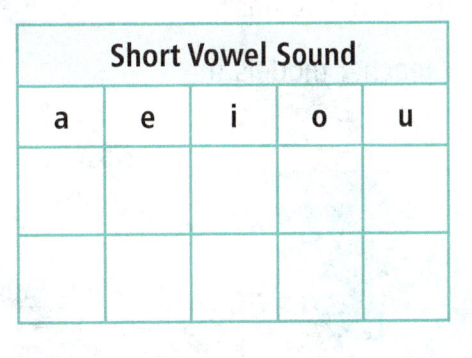

Short Vowel Sound				
a	e	i	o	u

READING 1

Reading 1

Informational Text
Science

More About THE BIG QUESTION

Why is it important for animals to take care of their young?

🎧 **Listen to the Audio.**
Listen for the general meaning. Use the pictures to help you understand the selection.

Reading Strategy
Use Prior Knowledge

Before you read, answer the following in your notebook.

- What do I already know about animals taking care of their young?
- What do I want to find out about animals taking care of their young?
- Copy the chart on page 23. Fill in the first two columns.

Listen as your teacher models the reading strategy.

Taking Care of the Young

Adult penguins watch their chicks.

12 UNIT 1

> **Reading Skill**
>
> The yellow highlighted word **protect** is a key word.

Penguins

Human babies need adults to protect them. Animal babies need parents, too.

Both male and **female** emperor penguins take care of their babies. The mother lays an egg. Then the father keeps the egg warm while the mother looks for food.

Emperor penguin chicks stay close to their parents at all times. One parent will stay and watch the chicks. The other will go find food. Then he or she will bring the food back for the babies to eat. The parents work together to keep their babies safe.

---

human	person
female	girl or woman

> **Before You Go On**
>
> The penguin parents work together toward what **goal**?

READING 1

Swans

Swans also take care of their young. One parent stays with the babies at all times. This keeps them safe and secure. The babies cannot fly for many months after they are born. It is hard for them to escape **danger** when they cannot fly.

The adult swans work hard to keep other animals away from their babies. They also teach their babies how to take care of themselves. Soon, they will be old enough to fly. Then they will leave their parents.

---

danger something that can cause harm

This mother swan watches her babies.

Baby raccoons wait for their mother.

Reading Skill

To understand the boldfaced words, read the definitions below the paragraphs. Later, use the word in a sentence.

Raccoons

Raccoon babies are very small when they are born. They cannot stand or open their eyes. Only female raccoons take care of the babies. A mother might have four babies to take care of alone. She must leave them in the **den** when she looks for food. In the den, the raccoon babies are safe from danger.

The mother raccoon worries that other animals might find her den. So after a few months, the family moves. By then, the babies can walk and climb. Their mother has taught them to take care of themselves.

---

den home for animals that is hidden

Before You Go On

What **challenges** does the mother raccoon have?

READING 1

This baby wallaby is protected in its mother's pouch.

Wallabies

Mother wallabies have an unusual way to protect their babies. They carry their babies in a **pouch**. A baby wallaby, called a joey, has no fur when it is born. The baby climbs into its mother's pouch to stay warm. The wallaby's pouch also **guards** the joey from danger.

When a joey gets older, it will sometimes leave its mother's pouch. But mother wallabies still try to keep their babies safe. If a mother wallaby senses trouble, she communicates with her baby. She stomps on the ground. This tells her joey to return to her pouch.

Reading Skill

Read the caption that goes with each picture. This will help you to understand both the words and the pictures.

---

pouch a pocket-like skin where some female animals, like wallabies and kangaroos, carry their babies.

guards protects or keeps safe

Clownfish

All animal parents have to be careful. Even fish parents watch for danger in the water. Clownfish fathers guard their eggs carefully to keep them safe. They keep other fish away from their eggs. They also keep the eggs clean.

After the eggs **hatch**, the babies will swim away from their parents. Now they are on their own. Soon, they will find a place to live. Later, they will become parents themselves. They will have their own eggs to protect.

---

hatch   come out of an egg

Baby fish leave their parents after they hatch.

Before You Go On

How does a mother wallaby communicate with her baby?

People

Human mothers and fathers take care of their young. They must watch their children carefully. When it is cold, they put hats and sweaters on their children to keep them warm. Sometimes, they carry their young in their arms or on their shoulders.

Human children and animal babies keep their parents busy! How are these animals just like people?

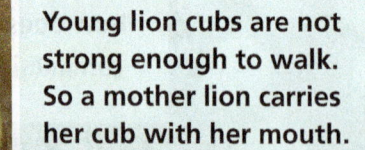

Young lion cubs are not strong enough to walk. So a mother lion carries her cub with her mouth.

A penguin keeps its chick warm in the cold.

Bear cubs like to play and run. Their mother needs to watch them carefully.

Reading Strategy
Use Prior Knowledge

- How did your knowledge of animals and people help you understand the reading?
- What have you learned about taking care of the young?
- What else would you like to learn?
- Ask your teacher or classmates if you don't understand.

Think It Over

1. **Recall** Where does the mother wallaby carry her babies?
2. **Comprehend** What is involved with caring for the clownfish eggs?
3. **Analyze** How do human children keep their parents busy? Explain.

READING 1

A Closer Look at... Animals and Their Young

▲ **Goose and goslings**
This mother goose has two goslings.

▲ **Lion and cub**
A mother lion keeps her cub clean.

◀ **Horse and foal**
A horse runs with her new foal.

▲ **Eagle and chick**
An eagle feeds its chick. They live in a nest high in a tree.

▲ **Hyena and pups**
A hyena looks a little like a dog. Its babies are called pups.

▲ **Deer and fawn**
A young deer is called a fawn. It has spots to help it hide in the woods.

Cow and calf ▲
This young calf stands in a field with two cows.

Activity to Do

These two pages tell you more about adult animals and their babies.

- Choose an animal.
- Research the animal online or in the library.
- Tell about the animal's babies using pictures and words.

Reading 1

Learning Strategies

Reread for Details

You can reread a selection to find information.

Practice

Tell if each statement below is TRUE or FALSE. Tell the page number you found the answer on.

1. Only the male emperor penguin takes care of penguin chicks.
2. Baby swans leave their parents when they can fly.
3. Only female raccoons take care of baby raccoons.
4. The father clownfish shows the babies how to swim.

Use a K-W-L Chart

A K-W-L Chart helps you remember three kinds of information:

1. What you **Know** about a topic before reading
2. What you **Want** to learn about the topic
3. What you **Learned** about the topic

Practice

Before reading, you completed the first two columns. Now complete the third column: What I Learned.

- Begin by adding new details you remember.
- Then look back in the selection to recall other details.

Topic: Taking Care of the Young		
What I Know	What I Want to Learn	What I Learned

1. What is something that you still want to learn about how animals care for their young?
2. Where might you look to find this information?

Apply

Choose an animal from the lesson. Explain to a partner how that animal takes care of its baby. Use some of the key words.

Extension

Form a small group and choose a favorite animal. Write a skit about that animal and its babies. Be sure to listen carefully to your classmates and work together. Use informal language in your skit. You can speak using simple sentences and slang.

Reading 1

Grammar

Simple Present *Be* and Regular Verbs

The simple present of **be** has three forms: **am**, **is**, and **are**. Use the simple present to talk about things that happen regularly.

> We**'re** always busy at school.   I **get up** every day at 6 A.M.

The verb should agree with the subject. Study these examples.

SUBJECT	Be verb	
I	am	happy.
He/She/It	is	happy.
You/We/They	are	happy.

SUBJECT	Regular verb	
I	protect	the baby.
He/She/It	protects	the baby.
You/We/They	protect	the baby.

Use **not** to make negative statements with **be** and regular verbs.

> I'm **not** sad. They **aren't** sad. She **doesn't** like it. They **don't** have pets.

For negative statements with regular verbs, use **do not** and **does not**.

> She **doesn't stay** with the egg. I **don't have** a pet.
> They **don't stay** with their parents.

To ask questions with **be** verbs, begin the questions with **Am**, **Is**, or **Are**.

> **Am** I late? **Are** they happy? **Is** he a parent?

To ask questions with regular verbs, begin with **Do** or **Does**.

> **Do** I **know** you? **Does** he **guard** the egg?

Practice A

Complete each sentence with the correct form of the verb.

1. The mother ____carries____ her young. (carry)
2. It _____ safe and secure. (be)
3. I _____ with my parents every day. (communicate)
4. She always _____ the joey from danger. (protect)
5. They _____ for food at night. (not look)

Practice B

Complete each question with the correct form of the verb.

1. ____Does____ the father ____guard____ the egg? (guard)
2. _____ you _____ any goals? (have)
3. _____ the babies safe and secure? (be)
4. _____ he _____ with his parents? (communicate)
5. _____ English a challenge for you? (be)

Apply

Reading Skill
Look back at the reading to help you answer the questions.

Work with a partner. Ask and answer the questions about *Taking Care of the Young*.

Example: A: Why do animal babies need parents?
B: They need parents to protect them.

Grammar Check ✓
What are the contractions for *do not* and *does not*?

- What does a mother penguin look for?
- Where are baby raccoons safe from danger?
- Does a clownfish mother guard the eggs?

READING 1

Reading 1

Writing

Describe an Animal

A description is a picture made up of words. When you describe something, you include details that tell how it looks and acts. You can also describe how it sounds, smells, tastes, and feels to help your reader experience it.

Writing Prompt

Write a description of an animal. The animal can be real or from your imagination. Be sure to use the present form of verbs correctly, including forms of *be* and regular verbs.

① Prewrite
GO 13

Choose an animal to write about. Think about the words you will use to describe the animal. Write the name of the animal in the center of a word web. In the squares, write words that describe the animal.

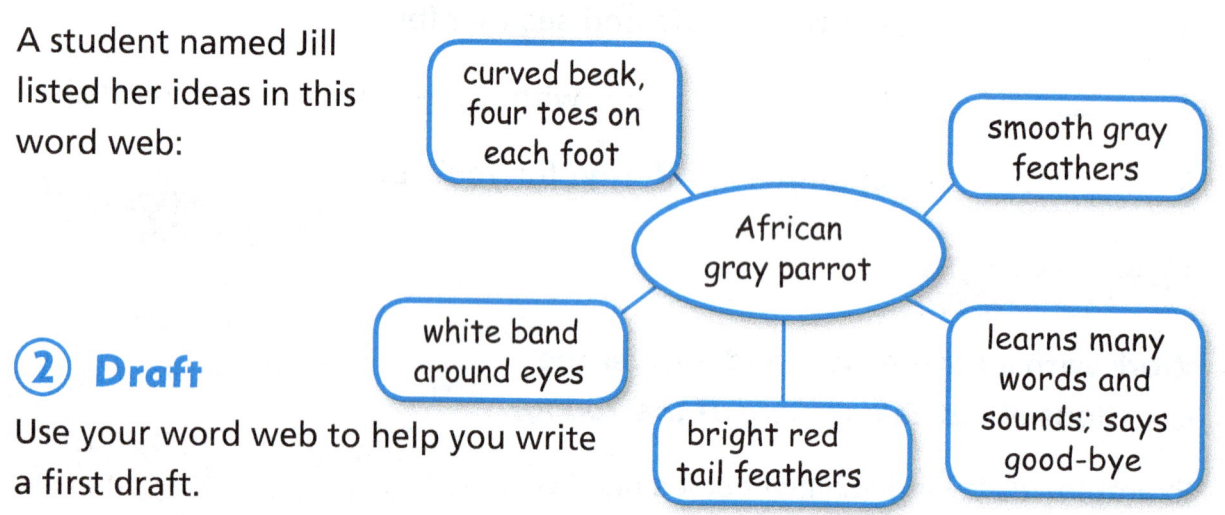

A student named Jill listed her ideas in this word web:

- curved beak, four toes on each foot
- smooth gray feathers
- white band around eyes
- bright red tail feathers
- learns many words and sounds; says good-bye

Center: African gray parrot

② Draft

Use your word web to help you write a first draft.

- Keep in mind your purpose for writing—to describe.
- Use words that describe how the animal looks, acts, sounds, and feels.

26 UNIT 1

③ Revise

Read over your draft. Look for places where the writing needs improvement. Use the Writing Checklist to help you identify problems. Then revise your draft.

④ Edit

Check your work for errors. Trade papers with a partner to get feedback. Use the Peer Review Checklist on page 402. Edit your final draft in response to feedback from your partner and your teacher.

> **Writing Checklist**
>
> ✓ **Ideas**
> I told how the animal looks, acts, and sounds.
>
> ✓ **Sentence Fluency**
> I used sentences of different lengths and types.
>
> ✓ **Conventions**
> My nouns, pronouns, and verbs agree.

⑤ Publish

Prepare a clean copy of your final draft. Share your paragraph with the class. Save your work. You'll need to refer to it in the Writing Workshop at the end of the unit.

Here is Jill's paragraph:

Jill Lee

I am at the children's zoo with my class. The zookeeper shows us an African gray parrot. The bird is beautiful. It has a powerful curved beak. On each foot it has four toes with long claws. Its feathers are smooth and gray. There is a white band around the bird's eyes. Its eyes look smart. The parrot's bright red tail feathers gleam in the sunlight. This amazing bird learns many words and other sounds. When our class leaves, the parrot says good-bye.

Reading 2
Prepare to Read

Key Words

The Star Llama is about a boy and his llama.

Words in Context 🎧

① See the sunlight **shimmer** on "top of" the water.

② Many young animals are **frisky**. Just like human children, they love to play.

③ The fireflies **glowed** in the jar.

What You Will Learn

Reading
- Vocabulary building: *Context, word study*
- Reading strategy: *Identify fantasy and reality*
- Text type: *Literature (fable)*

Grammar
Simple past: *be* verbs

Writing
Describe yourself

These words will help you understand the reading.

Key Words
- shimmer
- frisky
- glowed
- warm
- breath
- companion

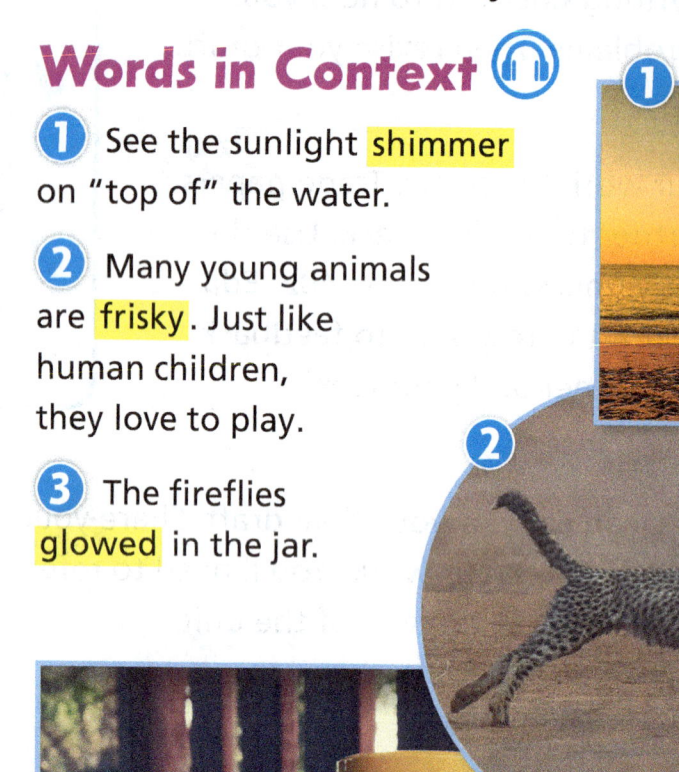

28 UNIT 1

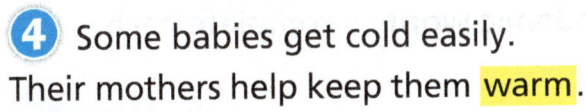

4 Some babies get cold easily. Their mothers help keep them warm.

5 You can see an animal's breath when it is cold outside.

6 A pet can be a good companion. This puppy will keep these people company on a picnic.

Practice

Create a vocabulary notebook.
- Divide your page into three columns: the new words, their definitions, and drawings of the words when possible.
- Test yourself by covering one of the columns.

Make Connections

In the next story, a boy is helped by a special friend. Narrate a story about how a friend helped you. How did it make you feel?

WB 13

READING 2

Reading 2

These words will help you talk about the reading.

Academic Words

bond
special relationship or connection

encounter
a meeting

occur
to happen or take place

Academic Words

Words in Context

Children and animals often form strong **bonds**.

An **encounter** between a dog and a cat can be very noisy.

When it rains for a long time, floods can **occur**.

Practice

Choose an academic word to complete each sentence.

1. When storms _____, the ball games stop.

2. The girls saw their teacher at the movies. The _____ surprised them all.

3. Students can form a _____ of friendship by playing on the same team.

Apply

Write the answers in your notebook. Use the academic words. Then ask and answer with a partner.

1. With what friend do you have a strong **bond**?

2. In a first **encounter** with a new teacher, many students are shy. Are you?

3. What are some activities that **occur** in your school?

Word Study

Endings: -s, -es, -ed 🎧

A **verb** names an action. The ending of a verb tells when the action happened. Listen. Then read each sentence aloud.

Today the boy **walks** many miles without his llama.

Now the boy **searches** for the star llama.

Yesterday, the boy **walked** many miles.

> **Reading Skill**
> Looking for patterns in English will make you a better reader.

Rule

Look for this pattern in English: The endings -s and -es tell what the boy does now. The ending -ed tells what the boy did in the past.

walk**s** = walk + **s**   search**es** = search + **es**

walk**ed** = walk + **ed**

Practice

Work with a partner. Take turns reading the sentences aloud.

- Charlie the llama plays in a field.
- His hair reaches down to the ground.
- Charlie wanted to visit new places.
- He runs around the yard.

Verbs with Endings		
-s	-es	-ed

1. List each verb in the correct column.

2. Look in the story. Find three words ending in -ed.

Reading 2

Literature
Fable

More About THE BiG QUESTION

In what ways can animals help the people who care for them?

🎧 **Listen to the Audio.**
Listen for the general meaning. Use the pictures to help you understand the selection.

Reading Strategy
Identify Fantasy and Reality

Many stories describe events that can happen in real life. But sometimes, stories describe things that could never happen in reality.

- Read the title.
- Look at the pictures.
- Think about parts of the story that could be real.
- Think about parts of the story that must be fantasy.

Listen as your teacher models the reading strategy.

The Star Llama

by Jan Mike
illustrated by Theresa Smith

Once there was a young **Inca** boy. He had no family except for an old **llama**. Each day, the boy and his companion walked many miles, looking for a home. Each night, they curled up together and slept. But one starry evening, the old llama died.

Inca — person from an ancient culture in the Andes mountains in South America

llama — South American animal with thick hair like wool and a long neck

32 UNIT 1

Before You Go On

Could the event in this picture really occur?

The boy buried his friend next to an icy **stream**. Then he sat under a tree and cried. What would he do, he thought. He had no family and no home.

The boy cried for a very long time. But there was no one to comfort him. There were only the stars in the sky.

---

stream   flow of water that moves across the land and is narrower than a river

Suddenly, the sky filled with bright light. The boy held his breath. He was afraid to move. One star began to shimmer. Then it floated to the ground beside the stream. Slowly, the star took the shape of the old llama. The llama bent her head and drank from the stream.

Before You Go On

Could the event in this picture really occur?

The star llama drank for a very long time. Then she looked at the sad Inca boy and smiled. When she jumped back into the sky, bits of llama wool fell. The boy felt the silver wool. It was soft and warm.

As the sun began to rise, the boy **gathered** the llama wool. It glowed in his hands like starlight. He carried the wool to the city and sold it. With the money, he bought a house and two frisky young llamas. He never forgot the star llama. And he was never lonely again.

---

gathered collected

Reading Strategy

Identify Fantasy and Reality

- Which parts of the story could be real?
- Which parts are fantasy?
- Did telling fantasy from reality help you understand the story? How?

Think It Over

1. **Recall** Where does this story take place?
2. **Comprehend** Describe the bond between the boy and the old llama.
3. **Analyze** How did the encounter with the star llama change the boy's life?

READING 2   37

Reading 2

Learning Strategies

Fantasy and Reality

Some stories are **fantasy**, or make-believe. The characters or the settings are not real. The events could never happen.

Other stories are real. They are based on **reality**, or the real world. The events could happen. Some stories have both fantasy and reality in them.

Practice

Read each sentence. Ask yourself, *Could this really happen?*

- If the answer is *yes*, write R for reality.
- If the answer is *no*, write F for fantasy.

1. A boy and a llama walk many miles in the Andes Mountains. _____
2. The boy goes to sleep next to his llama. _____
3. The boy sits under a tree and cries. _____
4. A star takes the shape of a llama. _____
5. The star llama drinks from the stream. _____

Use a T-Chart

A T-chart helps readers understand a story that has both fantasy and reality. It also helps readers look more closely at the characters, setting, or plot of a story.

Practice

Complete the chart.

- Write the sentences from the previous page in the correct column.
- Then reread the story.
- Find another sentence for the Fantasy column and another sentence for the Reality column.

Fantasy	Reality
	A boy and a llama walk many miles in the Andes Mountains.

Compare your chart with a partner's. Discuss what makes *The Star Llama* a fantasy story and not realistic fiction.

Apply

Using the pictures in the reading, retell the story to a partner.

Reading 2

Grammar

Simple Past: *Be* Verbs

The simple past forms of **be** are **was** and **were**. Use **was** with **I**, **he**, **she**, or **it**. Use **were** with **you**, **we**, or **they**.

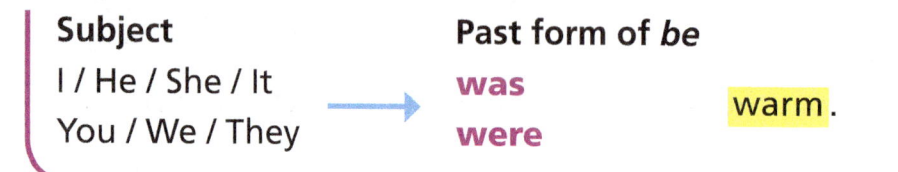

Subject	Past form of *be*	
I / He / She / It	**was**	
You / We / They	**were**	warm.

To make negative statements with **be**, use **was** or **were** + **not**.

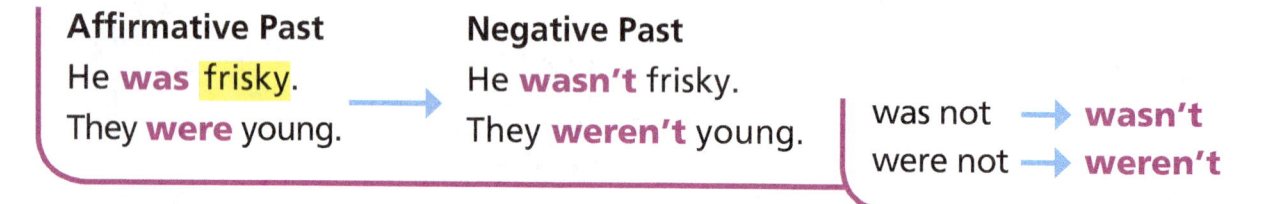

Affirmative Past	Negative Past		
He **was** frisky.	He **wasn't** frisky.	was not →	**wasn't**
They **were** young.	They **weren't** young.	were not →	**weren't**

To make *Yes/No* questions in the simple past, begin the question with **Was** or **Were** + the subject.

Was he here last night? Yes, he **was**. OR No, he **wasn't**.
Were they here last night? Yes, they **were**. OR No, they **weren't**.

For **Wh-** questions, start with **Who, What, Where, When, Why** + **was/were** + the subject.

Where **were** they? They **were** at the movies.
Who **was** that? That **was** my brother.

Practice A

Change each simple present *be* verb to the past. Write the sentences in your notebook.

1. The boy is not here. The boy was not here.
2. The boy and his horse are **companions**.
3. There is a special **bond** between them.
4. The **encounter** with the bear is a fantasy.
5. They aren't lonely at their grandmother's house.

Practice B

Reorder the words to make questions. Write the questions in your notebook.

1. sad / the / boy / ? / was   Was the boy sad?
2. ? / sky / many / there / the / in / were / stars
3. where / boy / the / were / ? / and / llama / the
4. the / warm / wool / was / soft / ?
5. was / the / star llama's / what / present / ?

> **Grammar Check ✓**
>
> Name the past negative contractions for the verb *be*.

Apply

Work with a partner. Ask and answer the questions about what you were like when you were younger.

Example: A: What were you like when you were six?

B: When I was six, I was shy.

- What was your favorite animal?
- What were your favorite foods?
- What was your favorite toy?

Reading 2

Writing

Describe Yourself

How would you describe yourself as a younger person? Answer these questions: *What did you look like? How did you act? What did you like and dislike?* Writers use the pronouns *I, me,* and *my* when they write about themselves.

> **Writing Prompt**
> Write a paragraph that describes a photograph of yourself when you were younger. Be sure to use the past form of *be* verbs correctly.

① Prewrite

Find a photograph of yourself that was taken when you were younger. Then write a short description of how you look in the photograph. List your ideas in a word web.

A student named Ricky listed his ideas in this word web:

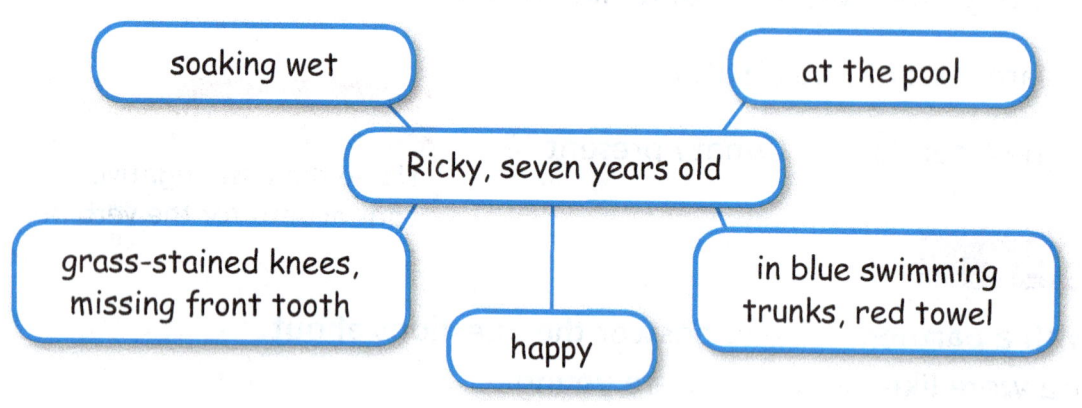

- soaking wet
- at the pool
- Ricky, seven years old
- grass-stained knees, missing front tooth
- in blue swimming trunks, red towel
- happy

② Draft

Use your word web to help you write a first draft.
- Keep in mind your purpose—to describe.
- Use words to show how you acted, looked, thought, and felt.

③ Revise

Read your draft. Look for places where the writing is uninteresting or unclear. Use the Writing Checklist to help you identify problems. Then revise your draft.

④ Edit

Check your work for errors. Trade papers with a partner to get feedback. Use the Peer Review Checklist on page 402. Edit your final draft in response to feedback from your partner and your teacher.

⑤ Publish

Prepare a clean copy of your final draft. Share your paragraph with the class. Save your work. You'll need to refer to it in the Writing Workshop at the end of the unit.

Here is Ricky's paragraph:

Writing Checklist

✔ **Ideas**
I described how I looked and felt.

✔ **Conventions**
I used the past form of *be* verbs correctly.
My nouns, pronouns, and verbs agree.

Ricky Torres

When I was seven years old, I was at the swimming pool almost every day. I was soaking wet. My swimming trunks were blue, and my towel was red with yellow and green stripes. My knees were grass-stained and my front tooth was missing. I remember that I was very happy that day. It was a great day! To me, the pool was the best place in the world!

Reading 3
Prepare to Read

Key Words

Merazonia: Saving Wild Animals is about saving animals in the rainforest of Ecuador.

Words in Context

1 Many **volunteers** work in the Amazon **rainforest**. They don't work for money.

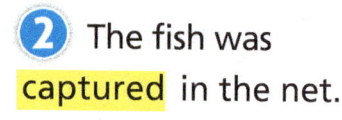

2 The fish was **captured** in the net.

What You Will Learn

Reading
- Vocabulary building: *Context, phonics*
- Reading strategy: *Preview*
- Text type: *Informational text (science)*

Grammar
Simple past: regular verbs

Writing
Describe a place you visit

These words will help you understand the reading.

Key Words

volunteers
rainforest
captured
adopt
banned

44 UNIT 1

③ Many cats don't have a home. You can **adopt** one and give it a home.

④ Some countries have **banned** the use of plastic bags in supermarkets. Many animals die from eating plastic and from choking.

Practice

Add a page to your vocabulary notebook.
- Divide your page into three columns: the new words, the new words' definitions, and drawings of the words when possible.
- Test yourself by covering one of the columns.

Make Connections

Do you know someone who has **adopted** a pet? What kind of animal was it? Where did the pet come from? Do you think the pet was happy in its new home?

Reading 3

These words will help you talk about the reading.

Academic Words

establish
get something started, such as a company, system, or situation

recover
get back to a healthy condition

strategy
plan used to reach a goal

Academic Words

Words in Context

Volunteers wanted to **establish** an animal sanctuary to care for and save wild animals.

The doctor said the patient will fully **recover**.

Previewing is a **strategy** you can use to understand a reading selection.

Practice

Choose an academic word to complete each sentence.

1. _____ is important to win this game.

2. I was sick for two days, but on the third day I began to _____.

3. Tyrone is going to _____ a new club at school that helps animals.

Apply

Write the answers in your notebook. Use the academic words. Then ask and answer with a partner.

1. How might you **establish** a new club at school?

2. How do you **recover** from an illness?

3. What **strategy** could you use to prepare for a difficult exam?

Phonics

Long Vowels with Silent e 🎧

The words in the chart follow the CVCe pattern. Listen to your teacher say each word. Then sound out the words in the box.

a_e	i_e	o_e	u_e
cane	like	note	cube
made	time	home	cute
save	life	hope	mule

Rule

When the first vowel in a one-syllable word is followed by both a consonant and an e, the vowel is usually long. The final e is silent.

c a n e   l i k e   c u b e
C V C e   C V C e   C V C e

Practice

Work with a partner. Take turns.

1. Read the CVC words aloud.

2. Add an e to each word to write a CVCe word.

3. Read the CVCe words aloud.

4. Write a sentence using the new words.

CVC Words	CVCe Words
bit	
cod	
fad	
fin	

READING 3

Reading 3

Informational Text
Science

More About THE BIG QUESTION

How do people help and care for wild animals?

🎧 **Listen to the Audio.**
Listen for the general meaning. Use the pictures to help you understand the selection.

Reading Strategy
Preview

Before you read, preview the selection. Previewing helps you start thinking about what you will read. To preview, follow these steps:

- Read the title.
- Study the photographs and the captions.
- Predict what this section will be about.

Listen as your teacher models the reading strategy.

Merazonia: Saving Wild Animals

The Amazon **rainforest** in South America is the largest rainforest in the world. It is home to thousands of **species** of plants and animals. In fact, the rainforest contains more than ten percent (10%) of all the plants and animals in the world and covers more than 40% of South America.

There are many different kinds of monkeys, parrots, wild cats, and other animals living in the Amazon. Some of these wild animals are **captured** by people and sold as pets. Many countries, including the country of Ecuador, have **banned** this practice, but it is a continuing fight.

---

species   a kind of plant or animal

Wild parrots live in the Amazon rainforest.

Tamarin monkeys perch on a branch in the Amazon rainforest.

Reading Skill

Ask your teacher or classmates when you don't understand a word, phrase, or language structure.

The **government** of Ecuador tries to save as many wild animals from the pet business as it can, but it needs help. It works with organizations like Merazonia to return animals to the rainforest. Merazonia is an animal **sanctuary** in eastern Ecuador near the village of Mera. The World Wildlife Fund calls the area "A Gift to the Earth" because of its beauty and **biological** importance.

The founders and volunteers established Merazonia in 2004, but it didn't open right away. It took several years of hard work before the sanctuary was ready. Building in the rainforest was very difficult. Finally, the first animal arrived in 2009. It was a baby tamarin monkey named Lukas.

---

government the group of people who control a country
sanctuary a safe place
biological relating to living things

Before You Go On

Who established Merazonia? When was it established?

READING 3

Animals like Lukas can **recover** at Merazonia and, when they are strong enough, return to the rainforest. But some animals cannot return to the wild. These animals stay at the sanctuary and are taken care of by the volunteers. The volunteers try to give the animals that stay the best possible life. And that includes lots of delicious fruit to eat!

Volunteers come from all over the world and work with Ecuadorian people at the sanctuary. They feed the animals three times a day and clean the animal **cages**. They also do different **chores** to keep the sanctuary in good condition.

---

cage a place to keep birds or animals
chore regular work that needs to be done

Volunteers take care of the parrots.

The goal of Merazonia is to help the animals of the Amazon rainforest. It is not to make money. But taking care of hundreds of animals is expensive. One **strategy** the sanctuary uses to get money is asking people to <mark>adopt</mark> an animal. That means you choose an animal online to help and pay for its monthly costs.

People can visit the group's website and see pictures and read stories about the animals. And if you adopt an animal, they will send you news about how your animal is doing. They will also send you a Merazonia t-shirt. Let's hope Merazonia can help as many animals as possible!

You can adopt a cute animal like Carlito the woolly monkey.

Reading Strategy
Preview

- How did previewing the title help you prepare for reading?
- What did previewing the photos and their captions tell you about the selection?
- Did previewing help you when you read? How?

Think It Over

1. **Recall** Who **established** the Merazonia animal sanctuary?
2. **Comprehend** What is Merazonia's **strategy** for getting money?
3. **Analyze** Why do animals stay at Merazonia before returning to the <mark>rainforest</mark>?

READING 3 51

Reading 3

Learning Strategies

Preview

Before you read the selection, you previewed it. When readers preview a story, they look at:
- titles
- subtitles
- photos or illustrations
- captions

Previewing helps readers understand a story. It tells you a little about the topic. Then you have some information about the topic before you start reading.

What can you predict about the reading in Unit 2 based on this image?

Practice

Answer the following questions.

1. When you previewed this selection, what did the pictures and captions tell you?

2. Turn to page 78. Preview the text. What do you think it will be about?

3. Now turn to pages 94–95. Preview the text. What will this text be about?

Use a Details Chart

You can use a Details Chart to collect specific information from a text.

Practice
GO 12

Look at each place in the first box. Add details about each place to the three other boxes.

Place		Detail 1	Detail 2	Detail 3
Amazon rainforest	→	largest rainforest in the world	thousands of species of plants and animals	
the area of Mera, Ecuador	→			
Merazonia	→			

1. How does the Details Chart help you find details?
2. Check your chart. Why was the area of Mera called "A Gift to the Earth"?

Apply

Retell the selection to a partner using the photographs. Be sure to use the key words.

WB 29

Extension

Talk with your partner about things that you are good at. How could you use those skills to help or care for animals? Present your ideas to the class using visuals.

READING 3

Reading 3

Grammar

Simple Past: Regular Verbs

Use the simple past for actions that have already happened.

To change regular verbs to the simple past, follow these rules:

Rule	Example
Most verbs, add **-ed** to the base form	work → **worked**
Verbs ending in **-e**, add **-d**	bake → **baked**
Verbs ending in consonant and **-y**, change the **-y** to **-i** and add **-ed**	carry → **carried**
Verbs ending in a vowel and **-y**, add **-ed**	stay → **stayed**
Verbs that end with consonant-vowel-consonant, double the final consonant and add **-ed**	stop → **stopped**

To make negative statements with regular verbs in the simple past, use **did not** + the base form of a verb.

We **didn't play** football last Saturday.

did not → **didn't**

To ask *Yes/No* questions, use **Did** + subject + the base form of a verb.

Did you **play** tennis last Saturday? Yes, we **did**. OR No, we **didn't**.

For *Wh-* questions, use **Who, What, Where, When, Why** + **did** + subject + the base form of a verb.

Where **did** volunteers establish Merazonia? They **established** it near Mera.

Practice A

Change the regular verbs to the simple past. Write the sentences in your notebook.

1. I stay after school. *I stayed after school.*
2. They permit the horses to graze.
3. We don't play soccer after school every day.
4. I prefer to do it myself.
5. The students don't study an hour a day.

Practice B

Change each sentence to a simple past *Yes/No* question.

1. He went home yesterday. *Did he go home yesterday?*
2. They visited the Amazon rainforest two years ago.
3. He didn't play basketball last weekend.
4. I recovered from my illness.
5. My family adopted a kitten.

> **Grammar Check ✔**
>
> How do you form the negative past of a regular verb?

Apply

Work with a partner. Ask and answer the questions.

Example: A: What did you do last summer?
B: Last summer, I traveled with my family.

- What did you do last night?
- When did you start studying English?
- What time did you arrive at school?

Reading 3

Writing

Describe a Place You Visit

Writers often describe places they have visited. Their descriptions create exciting word pictures so other people can imagine these places. These descriptions answer the questions: How does the place look and smell? What do I think or how do I feel about the place?

Writing Prompt

Write a paragraph that describes a place you have visited. Be sure to use past forms of regular verbs correctly.

① Prewrite
GO 13

Choose a place that you have visited to write about. Think about the words you will use to describe the place. Write the name of the place in the center of a word web. Write five words or phrases that describe the place in the squares.

A student named Linda listed her ideas in this word web:

- beach sparkled in bright sunlight
- sharp smell of salt water
- cold ocean water, roaring waves
- wet, smooth sand
- amazing day

Beach

② Draft

Use your word web to help you write a first draft.
- Keep in mind your purpose for writing—to describe.
- Use words to show how the place looked or smelled and what you thought or how you felt about the place.

③ Revise

Read over your draft. Look for places where the sentences begin the same way or the writing is not interesting. Use the Writing Checklist to help you identify problems. Then revise your draft.

④ Edit

Check your work for errors. Trade papers with a partner to get feedback. Use the Peer Review Checklist on page 402.

⑤ Publish

Prepare a clean copy of your final draft. Share your paragraph with the class. Save your work. You will need to refer to it in the Writing Workshop.

Here is Linda's description:

> **Writing Checklist**
>
> ✓ **Ideas**
> I created an exciting word picture of the place.
> I described how I felt and thought about the place.
>
> ✓ **Conventions**
> I used regular past forms of verbs correctly.

Linda Wu

Last summer my family visited a beautiful beach near our home. When we got closer to the ocean, I recognized the sharp smell of the salt water. As soon as we arrived, my sisters and I jumped from the car and raced along the shore. The beach sparkled in the bright sunlight. Then we rushed into the cold ocean water. Suddenly the roaring waves carried us back to shore. To warm up, we buried our feet under the wet, smooth sand. What an amazing day!

Put It All Together

Apply and Extend

Link the Readings

Read the words in the top row.

- For *Taking Care of the Young*, put an X under the words that remind you of the selection.
- Repeat the same activity for the other readings.

	Informational text	Literature	Animals helping others	People helping others
Taking Care of the Young				
The Star Llama				
Merazonia: Saving Wild Animals				

Discussion

1. Why doesn't the clownfish stay with its young like other animal parents do?
2. How is the star llama different from the llamas the boy buys at the end of the story?
3. How does Merazonia help wild animals?

How do animals and people show they care?

THE BiG QUESTION

Listening Skills

If you want to hear something a speaker said again, you can say, "Would you repeat that, please?"

Projects

Your teacher will help you choose one of these projects.

Written ✏️	Oral 💬	Visual/Active 👏
Science Article Research an animal. Write information about how that animal cares for its young. Include pictures or photographs from magazines.	**Presentation** Prepare a lesson to share what you learned about an animal and its young. Present your lesson to classmates.	**Picture Book** Create a picture book. Find photos that show how human parents and animal parents are similar.
Adventure Story Write a story about a young animal that gets into trouble. Tell how its parent saves it. Make sure your story is based on facts about the animal.	**Interview** Interview someone who has a pet. Find out how that person cares for the animal. Record your interview.	**Animal Playing Cards** Create matching cards: one set for adult animals; the other for their young. Write the animal names. Use your cards to play games.

Put It All Together

Listening and Speaking Workshop
Play a Description Guessing Game 🎧

You are going to describe how animal parents care for their young. Then you will listen as your classmates talk about how animal parents care for their young.

① Prepare

A. Choose an animal. You will describe in five or more sentences how the parents take care of their young without naming the animal. Your classmates will have to guess the animal you are describing. You can decide if you need to use formal or informal language.

B. Write down some details to use in your description. It may help to reread the selections in the unit to find information and details for your description.

> These parents have one baby at a time. The baby is very, very small when it is born. The mother keeps it warm and safe in her pouch. The baby leaves its mother's pouch when it gets bigger. The baby jumps back into the pouch when there is danger.

Useful Language
🎧 Listen and repeat.

This baby comes from/does not come from an egg.

This baby animal's parents stay with it for a long/short time.

The baby has/does not have fur when it is born.

The baby and its parents live in a nest/den.

② Practice

Practice your description in front of your family or friends. If possible, record your description. Then listen to yourself. How do you sound? Record yourself again and try to improve.

③ Present

As you speak, do the following:
- Speak clearly and loudly enough for everyone to hear.
- Don't be nervous. Have fun. Remember, this is a game.

As you listen, do the following:
- Listen quietly to your classmates. Don't call out any guesses until your classmates ask for them.
- If you don't understand something a speaker says, you can say, "Excuse me. Could you repeat that, please?"

Speaking Skills
Include important details. This helps your listener picture what you are describing. You can use informal or formal language in your descriptions.

Listening Skills
Listen carefully for important words and details.

④ Evaluate

After you speak, answer these questions:
- ✓ Did you understand the game rules?
- ✓ Did you choose important details?
- ✓ Did you say at least five sentences?

After you listen, answer these questions:
- ✓ Did you guess the animal?
- ✓ If you were describing how this animal cares for its young, would you have described it the same way? What details would you have included?
- ✓ Did the speaker use formal or informal language?

UNIT 1 61

Put It All Together

Writing Workshop
Write a Descriptive Essay

Writing Prompt
Write an essay that describes a memorable event. Use sensory details, or details that appeal to any of the five senses, to give your reader a mental picture of your description.

① Prewrite
Review the writing you have done in this unit. Then choose a topic. Think about school or community events that you have enjoyed. What sights, sounds, tastes, and smells did you experience? List your ideas in a graphic organizer.

Listening Skills

Writing an essay is a process. Listen carefully to your teacher's instructions and requests.

A student named Alex listed his ideas in this chart:

sight	sound	taste	touch	smell
crowded street	salsa music, people clapping	tangy mustard, fresh tomatoes	soft angora blankets	spicy stews, freshly baked bread

② Draft
Use your graphic organizer to write a draft.
- Keep your purpose in mind—to describe an event.
- Use sensory details in your description.

③ Revise

Read your draft. Look for places where the writing needs improvement. Use the Writing Checklist to help you. Then revise your draft.

Here is how Alex revised his essay:

Six Traits of Writing Checklist

✓ **Ideas**
Did I include sensory details?

✓ **Organization**
Are my ideas presented in order?

✓ **Voice**
Does my writing show energy and feeling?

✓ **Word Choice**
Did I choose specific words?

✓ **Sentence Fluency**
Did I vary my sentence lengths?

✓ **Conventions**
Did I use past tense verbs correctly?

Alex Romero

The Street Fair

Last Saturday my sister and I spent the day at a street fair. We strolled along the street and looked at all the interesting items for sale. The crowded street was lined with stalls selling everything from roasted corn to baby-soft angora blankets.

Revised to make the meaning clearer.

When we turned the corner, the excited beat of a salsa band greeted us. Immediately, people started dancing. They twirled their partners, and ~~They~~ clapped their hands. My sister and I had to join in the fun.

Revised to combine sentences.

After dancing for a while, we stopped at a stall for lunch. The smells of spicy, hot stew and freshly baked bread reminded us that we were hungry. My sister tried the stew, and ~~I~~ I had a cheese sandwich with tangy mustard and fresh tomatoes.

Revised to combine sentences.

By evening we left the sights and sounds of the street far behind us. It was a great afternoon. I can not wait till next year!

Revised to correct spelling error.

UNIT 1   63

Put It All Together

④ Edit

Check your work for errors. Trade papers with a partner. Use the Peer Review Checklist to give each other feedback. Edit your final draft in response to feedback from your partner and your teacher.

⑤ Publish

Prepare a clean copy of your final draft. Share your essay with the class.

WB 35–36

Peer Review Checklist

- ✓ The sensory details are vivid.
- ✓ The writing is interesting.
- ✓ The main ideas and details are clearly organized.

Spelling Tip

You cannot form the past of irregular verbs by adding *-ed* to the end of the word.

blow → **blew**

say → **said**

Put It All Together

Fluency 🎧

Listen to the sentences. Pay attention to the groups of words. Read aloud.

1. Different kinds of animals try to keep their young secure.
2. A boy cares for his llama, and his llama companion helps him in return.
3. Animals like Lukas can recover at Merazonia and, when they are strong enough, return to the rainforest.

Work in pairs. Take turns reading the passage below aloud for one minute. Count the number of words you read.

Human babies and animal babies need adults to protect them.	10
Mother wallabies have an unusual way to protect their babies.	20
They carry their babies in a pouch. A baby wallaby, called a	32
joey, has no fur when it is born. The baby climbs into its	45
mother's pouch to stay warm. The wallaby's pouch also guards	55
the joey from danger.	59
When a joey gets older, it will sometimes leave its mother's	70
pouch. But mother wallabies still try to keep their babies	80
safe. If a mother wallaby senses trouble, she stomps on the	91
ground. This tells her joey to return to her pouch.	101

With your partner, find the words that slowed you down.

- Practice saying each word and then say the sentence each word is in.
- Take turns reading the text again. Count the number of words you read.

WB 37–38

UNIT 1

Test Preparation

Taking Tests

You will often take tests that help show what you know. Follow these tips to improve your test-taking skills.

Coaching Corner

Answering Test Items That Are Cloze Items

- Cloze items ask you to fill in a blank.

- Sometimes you will be asked to complete a sentence. Other times you will be given a selection with some words left out.

- First read the questions and answer choices. Sometimes there is no question, just a list of words.

- Read the entire selection carefully. Try to think of words that might fit in the blanks as you read.

- If you don't know what a word means, use the words around it to help you.

- Silently, read the cloze with each answer choice. Then choose the answer that makes the most sense.

Practice

Read the selection. Then choose the correct words to fill in the blanks.

I spent a week at the Old River Ranch last summer. Mr. and Mrs. Lopez treated us like we really worked there. They had animals like horses, cattle, chickens, and goats on the ranch. Each morning, we woke up very early to help feed all the __1__. I liked watching the __2__ colt the best. It was days-old and still very wobbly. It looked a little nervous. The colt stood right next to its mother so she could __3__ it. I hope I can spend some __4__ on a ranch again. It was great!

1. A geese
   B livestock
   C chicks
   D colts

2. F warm
   G young
   H feral
   J banned

3. A protect
   B shimmer
   C capture
   D recover

4. F work
   G food
   H time
   J money

Tips

✓ Look through the selection to figure out the answer.

✓ Be careful. Make sure you read the whole passage before choosing your answers.

UNIT 1

Unit 2
Powerful Forces of Nature

Thunder and lightning! Floods! Hurricanes and erupting volcanoes! Powerful forces of nature change our world.

Reading 1
Nonfiction

Lava Boat Tour!

Reading 2
Article

Thunder and Lightning

Reading 3
Short Story

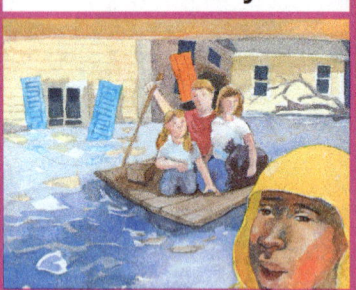

Hurricane!

THE BIG QUESTION

How do people protect themselves from powerful forces of nature?

Listening and Speaking
You will discuss the powerful forces of nature and what to do in an emergency. In the Listening and Speaking Workshop, you will give a how-to presentation.

Writing
You will practice expository writing. In the Writing Workshop, you will write a how-to essay.

Quick Write
Use a T-chart to compare a stormy day and a nice day.

View and Respond
Talk about the poster for this unit. Then watch and listen to the video and answer the questions at Pearson English Portal.

Build Unit Vocabulary

What do you know about weather?

Words to Know 🎧

Listen and repeat. Use these words to talk about weather.

sunny

snowy

cloudy

rainy

windy

foggy

Practice

Work with a partner. Ask questions using the words above. Answer them using the words from the box or your own ideas.

| summer | fall | winter | spring |

Example: A: When is the weather <u>rainy</u>?

B: It is <u>rainy</u> in the <u>spring</u>.

Write

Read the questions. Write your response in your notebook.

What kind of weather do you like? Why?

Make Connections

Complete the sentences with the following words.

a blizzard **a hurricane** **a flood**

1. During _____ it is very windy and rainy. Sometimes trees could fall down.

2. When there is too much rain in a bad storm or the river overflows with water, there could be _____.

3. There is a lot of snow in _____. It could also be very windy, too. Most of these storms take place in the winter.

What about you?

Talk with a partner. Which one is the scariest—a flood, a hurricane, or a blizzard? Why?

UNIT 2   71

Build Unit Background

Kids' Stories from around the World

U.S.A.

Dominican Republic

Jennifer

I live in Colorado, in the United States. Last year we had a very strong blizzard. Our lights went out, and our car was buried in snow. Our house became cold, and we needed food. We had to go to the local high school to get warm and to get something to eat.

Alberto

I live in the Dominican Republic. My country is part of an island in the Caribbean Sea. Almost every year the island is hit by powerful hurricanes. You shouldn't go outside during hurricanes. They are very dangerous.

Atsuo

In Japan we sometimes have typhoons. Typhoons can cause flooding and mudslides because of heavy rains and very strong winds. They can destroy roads, houses, and trees. It is important to be prepared for this kind of emergency.

Bani

We have many floods in Bangladesh. In the spring, the snow on the mountains melts. We also have lots of rainstorms in my country. Our rivers often fill with too much water. The floods destroy towns and crops.

What about you?

1. What kind of weather do you have where you live?
2. Do you know of any stories about forces of nature? Share them with the class.

Reading 1
Prepare to Read

What You Will Learn

Reading
- Vocabulary building: *Context, word study*
- Reading strategy: *Predict*
- Text type: *Informational text (literary nonfiction)*

Grammar
Simple past: irregular verbs

Writing
Organize ideas by cause and effect

These words will help you understand the reading.

Key Words
- volcano
- lava
- crater
- erupts
- ash

Key Words

Lava Boat Tour! is about an exciting boat trip to see lava flowing from a volcano.

Words in Context

1 A **volcano** is where melted rock, or **lava**, escapes through an opening in the Earth's surface.

2 The **crater** is the opening.

3 The lava **erupts**, or escapes, through the crater.

4 **Ash**, or tiny pieces of burned lava and gas, also escapes in a volcanic eruption.

gas and ash

crater

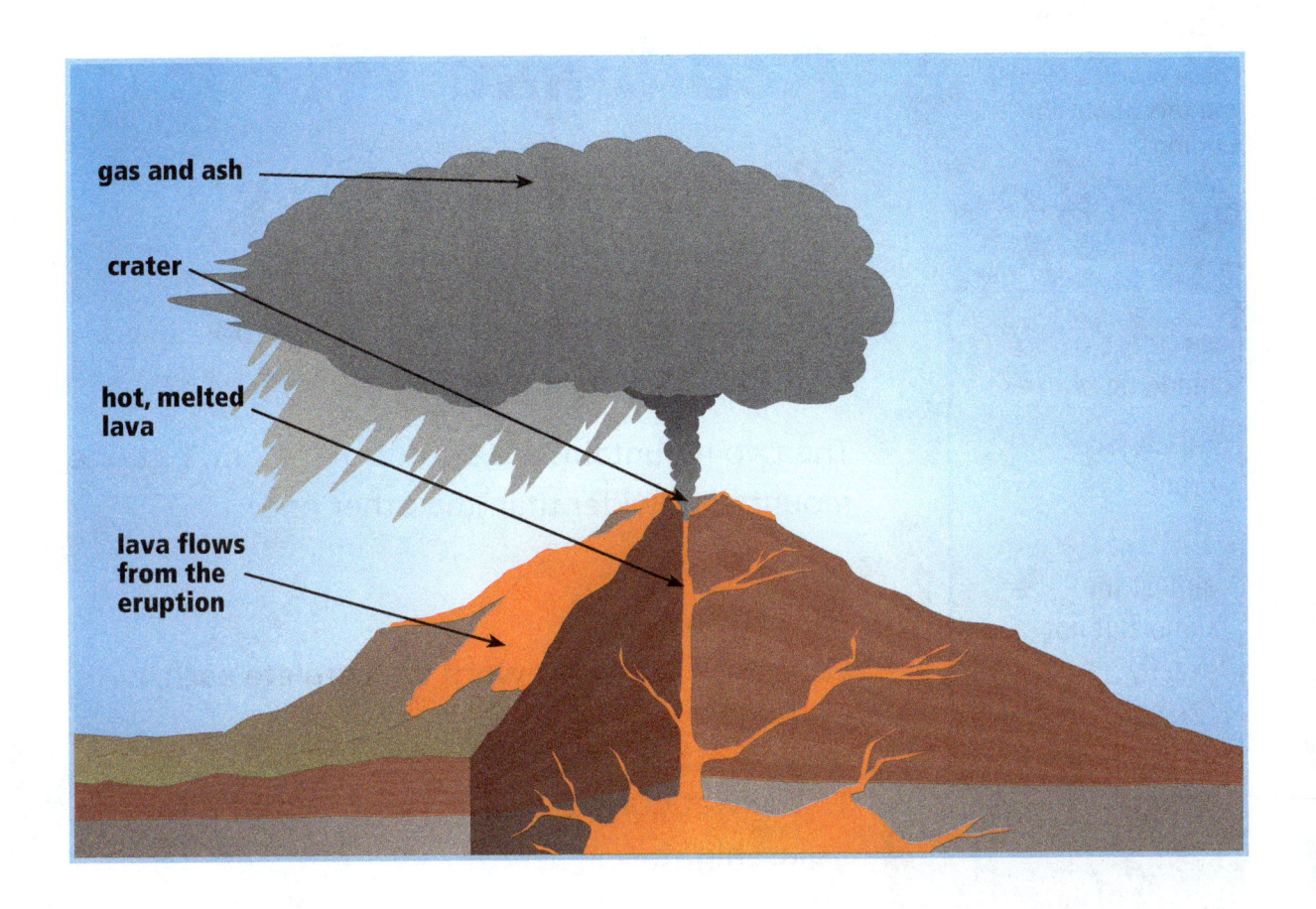

hot, melted lava

lava flows from the eruption

Practice

Draw a picture of a volcano in your notebook. Label the picture using sentences that contain the key words.

Make Connections

An eruption usually occurs suddenly. Do you remember something that happened very suddenly? How did you feel? What did you do?

Speaking Skills

When you don't know the right word to use, explain or describe the idea using words you know.

Reading 1

These words will help you talk about the reading.

Academic Words

consist of
made up of

evidence
proof

similar
almost the same, but not exactly

Academic Words

Words in Context 🎧

Mud **consists of** soil and water.

The scientists found **evidence** that people lived near the volcano a long time ago.

The two mountains are **similar** in height, but one mountain is wider than the other one.

Practice

Choose an academic word to complete each sentence.

1. The wet grass is _____ that it rained last night.

2. The books _____ different stories about volcanoes.

3. Lions and pet cats are _____, but lions are very big and pet cats are small.

Apply

Ask and answer with a partner.

1. How are books and movies **similar**? How are they different?

2. What does a good lunch **consist of**?

3. Why is **evidence** important to scientists?

WB 42

76 UNIT 2

Word Study

Pronunciation of Ending -ed

The words in purple below name actions that happened in the past. They end in -ed. Listen. Then read the sentences aloud.

Present
The girls **walk** every day. → The girls **walked** yesterday.
Ice cubes **melt**. → The ice cubes **melted** yesterday.

Past

Adding the -ed ending to **melt** adds a syllable.
Adding the -ed ending to **walk** does not add a syllable.

Rule

If the letter *t* or the letter *d* comes before the -ed ending, then -ed is pronounced as a separate syllable.

Practice

Work with a partner. Sound out the words in the box.

melted	stayed
filled	decided
started	waited
called	helped

- Circle the word if the -ed adds another syllable.
- Cross out the word if the -ed does not add another syllable.
- Take turns reading the words aloud.
- List other words that end in -ed. Have your partner tell if the -ed adds another syllable.

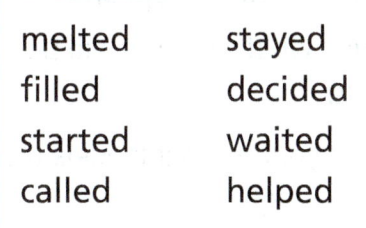

READING 1

Reading 1

Informational Text
Literary Nonfiction

More About THE BIG QUESTION

Can people protect themselves from lava flows? How?

🎧 **Listen to the Audio.**
Listen for the general meaning. Use the pictures to help you understand the selection.

Reading Strategy
Predict

Before you read, guess, or predict, what the story will be about. Follow these steps:

- Read the title.
- Look at the illustrations and photos. Read the captions.
- Predict what the story will be about.

Listen as your teacher models the reading strategy.

Lava Boat Tour!

Lava boat tours take people to see the lava flowing from the volcano.

We saw the **steam** from far away. "Is that smoke from lava?" I asked the **tour** guide, Kala. Our tour boat was still far away from the volcano.

"Actually, it's **steam**," she said. "Hawaii is a **chain** of islands that are ancient volcanoes. Some of them still erupt, like this one, Kilauea. They're actually mountains that are so tall they reach up from the bottom of the ocean. They're very, very old."

"But what causes the steam?" Mom asked.

Kala said, "Lava is very hot. It consists of **melted** rock. In fact, the lava is so hot that it makes the seawater boil when it reaches the ocean."

"Just like when dad makes spaghetti!" said my little brother.

Kala smiled. "That's right. When water gets hot, it changes to steam, whether it's on your stove or at the foot of a volcano."

Hawaii is a chain of eight volcanic islands in the Pacific Ocean.

---

tour   a short trip to see a place

steam   water in hot gas form

chain   things that are connected to each other, forming a line

melted   in liquid form

Before You Go On

Why did the family choose to visit the Big Island of Hawaii?

The boat drew closer, and we could see the hot red lava **flow** off the land and into the water. It changed from bright red to black as it cooled. "This lava came all the way from the crater at the top of the volcano, traveling miles to get here. Sometimes lava covers roads that are in its path."

From her pocket Kala took a gray stone and a shiny lump of black glass. "This isn't glass from a window. This is volcanic glass. It forms when lava cools really fast. This other stone is called pumice." She handed it to me; it was scratchy and rough, and full of holes. "It shows that the lava cooled slowly. The holes are evidence that the lava contained a lot of gases trapped inside it."

---

flow to move along steadily

The Kilauea volcano on the Big Island of Hawaii.

Tourists can see lava flowing into the ocean from the lava boat.

I turned the rough rock over in my hands. "What happens after the lava cools?"

"The lava becomes new land. That's how the Hawaiian Islands have grown. When the rock is cool enough, plants will start growing. Old lava and ash **form** very good soil. That's why Hawaii's farms are so productive."

Dad said, "I thought all volcanoes erupted with a lot of explosions. I've read about other eruptions that threw big rocks high into the air."

Kala nodded. "Some volcanoes have explosive eruptions. They release a lot of rocks and ash. Others, like this one, produce smoother lava that flows, similar to chocolate **syrup**."

"I wouldn't want that on my ice cream," I said. Everyone laughed.

---

form to make
syrup a thick, sweet liquid

Lava flows from the volcanic crater of Kilauea.

evidence of old lava flows

WB 44–46

Strategy
Predict

Before reading, you predicted what the story would be about.
- Were your predictions correct?
- Did making predictions help you to understand the story? How?

Think It Over

1. **Recall** What does the lava that flows from the crater consist of?
2. **Comprehend** How are syrup and lava similar?
3. **Analyze** What can we learn from the evidence of old lava flows?

READING 1   81

A Closer Look at... Lava Flows

▲ **Aerial photo**
This aerial photo of Kilauea's crater was taken from an airplane.

▲ **Lava flows**
When Kilauea erupts, lava flows out of the volcanic crater.

▲ **Destructive power**
Lava flows can destroy houses and roads.

▲ **Fire and water**
Sometimes the lava reaches the ocean. It's amazing!

▲ **New life**
New plants appear after the lava cools and becomes black lava rock.

▲ **New land**
The lava that reaches the ocean makes the island bigger. The Big Island is growing!

Activity to Do

These two pages tell you more about Kilauea's lava flows.

- Choose another volcano in the world.
- Research the volcano online or in the library.
- Create two pages, using pictures and words, to tell about the volcano.

READING 1

Reading 1

Learning Strategies

Sequence of Events

In many stories, events happen in a certain order. This order is called the **sequence** of events.

Practice

Read this series of events from *Lava Boat Tour!* List the events in the order in which they happen.

a. Sometimes the hot lava flows all the way to the ocean. _____
b. The lava is so hot that the ocean water boils, and there are big clouds of steam. _____
c. The lava flows across the island, destroying everything in its path. _____
d. Lava forms under the volcano, deep inside the Earth. __1__
e. When the volcano erupts, some of the lava flows out of the volcano's crater. _____

Use a Sequence of Events Chart

A Sequence of Events Chart can help you summarize the main events in a story in the order they happened.

Practice

Answer the questions below to complete the Sequence of Events Chart.

1. Which event would you add to the middle of the chart?
   a. The lava fills the volcano's crater.
   b. The lava flows across the island.
   c. The lava cools and becomes black rock.
   d. The island gets bigger and bigger.

2. Which sentence could be added to the end of the chart?
   a. The lava can burn houses and buildings and destroy roads.
   b. The lava is similar to thick chocolate syrup.
   c. The lava cools and becomes rock, making the island bigger.
   d. The lava is so hot that it can turn solid rocks into liquid.

Apply

Retell the selection to a partner. Use some of the key words.

Lava forms under the volcano, deep inside the Earth.

↓

When the volcano erupts, some of the lava flows out of the volcano's crater.

↓

[ ]

↓

Sometimes the hot lava flows all the way to the ocean.

↓

The lava is so hot that the ocean water boils and there are big clouds of steam.

↓

[ ]

Extension

Old lava flows are **evidence** of past volcanic eruptions. Find other evidence that tells us about the past. Share it with your class and explain.

Reading 1

Grammar

Simple Past: Irregular Verbs

Simple past irregular verbs do not end in **-d** or **-ed**. Here are some examples:

become	→	**became**	give	→	**gave**	rise	→	**rose**
begin	→	**began**	go	→	**went**	sing	→	**sang**
choose	→	**chose**	have	→	**had**	take	→	**took**

Simple present
Tourists often **take** pictures.

Simple past
We **took** pictures in Hawaii last year.

For negative statements, use **did** + **not** + the base form of a verb.

Affirmative past
We **had** fun yesterday.

Negative past
We **didn't have** fun yesterday.

did not → didn't

To make **Yes/No questions**, begin the question with **Did** + subject + the base form of a verb.

Did lava **begin** to flow this morning? Yes, it **did**. OR No, it **didn't**.

To make **Wh- questions**, begin the question with a question word such as **When** + **did** + the base form of a verb.

When did lava **begin** to flow? It **began** to flow this morning.

Don't use **did** if **Who** is the subject of the question.

Who saw the volcano erupt? We all **saw** the volcano erupt.

Practice A

Complete the sentences with the irregular past form of the verb in parentheses.

1. The tourists _____ during the boat tour yesterday. (sing)
2. We _____ to stay on the Big Island last year. (choose)
3. The eruption _____ a lot of noise. (make)
4. Clouds of steam _____ from the ocean. (rise)
5. The lava _____ a hard, black rock. (become)

Practice B

Use the sentences from Practice A to make negative simple past statements. Write in your notebooks.

1. The tourists didn't sing during the boat tour yesterday.

Apply

Work with a partner. Ask and answer the questions about *Lava Boat Tour!* Use regular and irregular past verbs.

> **Grammar Check ✔**
> Name some irregular past verbs.

Example: A: Did they go to Indonesia on their vacation?

B: No, they didn't. They went to Hawaii on their vacation.

- What did the narrator's brother compare to water for making spaghetti?
- What did the tour guide explain?
- Did the child have a good time?

Reading 1

Writing

Organize Ideas by Cause and Effect

Expository writing informs or explains. One way to organize expository writing is by cause and effect. A cause is something that makes something else happen. An effect is what happens as a result of the cause.

Writing Prompt

Write a paragraph explaining the causes and effects of an event. The event can be from real life or from books, movies, or television. Be sure to use irregular past verbs correctly.

① Prewrite

Choose an event to write about. Ask yourself why things happened as they did. List the causes and effects in a graphic organizer.

A student named Barbara listed her ideas like this:

② Draft

Use your graphic organizer to write a draft.

- Explain the causes and effects of an event.
- Show how each cause leads to an effect.

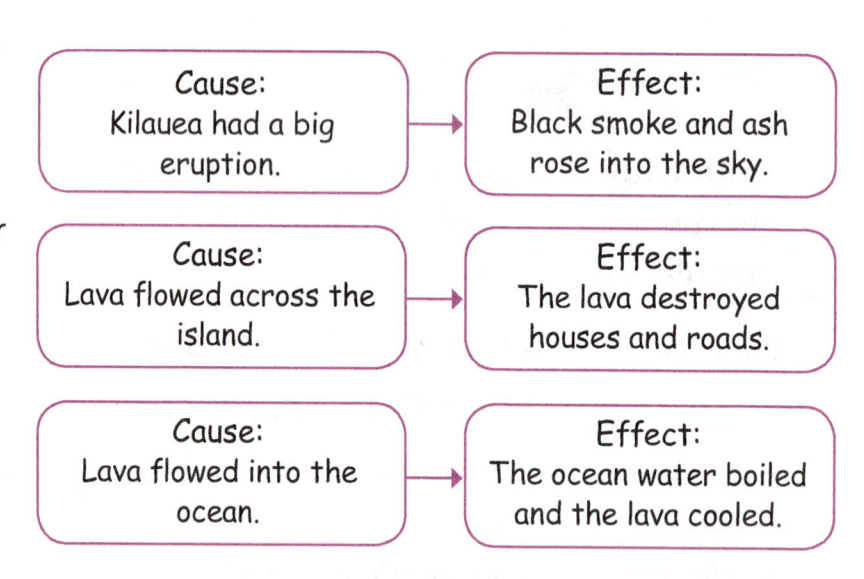

Cause: Kilauea had a big eruption.	→	Effect: Black smoke and ash rose into the sky.
Cause: Lava flowed across the island.	→	Effect: The lava destroyed houses and roads.
Cause: Lava flowed into the ocean.	→	Effect: The ocean water boiled and the lava cooled.

88 UNIT 2

③ Revise

Read your draft. Look for places where the writing needs improvement. Use the Writing Checklist to help you find problems. Then revise your draft.

④ Edit

Check your work for errors. Trade papers with a partner. Use the Peer Review Checklist on page 402. Edit your final draft in response to feedback from your partner and your teacher.

⑤ Publish

Make a clean copy of your final draft. Share it with the class. Save your work. You'll need to refer to it in the Writing Workshop at the end of the unit.

Here is Barbara's cause-and-effect paragraph:

> **Writing Checklist**
>
> ✓ **Ideas**
> I showed how causes led to effects.
> I expressed my ideas clearly.
>
> ✓ **Conventions**
> I used irregular past verbs correctly.

Barbara Torres

Kilauea volcano had a huge eruption in 1969. Black smoke and ash rose high into the sky. Lava flowed from the volcano and down the mountain. The lava covered large areas of land. It destroyed many buildings and roads. After some time, the lava reached the ocean. The hot lava boiled the ocean water. Big clouds of steam rose into the air. The lava cooled in the ocean water and became hard, black rock. The new lava rock made the island bigger. The eruption lasted five years!

Reading 2
Prepare to Read

What You Will Learn

Reading
- Vocabulary building: *Context, word study*
- Reading strategy: *Identify genre*
- Text type: *Informational text (Internet article)*

Grammar
Imperatives and time-order transitions

Writing
Explain how to do something

These words will help you understand the reading.

Key Words
lightning
thunder
electricity
temperature
evaporate

Key Words

You will read three passages about thunder and lightning. Each passage gives information in a different format.

Words in Context

Lightning is a flash of light in the sky. It happens during a storm. It is usually followed by a loud sound called **thunder**.

Electricity is a kind of energy. Lightning in the sky is electricity.

Which of these three pictures show items that use electricity?

90 UNIT 2

Temperature is a measure of how hot or cold something is.

These two pictures show water. Which picture shows water at a hotter temperature?

When water gets hot, it boils. Then, water will **evaporate** and change into a vapor or gas.

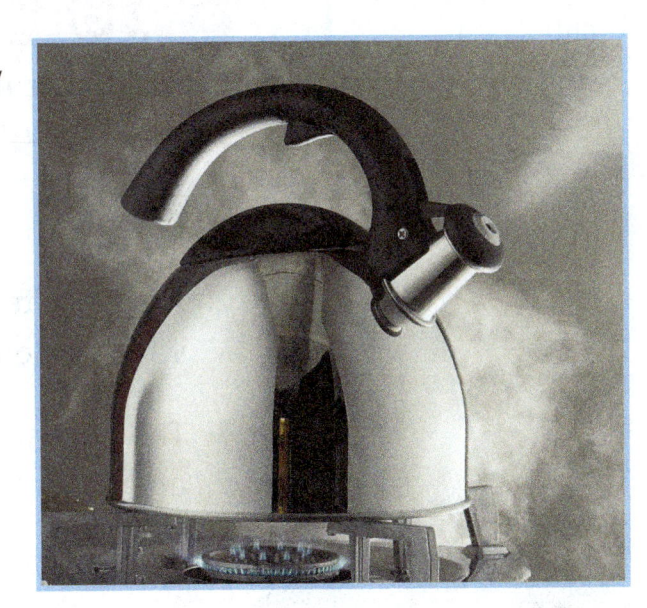

Practice

Make flashcards to help you memorize the words.
- Write a key word on the front.
- On the back, write the meaning.

Make Connections

What things in your home use **electricity**? How are they important in your life?

Reading 2

These words will help you talk about the reading.

Academic Words

appropriate
fitting; suitable

demonstrate
show how to do something

feature
a part that stands out

Academic Words

Words in Context

It is **appropriate** to raise your hand when you ask a question in class.

The scientist is going to **demonstrate** how to create electricity.

The newspaper's photographic essays are one of its most interesting **features**.

Practice

Choose an academic word to complete each sentence.

1. The best _____ of the cell phone is the camera.

2. A firefighter came to our class to _____ what to do during a fire drill.

3. The new action movie is _____ for families and children.

Apply

Ask and answer with a partner.

1. What **feature** of your textbook do you like the best?

2. What are some **appropriate** ways to act in your classroom?

3. Can you **demonstrate** how to make a paper airplane? Show your partner.

Word Study
Compound Words

A **compound word** is formed when two words are combined to form a new word.

class + room = **classroom**
thunder + storm = **thunderstorm**

Rule

This is a pattern in English: look for the shorter words that make up a compound word. They can help you pronounce and understand the compound word. For example, *thunderstorm* is a storm with thunder.

Practice

Work with a partner.

- Circle all of the shorter words you see.
- Compare your list to your partner's. Did you find the same words?
- Add more compound words to your list.
- Read your lists aloud.

| sunshine | lookout | daytime |
| flashlight | anywhere | raincoat |

Reading Skill

Looking for patterns in English will make you a better reader.

READING 2 93

Reading 2

Informational Text
Internet Article

More About THE BIG QUESTION

What can you do to stay safe during thunderstorms?

🎧 **Listen to the Audio.**
Listen for the general meaning. Use the pictures to help you understand the selection.

Reading Strategy
Identify Genre

A genre is a type of writing. Stories, poems, articles, plays, and letters are some genres.

- What do you notice about the genres of the readings that follow?

Listen as your teacher models the reading strategy.

Thunder and Lightning

Electricity in the Sky

Lightning is a big **flash** of electricity. It is released during a storm. Lightning strikes more often in the summer than in the winter. That's because there are more storms in the summer. Sunny weather and hot temperature heat the air and make water evaporate. The hot air and water **vapor** rise into the sky. As they rise, they meet the cold air.

---

flash   sudden, bright light
vapor   small drops that float in the air

❶

Cloud-to-cloud lightning

94   UNIT 2

② Cloud-to-ground lightning

Up in the Clouds

The cold air makes the water vapor turn back into water **droplets** or ice **crystals**. That forms a cloud. Inside the cloud, the droplets and crystals carry a tiny bit of electricity. The electricity builds until lightning suddenly forms.

Lightning can jump from one cloud to another (see image 1). It can move from a cloud to the ground (see image 2). Sometimes lightning can even move from the ground up to a cloud (see image 3).

Lightning is five times hotter than the sun. Lightning heats the air around it so quickly that the air explodes. Thunder is the noise we hear when the air explodes.

Catch Me If You Can!

③

Light moves faster than sound. This means we see the flash of lightning before we hear the thunder. It takes five seconds for the noise of the thunder to go one mile.

If you see lightning and then hear thunder five seconds later, the storm is one mile away. If thunder comes ten seconds after lightning, the storm is two miles away.

Ground-to-cloud lightning

droplets   very small drops of liquid
crystals   little pieces of ice

Before You Go On

Why do we see lightning before we hear the thunder?

Staying Safe in a Lightning Storm

Lightning can be dangerous. Here are some tips to stay safe.

Outdoors

1. Check if thunderstorms are in the **forecast**.
2. Find shelter in a strong building or in a car with a hard roof.
3. Do not stand under trees that are alone in the middle of a field. Do not stand under tall trees when there are shorter trees close by.
4. Do not stand near things that are made of metal.

Indoors

1. Close all the windows and doors.
2. Do not take a bath or shower. Stay away from water.
3. Turn off electrical appliances, including computers and TVs.

The Lightning Crouch

If you feel your skin tingle or your hair stand up, this could mean you are about to be hit by lightning. Get into the "Lightning Crouch." Crouch down low and curl into a small ball. Put your hands on your knees, and keep your head down. Try to be as small as you can, with very little touching the ground. DO NOT LIE ON THE GROUND!

---

forecast   description of weather that is likely to occur in the future

To: dotsummers@quickmail.com

Subject: Lightning!

Hi Grandma!

My class learned all about lightning at school today. Our teacher told us about this man, Roy C. Sullivan, who had very bad luck. From 1942 to 1977 he was struck by lightning seven different times! That's more than anyone else in the world!

Roy worked in a national park. He was standing on a high tower in the park when he was first hit with lightning. Years later, he was driving along a road when lightning struck him again. Lightning hit him five more times.

Roy was unlucky, but he was also lucky. It's very dangerous to be struck by lightning. He was never badly hurt, though. You and I can be even luckier than Roy. At school I learned how to protect myself from being struck by lightning. I'll tell you how in my next email.

Love,

Emilio

Reading Skill

The word **about** is a basic sight word. Sight words are words you see a lot when you read.

Reading Strategy
Identify Genre

- What are some **features** of an email?
- How is the email different from the how-to poster?
- Ask your teacher or classmates if you don't understand how to identify genres.

Think It Over

1. **Recall** How can you **demonstrate** the lightning crouch?
2. **Comprehend** What are the **appropriate** actions to take when you are indoors during a lightning storm?
3. **Analyze** Why was Roy C. Sullivan more lucky than unlucky? Explain.

READING 2

Reading 2

Learning Strategies

Compare Genres

Genres have different purposes and are organized in different ways.

Informational Articles are usually organized into paragraphs and have a title and headings. An article often has photographs or illustrations to make the facts clearer.

How-to Posters often have headings and numbered steps. The headings help you find information. The numbered steps tell the order you should follow.

Emails have a subject, a salutation (Hi Grandma!), a message, and a closing (Love, Emilio).

Practice

Write *article*, *poster*, or *email* in the final column of the chart. There can be more than one answer.

Feature	Genre
1. Purpose: It is written to one person.	email
2. Purpose: It is written to present information to many people.	
3. Subjects: It has a subject line.	
4. Headings: It has headings.	
5. Salutations/Closings: It has a salutation and a closing.	
6. Numbered Steps: It has steps that tell what order to follow.	
7. Information: It tells facts.	

Use a Venn Diagram

A Venn Diagram makes it easy to see what is the same or different about two items. Circle A represents one item. Circle B represents another. The part that overlaps represents things that are true for both.

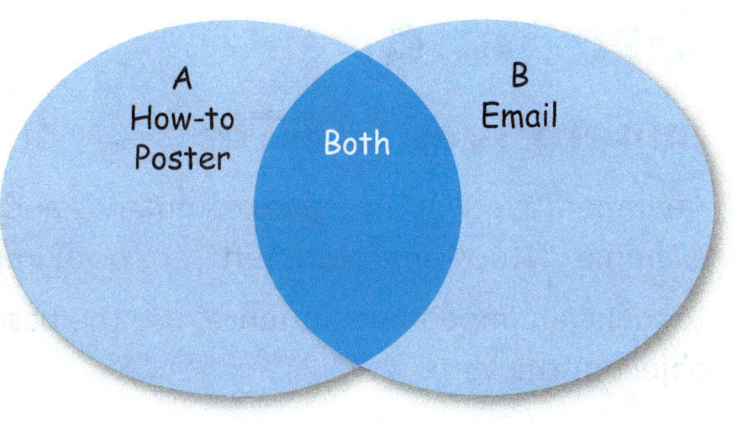

A How-to Poster

Both

B Email

Practice

GO 2

Create a Venn Diagram to compare two of the genres. Use the statements from the chart on the previous page.

- Choose two of the three genres from the selection.
- Draw a blank Venn Diagram. List one genre in Circle A. List the other genre in Circle B.
- Write statements that are true for one genre, but not for the other genre, in the big parts of Circle A or Circle B.
- Write statements that both genres have in common in the section labeled *Both*.

WB 57

Apply

Take notes about the article, informational poster, and email.

- Share them with a partner.
- Try to use the key words.

Extension

Work in small groups. Make a how-to poster warning people about a danger. Do research. Share the information with your group. Be sure to listen carefully to your classmates and work cooperatively.

READING 2

Reading 2

Grammar

Imperatives and Time-Order Transitions

An imperative sentence gives commands and directions. For example, "Stop" and "Turn left" are both imperatives.

To make an imperative sentence, use the base form of a verb + the object of the verb.

Verb	Object
Close →	the door.

To make a negative imperative use **Do not** or **Don't** + the base form of a verb + the object of the verb.

Don't take a bath or shower.

do not → don't

We also use the imperative to give instructions. Instructions usually include several steps in a sequence. To show sequence, use time-order transition words such as *first*, *then*, *next*, and *finally*.

Time-Order Transition Words
First, crouch down low.   **Next,** put your hands on your knees.
Then, curl into a ball.   **Finally,** do not touch the ground!

Other time-order transition words like *as soon as*, *immediately*, *meanwhile*, and *until* can be used to combine clauses.

As soon as you crouch down low, **immediately** curl into a ball. **Meanwhile,** do not touch the ground **until** the storm passes.

Practice A

Work with a partner. List five verbs used to give commands. Use the verbs to give your partner directions, or commands.

Example: Pick up your backpack.

Practice B

Complete the instructions with these time-order words.

| As soon as | Immediately | Finally | Then | ~~First~~ |

_____First_____, you need to see the lightning flash.

_____ after you see the flash, begin to count seconds slowly.

_____, keep counting while you listen for the thunder.

_____ you hear the thunder, stop counting.

_____, divide the number of seconds by five.

Grammar Check ✔

What are some time-order transition words?

Apply

Work with a partner. Choose an activity from the list. Explain how to do it to your partner. Your partner will repeat your directions. Then switch roles.

Example: First, address your email. Next, write a subject line. Then write a salutation....

- Make ice cubes
- Create a Venn Diagram

Reading 2

Writing

Explain How to Do Something

Writers explain how to do something in clear, step-by-step instructions. The verbs are in the command form. The steps are written in correct time-order. Often the writers introduce each step with time-order words, such as *first, next, then,* and *last.*

Writing Prompt

Write a paragraph that explains how to do or make something. Explain the steps in the correct order from first to last. Be sure to use the command form of verbs and time-order words.

① Prewrite

Choose a topic to write about, such as how to care for a pet or prepare a recipe. List the steps to follow in a Sequence of Events Chart.

A student named Omar listed his ideas in this Sequence of Events Chart:

② Draft

Use your sequence of events chart to help you write a first draft.
- Keep in mind your purpose for writing—to explain.
- Show the steps in clear order, from first to last.

STEP 1:
Cut hole in shoebox lid and glue four toothpicks on lid.

↓

STEP 2:
Slide two thick and two thin rubber bands around shoe box, across hole.

↓

STEP 3:
Slide pencil under four rubber bands, at the end of box near the hole.

102   UNIT 2

③ Revise

Read over your draft. Look for places where the writing is unclear and the steps are not in the correct order. Use the Writing Checklist to help you identify problems. Then revise your draft.

④ Edit

Check your work for errors. Trade papers with a partner to get feedback. Use the Peer Review Checklist on page 402. Edit your final draft in response to feedback from your partner.

⑤ Publish

Prepare a clean copy of your final draft. Share your paragraph with the class. Save your work.

Here is Omar's paragraph:

> **Writing Checklist**
>
> ✓ **Ideas**
> I clearly explained each step in the instructions.
>
> ✓ **Organize**
> I arranged the steps in order from first to last.
>
> ✓ **Conventions**
> I used imperatives and time-order transitions.

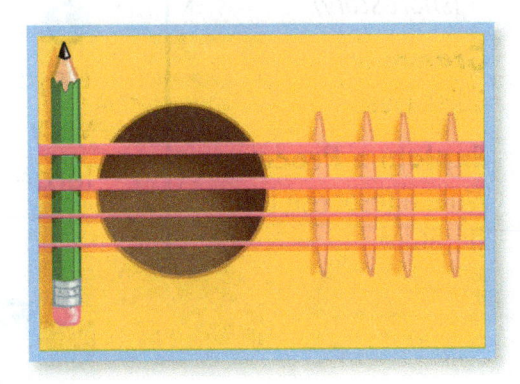

Omar Amari

First, cut a hole near one end of a shoebox lid. Then glue four toothpicks on the lid. Space the toothpicks evenly between the hole and the other end of the lid. Slide the two thickest rubber bands around the shoe box, so they go across the hole in the lid. Then slide the two thinnest rubber bands around the box in the same way. Finally, slide the pencil under the four rubber bands. Put the pencil at the very end of the box near the hole you cut. Now play the guitar by plucking the rubber bands.

Reading 3
Prepare to Read

What You Will Learn

Reading
- Vocabulary building: *Context, phonics*
- Reading strategy: *Visualize setting*
- Text type: *Literature (short story)*

Grammar
Adjectives

Explain a Process
Write a response to literature

These words will help you understand the reading.

Key Words

breeze
hurricane
shelter
bolt

Key Words

Hurricane! is a story about a family on vacation who lived through a hurricane.

Words in Context

1 A **breeze** is a light wind. When it is breezy, plants and trees may move a little.

2 A **hurricane** is a big tropical storm. It brings very strong winds and a large amount of rain.

104 UNIT 2

③ When a hurricane is coming, people can go to a **shelter**. A shelter is a place where people are protected from forces of nature.

④ A **bolt** of lightning looks like a white line in the sky.

Practice

Add a page to your vocabulary notebook.
- Divide your page into three columns: the new words, their definitions, and drawings of the words when possible.
- Test yourself by covering one of the columns.

Make Connections

What was the biggest storm you ever lived through? Discuss this question with a partner. Use the key words. Then write your response in your notebook.

READING 3

Reading 3

These words will help you talk about the reading.

Academic Words

assistance
help or support

impact
a strong effect

major
big; very important or serious

Academic Words

Words in Context

Emergency workers give **assistance** to people who are hurt.

Hurricanes cause a lot of damage and have a huge **impact** on a town.

Some people must leave their homes before a **major** storm comes.

Practice

Choose an academic word to complete each sentence.

1. Going to a new school is a _____ change.

2. The student needs _____ because his bag is very heavy.

3. The new president had a big _____ on the country.

Apply

Ask and answer with a partner.

1. What are some **major** storms you know about?

2. What **impact** could a storm have?

3. What kinds of **assistance** might people need in a storm?

Phonics

Digraphs: ch, sh, th 🎧

Sometimes two letters combine to make one sound. The letters *ch*, *sh*, and *th* are examples. These letters can come anywhere in a word. Listen. Sound out the words in the box.

ch	sh	th
chances	**sh**are	**th**ink
cheer	**sh**elter	**th**is
approa**ch**ing	**sh**ore	**th**under
wat**ch**ed	fla**sh**	wea**th**er
bea**ch**	spla**sh**ed	wi**th**

Practice

Work with a partner. Take turns.

- Choose a word from the chart. Say the word aloud.
- Without looking at the word, have your partner tell whether the word has the letters *ch*, *sh*, or *th*.
- List six more words that are spelled with *ch*, *sh*, or *th*.

1. _____
2. _____
3. _____
4. _____
5. _____
6. _____

Reading 3

Literature
Short Story

More About THE BiG QUESTION

Why is it important to know about dangerous weather?

🎧 **Listen to the Audio.**
Listen for the general meaning. Use the pictures to help you understand the story.

Reading Strategy
Visualize Setting

The setting of this story is important. As you read *Hurricane!*, picture each new setting in your mind.

- Think about how the author describes the setting.
- Look for descriptive words.

Listen as your teacher models the reading strategy.

Hurricane!

by Tracey Baptiste
illustrated by Amy Huntington

We went to the beach for our summer vacation. I splashed in the clear, blue sea. Mom and Dad sat on the shore. It was sunny, but not for long.

A man ran toward us. He worked at a nearby hotel.

"Señor! Señorita!" he called. "A big storm is coming. You must leave the beach now!" He told us that a hurricane was **approaching**. Everyone had to go to a shelter.

---

approaching   moving nearer

"But the water is so nice," I said sadly.

"Hurricanes are dangerous. We must leave," Dad said.

Mom smiled to make me feel better. Just then, I felt a breeze. Suddenly, the wind grew stronger and sand flew all around the beach.

"Let's go!" Dad said.

Before You Go On

What **impact** did the storm have on the people on the beach?

READING 3

Mom and I packed all of our bags. Dad nailed wood over the windows of the beach house. This would **protect** the house from wind and rain.

"Our vacation is **ruined**," I cried.

"Maybe the storm won't last for long," Mom said. "But we can't take chances. We have to go where it is safe."

"We'll be OK," said Dad. "Think of this as an adventure."

I tried to cheer up. I might have an exciting story to tell my friends. But soon my adventure did not seem to be so fun.

The hurricane came closer. Lightning flashed! I saw a bolt of lightning over the water. Thunder clapped! Rain fell like sheets of glass from the sky. It was hard to see out of the car windows.

---

protect shield from danger
ruined spoiled or destroyed

"The streets will flood soon," Dad said.

"We must drive carefully," Mom said.

The shore was pounded by angry waves. The waves were strong and high. It was the afternoon, but the sky was as dark as night.

People on the **coast** were leaving their homes. The roads were crowded with cars. Our car moved slowly down the wet road.

---

coast   where the land meets the ocean

Before You Go On

What kind of major damage can a storm do?

READING 3

Later that day, we stopped at a hotel. Usually, people on vacation stayed there. Now it was a shelter for travelers. Many people were in the lobby of the hotel. They were caught by the storm. They had nowhere else to go.

Mom and I watched the news on TV. The weather **forecaster** talked about the storm. She explained that soon it would be over. But some people were **trapped**. They were caught by the fast storm.

But my family was warm and safe inside the shelter. Outside, the wind and rain shook the trees and windows. People who were still outside needed help.

---

forecaster person who tells what the weather will be like
trapped not able to get out

One news reporter was in a boat. He saw a family on a raft. Their house was **flooded**, but they were fine. Emergency teams **rescued** these people. By that night, everyone was safe. I was happy now. And I had a story to share.

---

flooded covered in water
rescued helped or saved

Reading Skill

The word *fine* is a basic sight word. It's a word you recognize automatically. You don't have to sound it out.

64–66

Reading Strategy

Visualize Setting

- Describe the setting in your own words.
- Could this story have happened where you live? Why or why not?
- Did visualizing the setting help you to understand the story? How?

Think It Over

1. **Recall** Where does this story take place?
2. **Comprehend** How did the hotel offer assistance to the travelers?
3. **Analyze** What impact did the hurricane have on this family's vacation?

READING 3

Reading 3

Learning Strategies

Clues to Setting

To understand a story better, it helps to form a picture in your mind of the setting. The **setting** is where and when a story takes place. The setting of *Hurricane!* is near the beach during a hurricane.

Practice

Work with a partner. Look for clues to the setting.

- Reread pages 108–109.
- Copy the words, phrases, or sentences that help you get a clear picture of the setting of the story.

Use a Word Web

A Word Web helps you create a picture in your mind using just words.

Practice

GO 13

Copy and complete this Word Web to describe the setting of *Hurricane!*

1. Read the questions in each circle.
2. Write in each circle what you visualize, or picture, in your mind.
3. Compare your Word Web with your partner's. How are they alike? How are they different?

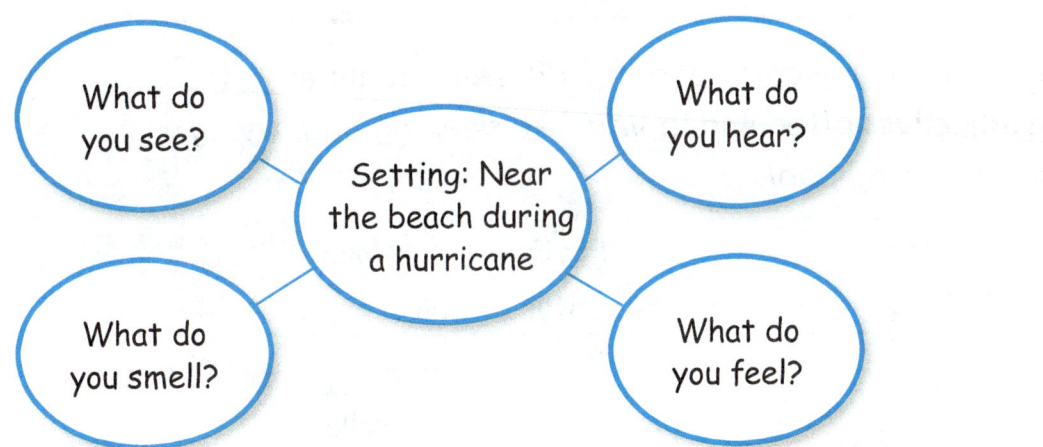

- What do you see?
- What do you hear?
- Setting: Near the beach during a hurricane
- What do you smell?
- What do you feel?

WB 67

Apply

Using the pictures in the story, make an outline of the events. Then narrate the story to a partner.

Extension

A setting can be drawn or even built in a model. Think of a setting that you know well. Picture how it might look during a big storm. Bring your setting to life in a description, drawing, or model. Share your setting with your class.

READING 3

Reading 3

Grammar
Adjectives

Adjectives are words that describe (or modify) nouns. They answer the questions *Which one? How many?* and *What kind?*

Usually, an adjective comes before the noun it modifies. An adjective can also come after the verb *be*. It modifies the subject noun.

Adjective	Noun	Noun	Adjective
It was a **big**	**balloon**.	The **balloon**	was **big**.

Different types of adjectives describe different qualities. **Purpose adjectives** often end in *-ing*, like *sleeping bag, frying pan,* and *swimming pool*.

Type	Adjective	Noun
opinion	beautiful	bird
size	small	desk
color	red	umbrella
material – what it's made of	brick	house
purpose – what it's used for	sleeping	bag

Sometimes we use more than one adjective before a noun. In sentences where two or more adjectives come before a noun, sequence the adjectives from opinion to purpose.

Adjective	Adjective	Noun
pretty (opinion)	blue (color)	flower
big (size)	wooden (material)	ship
metal (material)	frying (purpose)	pan

Practice A

Write adjectives before each noun. Choose adjectives from the box. Adjectives can be used more than once.

| warm | beautiful | plastic | green | sleeping |
| powerful | metal | brick | big | blue |

1. a ____big____ ____brick____ house
2. two _____ _____ paintings
3. a _____ _____ volcano
4. a _____ _____ bicycle
5. a _____ _____ bag
6. the _____ _____ sea

Practice B

Put the adjectives in the correct order. Write the sentences in your notebook.

1. There are yellow / small / birds in our backyard.
   There are small yellow birds in our backyard.
2. Mom bought me a camping / blue / cool / bag.
3. Elise slept in the brown / big / wooden / bed.
4. Did you see the swimming / blue / large / pool?
5. Let's meet at the stone / old / white / house.

Grammar Check ✔

Name the types of adjectives you learned in this lesson.

Apply

Work with a partner. Describe the things listed below. Use adjectives in your answers.

Example: A: A toy. A yo-yo is a small plastic toy.

B: A yo-yo has a long string. Yo-yos are fun.

- a toy
- a beach
- a kind of food
- an animal or pet

READING 3

Reading 3

Writing

Explain a Process

A process tells you how something happens. To explain a process, writers put the steps in order, from first to last. They include time-order words, such as *first*, *then*, *next*, and *last*. The steps in a process should be clear and include as many details as possible.

Writing Prompt
Write a paragraph that explains something you do in steps, such as growing a class plant or taking care of a pet. Be sure to use adjectives correctly.

① Prewrite

Choose a process to explain. Think about the steps that you follow. List the steps, from first to last, in a chart.

A student named Sandra listed her ideas in this chart:

② Draft

Use your chart to help you write a first draft.
- Keep in mind your purpose for writing—to explain.
- Present the information clearly and include as many details as possible.
- Include time-order words.

THE LIFE CYCLE OF A BUTTERFLY

STEP 1: Butterfly attaches egg to leaf or stem.

STEP 2: Long caterpillar feeds and grows. It has a pattern of stripes and patches on body. It sheds skin three or four times.

STEP 3: A pupa, or chrysalis, develops in a green or brown outer case, called a cocoon. Inside, the chrysalis turns into a butterfly.

STEP 4: Full-grown butterfly leaves the cocoon. It travels and lays eggs. Life cycle begins again.

③ Revise

Read over your draft. Look for places where there are not enough details and the steps are not in the correct order. Use the Writing Checklist to help you identify problems. Then revise your draft.

④ Edit

Check your work for errors in grammar, usage, mechanics, and spelling. Trade papers with a partner to get feedback. Use the Peer Review Checklist on page 402.

⑤ Publish

Prepare a clean copy of your final draft. Share your paragraph with the class. Save your work. You will need to refer to it in the Writing Workshop.

Here is Sandra's explanation:

> **Writing Checklist**
>
> ✓ **Ideas**
> I wrote the steps in a process, from first to last.
> I expressed my ideas clearly and included details.
>
> ✓ **Conventions**
> I included adjectives.

Sandra Miller

1. First, a butterfly attaches a tiny egg to a leaf or stem.
2. Next, a long caterpillar develops. It has an interesting pattern of stripes on its body. The caterpillar feeds and grows. It sheds its outer skin three or four times.
3. Next, a pupa, or chrysalis, develops. It is wrapped in a tough green or brown outer case called a cocoon. The pupa turns into a butterfly.
4. Finally, a beautiful butterfly leaves the cocoon. This colorful butterfly will travel to new places. It will lay eggs and the life cycle will begin again.

Put It All Together

Apply and Extend

Link the Readings

Read the words in the top row.
Then follow these steps:

- For *Lava Boat Tour!*, put an *X* under the words that remind you of the selection.
- Repeat the same activity for other readings.

	Informational text	Literature	Events caused by nature	Events caused by a storm
Lava Boat Tour!				
Thunder and Lightning				
Hurricane!				

Discussion

1. When Kilauea erupted in the past, the people of Hawaii were surprised. Do forces of nature today usually surprise people? Explain.

2. Describe the **impact** that the hurricane had on the town in *Hurricane!*

3. What is **similar** about volcanoes, thunder and lightning storms, hurricanes, and other **major** forces of nature?

THE BIG QUESTION How do people protect themselves from powerful forces of nature?

Listening Skills

If someone is speaking too quickly, you can say, "Can you speak more slowly, please?"

Projects

Your teacher will help you choose one of these projects.

Written	Oral	Visual/Active
Safety Guidelines Research what to do during a storm. Write school guidelines for students to follow in case of a terrible storm.	**Folktale** Long ago, people created folktales to explain the weather. Tell your own folktale to explain a form of extreme weather.	**World Map** Create a map of the world. Post photos on it showing types of extreme weather that are found around the world.
News Article Research on the internet or at the library to find a place that recently had severe weather. Write a newspaper article about the events.	**Vocabulary Hunt** Listen to daily weather reports for one week. Record as many weather words as you can. Create a collage to express the feelings of those words.	**Graphic Organizer** You learned about different types of lightning. Research and create a graphic organizer to show other types of weather, like rain, clouds, or storms.

Put It All Together

Listening and Speaking Workshop
Give a How-to Presentation 🎧

You are going to write and give a how-to presentation. Then you will listen as your classmates give their presentations.

① Prepare

A. Choose a dangerous situation or a sports activity. You will present how to stay safe or prepare for it. Then your classmates will ask you questions.

B. Think about the different steps. Decide on the sequence. Now write your how-to presentation. Remember to describe what you're going to demonstrate and then explain each step. Find props to use.

Useful Language

🎧 Listen and repeat.

Do you know how to . . . ?

First, find / buy . . .
Make sure you . . .
You will need . . .
Don't forget . . .

I am going to describe how to prepare for a blizzard. It is important to do these things before the snow arrives.

First, make sure you have food that does not need to be cooked. Peanut butter and bread are good. Also, you will need plenty of bottled water to drink. Next, make sure the batteries in your flashlights and radios work. Then find out if you have extra blankets.

Second, make a list of the things you need to buy.

Third, go to the store and buy the things you need.

② Practice

Find a partner. Practice your presentation in front of your partner. Your partner will act out or mime your instructions. Work with your partner to improve your presentation. Switch roles.

> **Speaking Skills**
>
> A presentation can use formal or informal language. Choose which to use based on the purpose of the presentation and its audience.

③ Present

As you speak, do the following:

- Speak clearly and slowly.
- Use your props while you speak.
- After your presentation, answer questions your classmates ask.

As you listen, do the following:

- Think about what you already know.
- Take notes.
- Think of questions to ask the speaker after the presentation.

> **Listening Skills**
>
> Be an active listener. Listen carefully to the spoken words. Watch for gestures and visuals.

④ Evaluate

After you speak, answer these questions:

- ✓ Did you describe what you demonstrated?
- ✓ Did you explain each step?

After you listen, answer these questions:

- ✓ Did you take notes?
- ✓ Did you ask any questions?
- ✓ What was the how-to presentation about?
- ✓ Did the speaker use formal or informal language?
- ✓ Think about the general meaning of the demonstration. Can you think of a title for it? Tell your idea to the class.

UNIT 2

Put It All Together

Writing Workshop
Write a How-to Essay

Writing Prompt
Write an essay explaining a process or how to do something. Present the steps of the process in order from first to last. To make the order clear, use words such as *first*, *next*, and *finally*.

① Prewrite

Review the writing you have done in this unit. Now choose a topic. Think about things you know how to do, such as downloading a song from the internet or making popcorn. List the steps of the process in a graphic organizer like the one below.

A student named Andy listed his ideas like this:

> **STEP 1:**
> Put emergency supplies in a safe place.

> **STEP 2:**
> Listen to weather reports. Watch for signs of a tornado.

> **STEP 3:**
> Find or go to a safe place.

② Draft

Use your graphic organizer to write a draft.

- Keep your purpose in mind—to explain how to do something.
- Present the steps in time order.

3 Revise

Read your draft. Look for places where the writing needs improvement. Use the Writing Checklist to help you. Then revise your draft.

Here is how Andy revised his essay.

Six Traits of Writing Checklist

✓ **Ideas**
Did I explain the steps clearly?

✓ **Organization**
Are the steps in time order?

✓ **Voice**
Does my writing sound like me?

✓ **Word Choice**
Did I choose precise words?

✓ **Sentence Fluency**
Did I vary my sentence patterns?

✓ **Conventions**
Do my pronouns agree?

Andy Wong

Tornado Safety

   ⟨You need to prepare for tornadoes before they hit.⟩ Tornadoes are powerful storms with fast winds. They can strike with little warning. They can destroy property and kill people. Here are things you can do to stay safe.

   First, gather emergency supplies and put them in a safe place. Choose a spot that is protected from the tornado's winds. Include water, canned foods, a first-aid kit, a radio, a flash light, and batteries.

   Then, listen to reports ⟨if a tornado is predicted⟩ and watch for signs of it coming. A tornado looks like a funnel. Sometimes you can hear it coming. A tornado sounds like a waterfall.

   Finally ~~Next~~, if a tornado is on its way, find or go to a safe place. Stay away from windows. Lie down and cover your head with your hands.

   Tornadoes move fast. ^so You need to be prepared in order to stay safe.

Revised to make the meaning clearer.

Revised to correct spelling errors.

Revised to make the meaning clearer.

Revised to choose a more effective transition word.

Revised to combine sentences.

UNIT 2 125

Put It All Together

④ Edit

Check your work for errors. Trade papers with a partner. Use the Peer Review Checklist to give each other feedback. Edit your final draft in response to feedback from your partner and your teacher.

⑤ Publish

Make a clean copy of your final draft. Share your essay with the class.

WB 73–74

> **Peer Review Checklist**
>
> ✓ The steps are clear.
> ✓ The steps in the correct order.
> ✓ All the information is related to the topic.

> **Spelling Tip**
>
> The letters *gh* are sometimes silent as in **sigh**, **high**, and **light**. Notice words with silent *gh* and learn their spelling patterns.

126 UNIT 2

Put It All Together

Fluency 🎧

Listen to the sentences. Pay attention to the groups of words. Read aloud.

1. It was erupting, and it was a gentle eruption.
2. We can follow tips to stay safe during thunder and lightning storms.
3. A family vacationing at the beach must find shelter when a hurricane hits.

Work in pairs. Take turns reading the passage aloud for one minute. Count the number of words you read.

One girl on the boat asked the tour guide how	10
the lava gets to the ocean. The guide explained	19
that the lava forms under the volcano, deep inside	28
the Earth. When the volcano erupts, some of the	37
lava flows out of the volcano's crater. Then	45
the lava flows down the side of the volcano.	54
The lava is similar to thick chocolate syrup.	62
It flows slowly.	65
The lava flows across the island. You can see evidence	75
of old flows everywhere. There are destroyed houses and	84
roads covered by black lava rock. Sometimes the lava gets	94
all the way to the ocean. That's what we saw. We were lucky.	107
It was awesome!	110

With your partner, find the words that slowed you down.

- Practice saying each word and then say the sentence each word is in.
- Then take turns reading the text again. Count the number of words you read.

WB 75

UNIT 2 127

Test Preparation

Taking Tests

You will often take tests that help show what you know. Follow these tips to improve your test-taking skills.

Coaching Corner

Answering Test Items for Revising and Editing

- Revising and Editing Tests often ask you to look for corrections and improvements that a writer should make.

- Before you read the written selection, preview the questions and answer choices.

- After reading the whole selection, go back and carefully reread the sentence mentioned in the question. Do you notice any mistakes in grammar or punctuation?

- Read each of the answer choices to yourself to see if one of them sounds better than the sentence in the selection. Choose the answer that does the most to improve the whole sentence.

- Remember that sometimes the sentence will not need any corrections or improvements.

Practice

Read the selection. Then answer the questions. Circle the correct answers.

(1) It stopped raining in the Southwest in the summer of 1931. (2) Crops died. (3) There was nothing left to hold the dirt on the ground. (4) Then the dust storms begin. (5) This event was called the Dust Bowl, and it lasted for 10 years. (6) There was dust everywhere. (7) There was dust in the food and in the water. (8) It is hard for animals and people to breathe. (9) Sometimes there was so much dust in the air, people couldn't see the sun. (10) The sky become so dark, it looked like night during the day.

1 What is the BEST way to revise sentence 4?

   A Then the dust storms end.

   B Then the dust storms begun.

   C Then the dust storms began.

   D No revision is needed.

2 What revision, if any, is necessary in sentence 8?

   F It was hard for animals and people to breathe.

   G It were hard for animals and people to breathe.

   H It are hard for animals and people to breathe.

   J No revision is needed.

3 What change, if any, should be made in sentence 10?

   A Change *looked* to **look**.

   B Change *become* to **became**.

   C Change *become* to **were**.

   D Make no change.

Tips

✓ Read sentence 4 in the selection again. What action is described?

✓ Read each answer choice to yourself. Think about how to form past tense verbs.

✓ Sentence 10 contains an irregular verb. Is it used correctly?

UNIT 2

Unit 3
Telling Tales

Everyone enjoys a good story. You will read two tales and a play. They are different genres, or types of literature. What stories do you like to tell or read?

Reading 1
Pourquoi Tale

Why Mosquitoes Buzz in People's Ears

Reading 2
Play

The Shoemakers and the Elves

Reading 3
Tall Tale

John Henry and the Machine

THE BIG QUESTION

What do the characters in tales have in common?

Listening and Speaking

You will talk about telling tales. In the Listening and Speaking Workshop, you will perform a play.

Writing

You will practice narrative writing. In the Writing Workshop, you will write a story.

Quick Write

What is your favorite story? Describe what happens.

View and Respond

Talk about the poster for this unit. Then watch and listen to the video and answer the questions at Pearson English Portal.

Build Unit Vocabulary

What do you know about reading?

Words to Know

Listen and repeat. Use these words to talk about reading.

- a magazine
- a newspaper 
- a recipe 
- a cereal box 
- a website 
- directions 

Practice

Work with a partner. Ask questions using the words above. Answer them using words from the box or your own ideas.

| see photographs | get information | learn how to do something | see illustrations |

Example: A: Why do you read <u>a newspaper</u>?

B: I read <u>a newspaper</u> to <u>get information</u>.

Write

Read the question. Write your answer in your notebook.

What do you like to read? Why?

132   UNIT 3

Make Connections

Complete the sentences with the following words.

a cookbook

a computer

a board game

photographs

1. It is fun to play _____ with friends. Before we play, we always read the directions so we can learn the rules.

2. I like to go on _____ to get information. There are a lot of interesting websites that help me with my homework.

3. My mom loves to cook. She reads recipes from _____. She always measures the ingredients.

4. When I go to the dentist I like to read a magazine. There are many things to read and lots of _____ to look at.

What about you?

Talk with a partner. Talk about other things you can read.

Build Unit Background

Kids' Stories from around the World 🎧

U.S.A.

Raymond

I live in the U.S.A. My father told me a tale about Johnny Appleseed. He was a kind man who had very little. But he did have apple seeds. Johnny traveled to many places. He planted apple seeds wherever he went. Apple trees grew and produced fruit for people to eat.

David

I live in the United Kingdom. My house is near the Natural History Museum. I like to visit the fossil of a giant dinosaur. We call him Claws. My favorite poem is *Bones to Stones*. It is about a dinosaur just like Claws.

Katya

I live in Germany. My favorite story is *Little Red-Cap*. In some countries, this story is called *Little Red Riding Hood*. The girl walks through the woods to visit her grandmother. She finds a surprise. A wolf is in her grandmother's bed!

Flora

I am from Burkina Faso. The summers here are hot and rainy. That means there are lots of mosquitoes. My grandmother tells a story about mosquitoes that buzz in people's ears.

What about you?

1. Do any of these stories sound familiar to you? Which ones?
2. Do you know of any stories or tales? Share them with the class.

UNIT 3

Reading 1
Prepare to Read

What You Will Learn

Reading
- Vocabulary building: *Context, phonics*
- Reading strategy: *Identify events in a plot*
- Text type: *Literature (pourquoi tale)*

Grammar
Singular and plural nouns

Writing
Retell a familiar story

These words will help you understand the reading.

Key Words
tidbit
mischief
nonsense
duty
satisfied
council

Key Words

Why Mosquitoes Buzz in People's Ears is a pourquoi tale. It explains why mosquitoes can't talk.

Words in Context

1 Sasha and Pedro put a **tidbit** of food in the fish tank.

2 My little brother is always getting into **mischief**.

3 Jessie likes to whisper **nonsense** in Rose's ear.

136   UNIT 3

4 Every citizen has a **duty** to vote. Voting helps cities and towns make plans.

5 Kelly was **satisfied** with the sandcastle she built.

6 This student **council** meets once a week. It is the school's government.

Practice

Make flashcards to help you memorize the words.
- Write a word on the front.
- On the back, write a sentence, but leave a blank where the key word should be.

Make Connections

What are your duties at home? What is a student's duty at school? After discussing these questions, write your responses in your notebook using the key words.

READING 1

Reading 1

These words will help you talk about the reading.

Academic Words

emerge
appear or come out from somewhere

react
say or do something because of something else

respond
answer

Academic Words

Words in Context 🎧

In spring, many animals **emerge** from their winter homes.

People often **react** to a mosquito by waving it away.

Students should always **respond** politely when a teacher speaks to them.

Practice

Choose an academic word to complete each sentence.

1. Please _____ to the test question. Write your answer neatly.

2. The soccer fans _____ to each goal with cheers.

3. Moths will _____ from their cocoons.

Apply

Ask and answer with partner.

1. How do you **react** when you do well on a test?

2. How do students **emerge** from their classroom on the last day of school?

3. How do you **respond** when a friend asks for a favor?

Phonics

Long Vowel Pairs 🎧

Long vowel sounds can be spelled with two vowels together making a pair. Listen. Then read each word aloud.

Long Vowel Pairs				
Long a	Long e	Long i	Long o	Long u
wait, day	bean, tree	cried	roam, toes	true, fruit

Did you notice that each word has two vowels together? Which vowel do you hear? Which vowel is silent?

Rule

When two vowels are together, the first vowel is usually long, and the second vowel is silent.

w **a** i   b **e** a n   t r **u** e

Practice

Work with a partner. Sound out the words in the box. Then write the word that has the vowel sound.

| road   skies   clue   fail   need |

1. long a _____
2. long e _____
3. long i _____
4. long o _____
5. long u _____

Reading 1

Literature
Pourquoi Tale

More About THE BIG QUESTION

How are animal characters like people?

🎧 **Listen to the Audio.**
Listen for the general meaning. Think about the situation or context. Use this to help you understand the story.

Reading Strategy
Identify Events in a Plot

A plot is made up of events from the story. Identifying the events can help you understand the story. As you read:

- Pay attention to the order in which events happen.
- Notice how one action leads to another action.

Listen as your teacher models the reading strategy.

Why Mosquitoes Buzz in People's Ears

by Pam Walker
illustrated by Gary Krejca

Have you ever heard a mosquito buzzing in your ear? Here's where that insect's **annoying** habit came from.

---

annoying   making you feel a little angry

140 UNIT 3

Reading Skill

Ask your classmates or teacher when you do not understand a word, phrase, or language structure.

One summer day, Mosquito saw Turtle sunbathing on a rock.

He flew over to his friend and whispered in her ear. "I have a tidbit of news!"

"You should not **gossip**," said Turtle.

"But wait until you hear this!" said Mosquito. "Farmer grew a carrot as large as an elephant!"

"That is nonsense!" Turtle cried. "I don't want to hear it!" She stuffed leaves in her ears and walked away.

Snake was in a tree branch when Turtle walked by.

"Hi, Turtle!" he hissed. "It'sssss me." But Turtle could not hear him.

---

gossip talk about someone in a way that is not nice

Before You Go On

Why didn't the turtle respond to the snake?

READING 1

"Turtle must be mad at me," Snake thought sadly. He **slithered** out of the tree to hide under a log. Mouse lived in the log. When she saw Snake coming, she ran from her home.

"What's wrong?" Rabbit asked the **timid** mouse.

"I have no time to talk," said Mouse. "Run! Danger!"

So Rabbit ran as fast as she could. "Run!" she cried. "Danger!"

Monkey heard Rabbit's cries. "Something bad is happening!" he thought. "It is my duty to tell the others!"

He jumped from tree to tree. "Run!" he called. "Danger!"

---

slithered moved by sliding along a surface

timid shy or scared

Monkey jumped to the tallest tree. He landed near Owl's nest. The nest began to shake. Then one egg fell to the ground.

When Owl returned, she saw that one of her eggs was missing. She was very sad, so she forgot to hoot the next morning. Because Owl did not hoot, the sun did not wake up.

The forest **remained** dark for days.

Finally, Lion asked Rabbit to **fetch** the others. The animal council had to talk about this problem.

"Everything is dark, and I am not happy," Lion roared. "Why won't you hoot, Owl?"

---

remained   stayed

fetch   get and bring back

Before You Go On

How did the monkey react after he heard the rabbit's cries?

READING 1

"I am too sad to hoot," said Owl. "Monkey broke one of my eggs!"

Lion looked at Monkey. "Rabbit said there was danger!" said Monkey. "I wanted to **warn** everyone!"

Lion looked at Rabbit. "Mouse told me to run!" Rabbit said.

Lion looked at Mouse. "Snake came to my house! I was afraid he would eat me!" cried Mouse.

"I wassss not hungry. I was sssssad," hissed Snake. "Turtle would not ssssspeak to me."

Just then, Turtle walked by.

"Turtle!" Lion roared. "Are you Snake's friend?"

"What?" Turtle removed the leaves from her ears. "Yes, I am Snake's friend."

---

warn   tell someone that something bad or dangerous may happen

"Then why didn't you speak when Snake said hello?" asked Lion.

"I did not hear him," said Turtle. "Mosquito gossips, so I put leaves in my ears."

"All this **mischief** started with you, Mosquito," the angry lion said. "You may never talk again."

All the animals were **satisfied**, but not Mosquito. Even today mosquitoes want to talk. But all they can do is buzzzzz!

Think It Over

1. **Recall** Who decides that the animal council must meet?
2. **Comprehend** How does Mouse **react** when she sees Snake?
3. **Analyze** Does the real story behind the animals' reactions finally **emerge** at the council's meeting?

Reading Strategy

Identify Events in a Plot

- What action started the events of the story?
- Did identifying the events in the plot help you understand the story? How?

READING 1

Reading 1

Learning Strategies

Sequence of Events

In many stories, events happen in a certain order. That order is called the **sequence of events**.

Practice

Read these events from *Why Mosquitoes Buzz in People's Ears*. List them in order from 1–5.

- Turtle told Mosquito that Mosquito should not gossip. _____
- Turtle stuffed leaves in her ears and walked away. _____
- Mosquito flew over to tell Turtle a tidbit of news. _____
- Mosquito whispered some gossip in Turtle's ear anyway. _____
- Mosquito saw Turtle sunbathing on a rock. __1__

Use a Sequence of Events Chart

A Sequence of Events Chart helps you put events in the correct order. Start with the first event. Then write each event that happens after that. Finish with the last event.

Practice

Complete this chart.

- Reread the story. List the tale's events in the correct order.
- Share your chart with a partner.
- Discuss what would happen if someone read the events in the wrong order.

Sequence of Events in *Why Mosquitoes Buzz in People's Ears*	
First	Mosquito sees Turtle sunbathing.
Then	
Next	
Next	Owl forgets to hoot.
Then	
Next	
Finally	Lion tells Mosquito he can never talk again.

Apply

Using the pictures in the reading, retell the story to a partner. Use some of the key words.

Extension

Do you know how to play Telephone? Form a circle with your classmates. The first person whispers a sentence to the next person. That person whispers the same sentence to the next person. The last person says the sentence aloud. Did the message change? How?

Reading 1

Grammar

Singular and Plural Nouns

A noun refers to a person, place, or thing. A plural noun refers to more than one person, place, or thing.
Review the spelling rules for making plural nouns.

Singular	Plural
a cat	three **cats**

Rules	Examples
Most nouns, add -s	turtle → turtle**s**
Nouns ending in -ch, -sh, -ss, or -x, add -es	bran**ch** → bran**ches**
Nouns ending in consonant + -y, change the -y to -i and add -es	ba**by** → bab**ies**
Nouns ending in vowel + -y, add -s	da**y** → da**ys**
Most nouns ending in consonant + o, add -es	mosquit**o** → mosquit**oes**
Most nouns ending in vowel + o, add -s	stud**io** → stud**ios**
Most nouns ending in -f or -fe, change the -f to -v and add -es	lea**f** → lea**ves** kni**fe** → kni**ves**

The plural form of irregular nouns varies. For example:

child → child**ren**; person → **people**; man → m**e**n; woman → wom**e**n.

Remember: Singular nouns take singular verbs. Singular verbs end in **-s**. Plural nouns take plural verbs. Plural verbs don't end in **-s**.

	Noun	Verb
Singular Subject	This **dog**	run**s** fast.
Plural Subject	These **dogs**	run fast.

148 UNIT 3

Practice A

Circle the singular subject nouns in the sentences.

1. The (flower) blooms in the summer.
2. A child often gets into mischief.
3. A tourist usually goes to a beach for a vacation.
4. The man **responds** to the fire alarm.
5. The wolf **emerges** in the evening.

Practice B

Change the subject nouns in Practice A into plural nouns. Be sure the subject agrees with the verb. Write the sentences in your notebook.

1. The flowers bloom in the summer.

Apply

Work with a partner. Say whether each noun is singular or plural and use it in a sentence. Then your partner will change it to its opposite form and use it in a sentence.

Example: A: Brushes is plural. That store sells many brushes.
B: Brush is singular. My dog chewed his brush.

brushes	shelves	women
hero	person	habit

Grammar Check ✔

How do you form the plural for most nouns ending in *-f* or *-fe*?

Reading 1

Writing

Retell a Familiar Story

When you retell a story, you explain what happened in your own words. Ask yourself: Did I retell the most important events or actions? Did I retell the events in the correct order? Did I use my own words?

Writing Prompt
Write a paragraph retelling a story that you know.

① Prewrite

Choose a familiar story to retell. Think about what happened in the beginning, middle, and end of the story. List these events in a sequence of events chart.

A student named Josh listed his ideas in this sequence of events chart:

Beginning
A little mouse woke up a sleeping lion. The lion caught the mouse.

Middle
The mouse asked the lion to free him. The mouse promised to help the lion. The lion freed the mouse.

End
The lion was caught in a hunter's trap. The mouse chewed a rope and freed the lion.

② Draft

Use your sequence of events chart to help you write a first draft.
- Keep in mind your purpose for writing—to retell.
- In your own words retell the events from the beginning, middle, and end of the story in order.

150 UNIT 3

③ Revise

Read over your draft. Look for places where the story events are out of order. Use the Writing Checklist to help you identify problems. Then revise your draft.

④ Edit

Check your work for errors. Trade papers with a partner to get feedback. Use the Peer Review Checklist on page 402. Edit your final draft.

⑤ Publish

Prepare a clean copy of your final draft. Share your paragraph with the class. Save your work. You will need to refer to it in the Writing Workshop.

Here is Josh's story:

> **Writing Checklist**
>
> ✓ **Ideas**
> I told the events from the beginning, middle, and end of the story.
> I used my own words.
>
> ✓ **Conventions**
> I used singular and plural nouns correctly.
> The subjects and verbs in my sentences agree.

Josh Snyder

The Lion and the Mouse

A great lion was sleeping in the forest. A little mouse ran over to the lion and woke him up. The lion grabbed the mouse with his large paw. "Please let me go and one day I will help you," the mouse said. "Help me?" the lion roared. "But you are only a tiny mouse," the lion laughed. Still, the lion was kind and let the mouse go.

The next day the lion was caught in a hunter's trap. He roared angrily. He could not break the hunter's ropes. The mouse heard the lion and came quickly. The tiny mouse chewed on one of the ropes until the lion was free.

Reading 2
Prepare to Read

Key Words

The Shoemakers and the Elves is a play about two elves and two shoemakers who help each other.

Words in Context

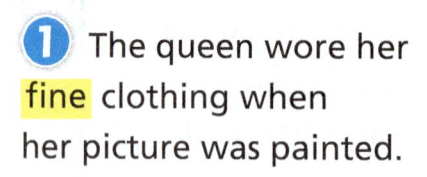

1 The queen wore her **fine** clothing when her picture was painted.

2 Taxis quickly **whisk** riders across town.

3 Many red **stitches** hold this baseball together.

What You Will Learn

Reading
- Vocabulary building: *Context, phonics*
- Reading strategy: *Make inferences*
- Text type: *Literature (play)*

Grammar
Possessives

Writing
Write a letter to a friend or family member

These words will help you understand the reading.

Key Words

fine
whisk
stitches
stroke
bare
wink

152 UNIT 3

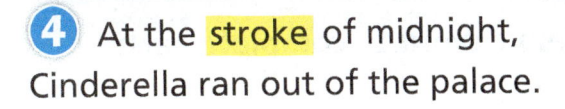

④ At the **stroke** of midnight, Cinderella ran out of the palace.

⑤ Old Mother Hubbard's cupboard was **bare**. There was no food inside.

⑥ Can you **wink** with your right eye?

Practice

Make flashcards to help you memorize the words.
- Write a word on the front.
- On the back, write a sentence, but leave a blank where the key word should be.

Make Connections

"As quick as a wink" means "very quickly." People use that expression even when something does not happen as quickly as a wink. What are some expressions you use? Explain what they mean.

Reading 2

These words will help you talk about the reading.

Academic Words

appreciate
be thankful or grateful for something

benefit
provide something helpful or good

infer
form an opinion based on information you have

Academic Words

Words in Context

The students **appreciate** the teacher's help.

Doing your chores will **benefit** the whole family because your home will stay tidy.

Mom could **infer** that Leo was home because she saw his backpack by the door.

Practice

Choose an academic word to complete each sentence.

1. They _____ everything the coach does for them.

2. When you read a story try to _____ how the characters get along.

3. All the students will _____ from the new computers in the classroom.

Apply

Ask and answer with a partner.

4. How do you show that you **appreciate** your friend's help?

5. How does your homework **benefit** you?

6. How could people **infer** that you like to help others?

154 UNIT 3

Phonics

Vowel Pair: *ea* 🎧

Each word below has the vowel pair *ea*. Listen to your teacher. Then read each word aloud.

Vowel Pair *ea*	
Long e	Short e
eat	bread
each	head
speak	ready

Rule

The vowel pair *ea* can have two sounds: the long e sound, as in *eat*, or the short e sound, as in *bread*. If you see a word you do not know, try saying the *ea* sound both ways.

Practice

Read the sentences with a partner. Take turns.

- They will sneak into the house.
- The mice will eat cheese instead of bread.
- Their shoes are made from leather.
- The girl thinks she is dreaming.

1. List the words in which *ea* has the long e sound.

   _____   _____

2. Then list the words in which *ea* has the short e sound.

   _____   _____   _____

READING 2

Reading 2

Literature
Play

More About THE BIG QUESTION

Why do tales often tell about characters that help each other?

🎧 Listen to the Audio.
Listen for the general meaning. Think about the situation or context. Use this to help you understand the story.

Reading Strategy
Make Inferences

When you make inferences, you are figuring out what the author means but doesn't say.

- Think about what you already know that the text doesn't tell you.
- Use the information in the text and your own experiences.

Listen as your teacher models the reading strategy.

The Shoemakers and the Elves

by Amanda Hong
illustrated by Sheila Bailey

Cast
Pixie, a female elf
Lumkin, a male elf
Amelia, a shoemaker and Diego's wife
Diego, a shoemaker and Amelia's husband

Scene 1: [*Two elves are looking into the window of a house. Two **elderly** shoemakers are inside. They are yawning. The elves wear **tattered** clothing. They are cold.*]

Lumkin: Let's play a trick on them!

Pixie: No, Lumkin. I think we have had enough fun for one day. We need a warm place to rest.

Lumkin: You're right. I don't want to get chased out of another house. I'm cold.

Pixie: [*She looks in the window again.*] Those people look tired.

Lumkin: And their shelves look bare. The shoemakers have nothing to sell.

Pixie: They're talking. Let's listen.

---

elderly old

tattered old and torn

Before You Go On

Why do you think Lumkin and Pixie were chased out of a house?

READING 2

[*The shoemakers are tired and worried. Tools for tomorrow's work are on a table.*]

Diego: I don't know how we can survive. We have no more leather to make shoes.
Amelia: What will we do?
Diego: Maybe we should close our shop.
Amelia: Then what will we do? Sell firewood?
Diego: Why not? I can chop down the walls to find wood.

[*They yawn as they walk upstairs.*]

Amelia: Let's sleep. We'll think about this tomorrow.

[*The elves enter the shoemakers' shop.*]

Pixie: This is sad, Lumkin.

Reading Skill

As you read, use the pictures to help you understand the words and ideas.

Lumkin: Yes, I am very sad. There is no bread here for us to eat.
Pixie: I think the shoemakers' problems are bigger than ours. We should help these people.
Lumkin: He wants firewood. Let's chop up the house!
Pixie: No tricks, Lumkin.
Lumkin: We could finish making the shoes. Then tomorrow the shoemakers will get a big surprise.
Pixie: Yes! We will make so many beautiful shoes. Everyone will want to buy them.
Lumkin: If you get that cheese on the **mousetrap**, I will make the shoes as quick as a wink.
Pixie: You always ask me to do the hard things.

---

mousetrap   trap that uses food to catch mice

Before You Go On

What could you infer about Lumkin wanting the cheese?

READING 2

[*The elves finish working.*]
Lumkin: Let's put away the tools and leather.
Pixie: Whisk the mess away. Let's go play!
[*The elves leave. The next morning, the shoemakers come downstairs. They find the new shoes. They are **speechless**.*]
Amelia: Look, Diego! Shoes! I must be dreaming!
Diego: Did you get up and work last night?
Amelia: No! I was going to ask you the same thing!
Diego: Then I must be dreaming, too! These shoes are beautiful.
Amelia: Look at these stitches! The **quality** is very fine.
Diego: Even we could not have made such special shoes.
Amelia: Let's put them in the window.
[*They embrace.*]

---

speechless   unable to speak
quality   degree to which something is good or bad

Reading Skill

The word *such* is a basic sight word. The more you read, the more words you'll recognize automatically.

[*One week later, the shoemakers sit at the table.*]

Diego: We are very lucky. Every night, someone makes shoes for us.

Amelia: And every day, we sell all those new shoes. We have so many **customers** now.

Diego: Who do you think is making the shoes, Amelia?

Amelia: I have no idea, Diego. But I would like to thank them. Wouldn't you?

Diego: Yes. But how?

Amelia: I have an idea!

[*That night, Diego and Amelia do not go to bed. Instead, they hide behind a curtain. At the stroke of midnight, the two elves appear at the window.*]

Diego: [*whispering*] Elves?

Amelia: [*whispering*] Elves! How **delightful**!

---

customers people who buy goods and services
delightful very nice

Before You Go On

How do the shoemakers show that they **appreciate** the new shoes?

[*The clock rings twelve times. Lumkin and Pixie **sneak** into the house through the window.*]

Pixie: Try to be quiet, Lumkin. We do not want to wake up the people.

[*Lumkin runs to the mousetrap. He grabs the **bait** and eats it.*]

Pixie: That cheese is for mice.

Lumkin: It's for hungry elves, too. I like to eat before I work.

Pixie: Well, there is a lot of work to do tonight.

[*The elves go to the table and begin working. The shoemakers watch from behind the curtain.*]

Amelia: We should do something nice for those hard workers.

Diego: I have an idea!

---

sneak go somewhere very quietly so as not to be seen or heard

bait food that is used to attract and catch animals

[*The next night, the shoemakers put two packages on the table. Then they hide and* **peek** *through the curtains.*]

Lumkin: It's midnight.

Pixie: That means it's time to go to work.

[*The elves look around. The table is bare except for the gifts.*]

Lumkin: Where is the leather? Where are the tools?

Pixie: What is this?

[*The elves open the packages.*]

Pixie: These beautiful things are for us!

[*They try on the clothes and shoes. Then they dance with joy.*]

Lumkin: Let's go outside and play!

Pixie: But what about our work?

Lumkin and Pixie: Ha ha!

[*The elves laugh as they dance. The shoemakers smile as the happy elves leave.*]

---

peek look secretly at something that you are not supposed to see

Reading Strategy

Make Inferences

- What time did the elves come?
- How can you make that inference?

Think It Over

1. **Recall** What problem do Amelia and Diego have?
2. **Comprehend** Do the elves **appreciate** the gifts from the shoemakers? How do they show it?
3. **Analyze** How do the elves and the shoemakers both **benefit** in this story?

Reading 2

Learning Strategies

Infer and Predict

To **infer** is to figure out something that the author doesn't directly tell you. To **predict** is to make guesses about what will happen.

Practice

Make inferences or predictions about the passage.

> The manager hired Manuel instead of Joe. He needed an experienced waiter, and he did not have time to teach Joe everything. Joe hoped to find a job soon. Summer vacation had already started. School would begin again in September. There were lots of "Help Wanted" signs on Main Street. Joe would keep looking for a job.

1. Has Joe been a waiter before?
2. Has Manuel been a waiter before?
3. Is Joe a student?
4. Will Joe return to school soon?
5. Does Joe want a job?
6. Will Joe get a job?

Use an Infer and Predict Chart

An Infer and Predict Chart helps you answer questions about a story or play.

Practice

Work with a partner. Read the dialogue in the first column.

- Discuss what you know about the elves and the shoemakers.
- Answer the questions in the second column.

Dialogue	Infer/Predict
Lumkin: Let's play a trick on them! **Pixie:** No, Lumkin. I think we have had enough fun for one day. **Lumkin:** You're right. I don't want to get chased out of another house. I'm cold.	**1. Infer:** Which elf seems more sensible? **2. Infer:** Have the elves been chased out of a house before?
Lumkin: If you get that cheese on the mousetrap, I will make the shoes as quick as a wink. **Pixie:** You always ask me to do the hard things.	**3. Predict:** What will Lumkin and Pixie do with the cheese? **4. Infer:** Which does Pixie think is harder, getting cheese or making shoes?
Pixie: These beautiful things are for us! **Lumkin:** Let's go outside and play! **Pixie:** But what about our work? **Lumkin and Pixie:** Ha ha!	**5. Infer:** Do the elves like their gifts? **6. Predict:** Will Lumkin and Pixie come back to work after they play?

Apply

Summarize the story to a partner. Use some key words.

Extension

Think of a chore you can do. Explain it to a partner. Ask your partner to follow the directions. Then switch roles and follow your partner's directions.

READING 2

Reading 2

Grammar

Possessives

Use the possessive form to show that someone or something "possesses," or owns, something. To form the possessive of singular or plural nouns that don't end in -s, add apostrophe s ('s).

Singular Noun	Object	Plural Noun	Object
the girl's	dress	the children's	books
the group's	notes	the women's	team

To form the possessive of plural nouns that end in -s, add an apostrophe (').

Plural Noun	Object
the students'	school
the Raines'	house

When two nouns (for example, two people) share ownership of something, add the apostrophe-s ('s) only to the second noun.

Compound Noun	Object	Meaning
Miguel and Wanda's	dog	The dog belongs to both Miguel and Wanda.

Possessive adjectives also show possession. A possessive adjective comes before a noun.

Possessive Adjectives	Object
my, your, his, her, its, our, their	cats

UNIT 3

Practice A

Change each phrase into the possessive form.

1. the clothing of the elves ___the elves' clothing___

2. the shoes belonging to customers _____

3. the horses belonging to Diego _____

4. the problems of the shoemaker _____

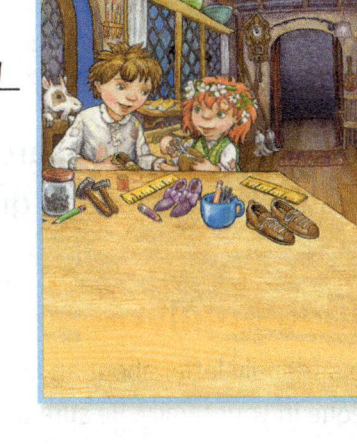

5. the dance of Lumkin and Pixie _____

Practice B

Answer the questions about *The Shoemakers and the Elves* in Apply. Write your answers in your notebook. Use possessive nouns.

1. Amelia is Diego's wife.

Apply

Work with a partner. Ask and answer these questions. Use your answers from Practice B.

Example: A: Who is Amelia?

B: She is a shoemaker. She is Diego's wife.

- Who is Amelia?
- Who is Diego?
- Whose shelves are bare?
- What is Pixie and Lumkin's problem?
- Whose problems are bigger? Why?

Grammar Check ✓

Why do we add 's to nouns?

Reading 2

Writing

Write a Friendly Letter

In a friendly letter, you share your experiences A friendly letter includes these parts: date, greeting, body, closing, and signature.

Writing Prompt

Write a friendly letter about an interesting event. You can write to a friend or to someone in your family. Be sure to use possessives correctly.

① Prewrite

Choose an event to write about. The event can take place in your school, home, or community. List your ideas in a graphic organizer.

A student named Kate used this graphic organizer:

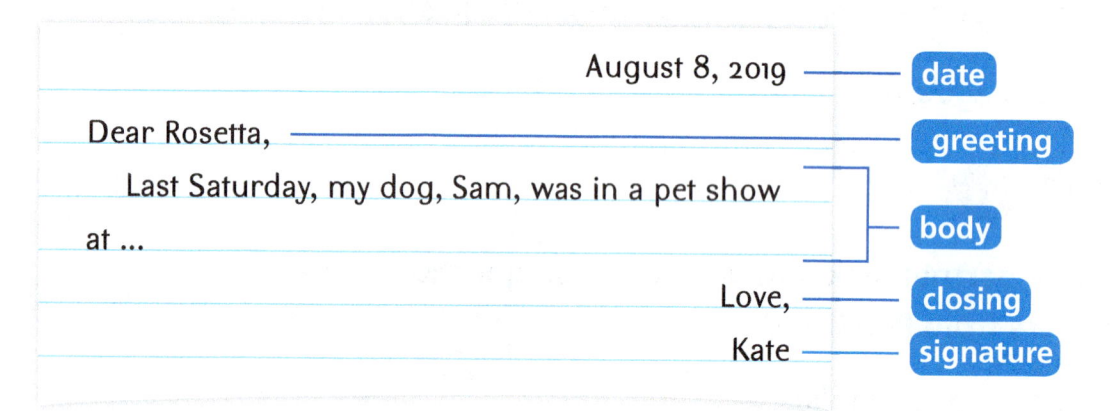

```
                          August 8, 2019  ——— date
Dear Rosetta, ———————————————————————————— greeting
    Last Saturday, my dog, Sam, was in a pet show
at ...                                          ┐— body
                                    Love, ——— closing
                                    Kate  ——— signature
```

② Draft

Use your graphic organizer to help you write a first draft.
- Keep in mind your purpose for writing—to write a letter.
- Write information in each part of the letter and include interesting details.

168   UNIT 3

③ Revise

Read over your draft. Look for places where the writing needs improvement. Use the Writing Checklist to help you identify problems. Then revise your draft.

④ Edit

Check your work for errors. Trade papers with a partner to get feedback. Use the Peer Review Checklist on page 402.

⑤ Publish

Prepare a clean copy of your final draft. Share your paragraph with the class. Save your work. You will need to refer to it in the Writing Workshop.

Here is Kate's personal letter:

Writing Checklist

✓ **Ideas**
I filled in all the parts of a friendly letter.

✓ **Word Choice**
I included interesting details.

✓ **Conventions**
I used possessives correctly.

---

32 First Avenue
Philadelphia, PA
August 8, 2019

Dear Rosetta,

　　Last Saturday my dog Sam was in a neighborhood pet show at Logan Park. Many of our neighbors' pets were in the show, too. People brought their dogs, cats, rabbits, birds, and fish. I didn't think most of the animals would get along. But they did, most of the time! Then, in the middle of a contest, Sam's collar fell off and he raced around the park. I guess he won't win prizes for being well behaved. It didn't matter. It was a wonderful day! Write soon.

Love,
Kate

Reading 3
Prepare to Read

What You Will Learn

Reading
- Vocabulary building: *Context, word study*
- Reading strategy: *Identify characters*
- Text type: *Literature (tall tale)*

Grammar
Quotations

Writing
Write a dialogue between two characters

These words will help you understand the reading.

Key Words

mighty
sledgehammer
machine
boasted
sputter

Key Words

John Henry and the Machine is about a contest between a man and a machine.

Words in Context

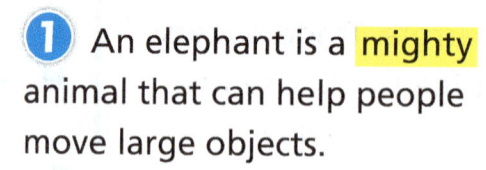

1 An elephant is a **mighty** animal that can help people move large objects.

2 A person can use a **sledgehammer** to break up rocks.

3 A **machine** can help people do work faster and with less effort.

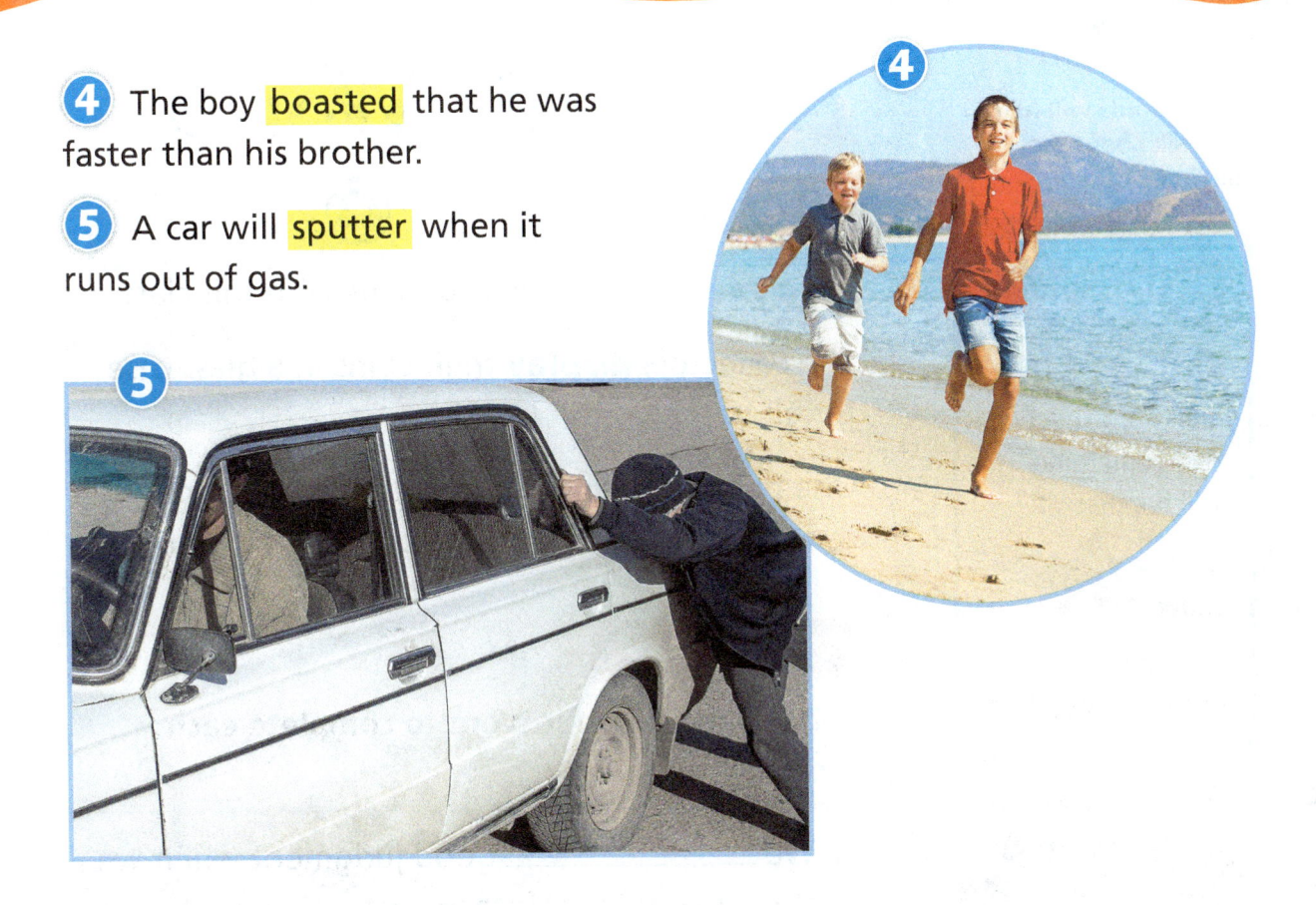

4 The boy **boasted** that he was faster than his brother.

5 A car will **sputter** when it runs out of gas.

Practice

Add a page to your vocabulary notebook.
- Divide your page into three columns: the new words, their definitions, and drawings of the words when possible.
- Test yourself by covering one of the columns.

Make Connections

Machines can't do everything that people can do. What is something you can do that a machine cannot? Draw a picture to show one of the skills you are good at. Then write a caption under your picture. Present your drawing and read your caption to the class.

Reading 3

These words will help you talk about the reading.

Academic Words

anticipate
guess or expect that something will happen

display
show

scenario
setting or situation

Academic Words

Words in Context

I don't **anticipate** any problems with this class.

The collectors **display** their coins in a glass case for all to see.

One possible **scenario** for the plot of our play could be a girl auditioning for a singing contest.

Practice

Choose an academic word to complete each sentence.

1. We _____ good judgment when we think carefully before we act.

2. This is a very familiar story. I can _____ the end of this story before it happens.

3. Here is the _____. You're just getting home from vacation. It's very late.

Apply

Ask and answer with a partner.

1. What is one thing that happened recently that you did not **anticipate**?

2. How would you **display** your favorite toy?

3. Can you imagine a **scenario** in which something surprising might happen? Describe it.

WB 100

172 UNIT 3

Word Study
Synonyms and Antonyms

Notice the words in purple. What do they mean?

> Wild horses are amazing! They have such **powerful** bodies and **strong** legs.

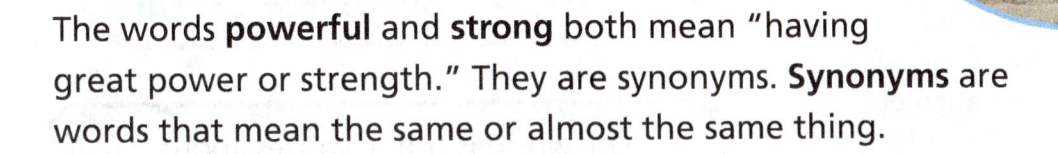

The words **powerful** and **strong** both mean "having great power or strength." They are synonyms. **Synonyms** are words that mean the same or almost the same thing.

The word **weak** means "not having strength or power." **Weak** and **strong** are antonyms. **Antonyms** are words that have opposite meanings.

Practice

Work with a partner. Replace each underlined word with a synonym or an antonym from the box. Write the new word.

later	roam
strong	talk

1. I'd love to chat some more. _____

2. The horse was weak. _____

3. Where did you wander? _____

4. Can we finish our work now? _____

Reading 3

Literature
Tall Tale

More About THE BIG QUESTION

How is John Henry similar to characters in other tall tales?

🎧 **Listen to the Audio.**
Listen for the general meaning. Think about the situation or context. Use the pictures to help you understand the selection.

Reading Strategy
Identify Characters

Characters are the people or animals in a story or poem. The main characters are the most important ones. The minor characters are less important. Think of a fairy tale you know well (for example, *Cinderella*). Then answer these questions:

- Who are the characters?
- Who is the main character? (There could be more than one in a story.)
- Who are the minor characters?

Listen as your teacher models the reading strategy.

John Henry and the Machine

by Michael Dunn Moriarty
illustrated by Nicole Laizure

The world is full of stories about the mighty John Henry. But he started out as a baby, just like the rest of us. The only difference was that even as a baby, John Henry could lift a sledgehammer over his head.

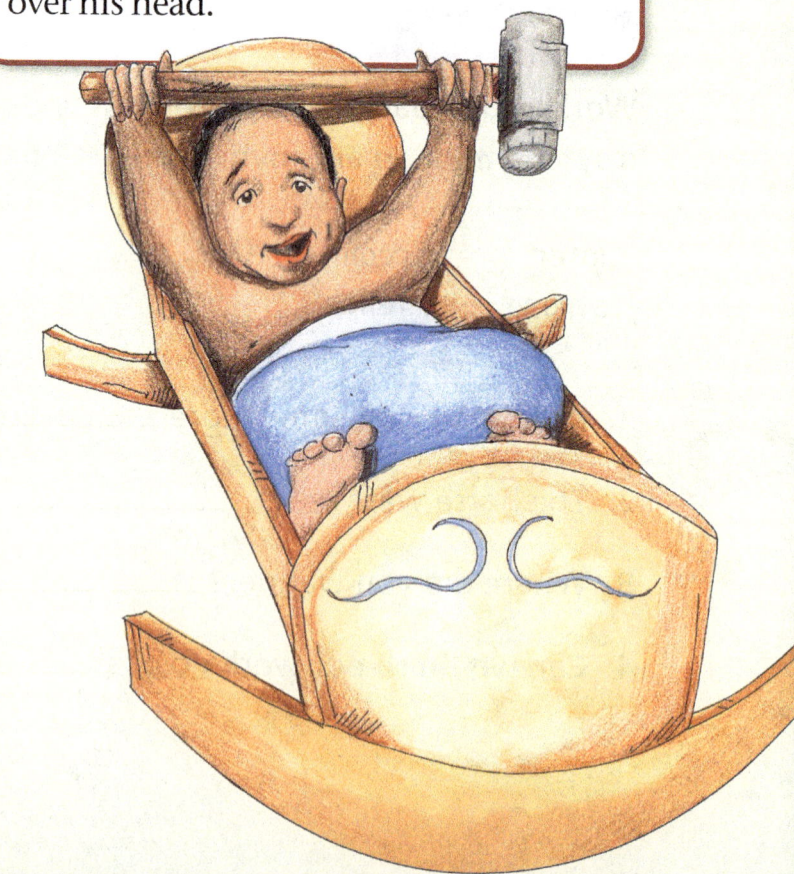

174   UNIT 3

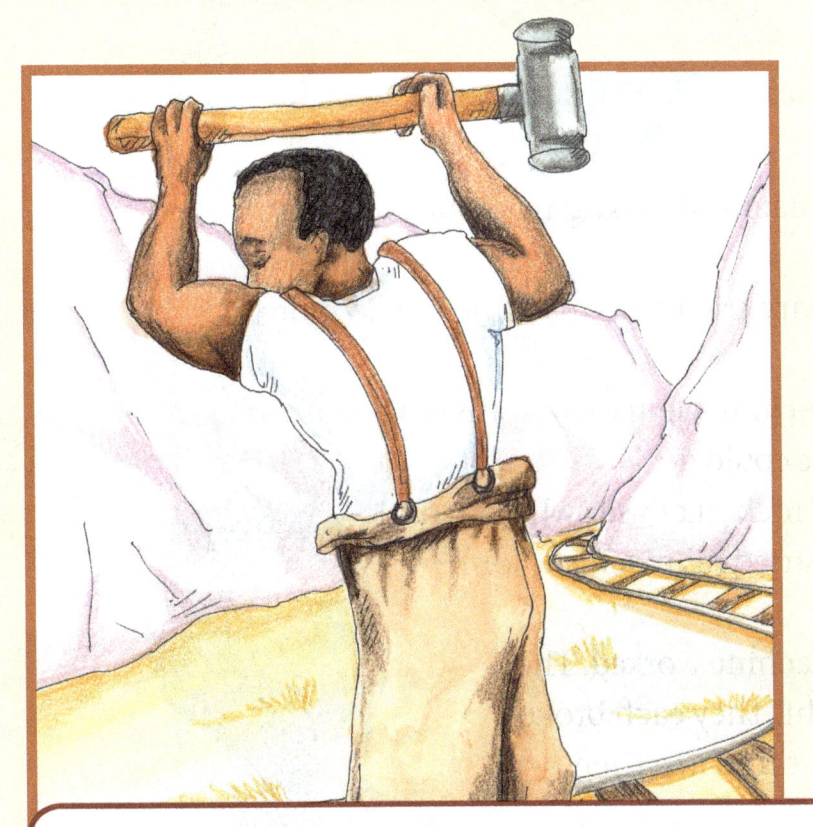

Reading Skill

As you read, use the pictures to help you understand the words and ideas.

Young John Henry loved that big hammer. He liked to **pound** on rocks. Up went the hammer, and then down it came. John Henry could turn big rocks into dust.

When he grew up, John Henry worked for the railroad. He was bigger and stronger than everybody else on the job. All day long, he hammered steel **spikes** into rocks. He broke every rock that was in the way of the railroad.

John Henry was as happy as a man could be. Then a stranger brought a new machine to town.

---

pound   to hit very hard

spikes   pointed metal objects that can be hammered into rocks to break them apart

Before You Go On

What do you think the stranger's machine can do?

READING 3

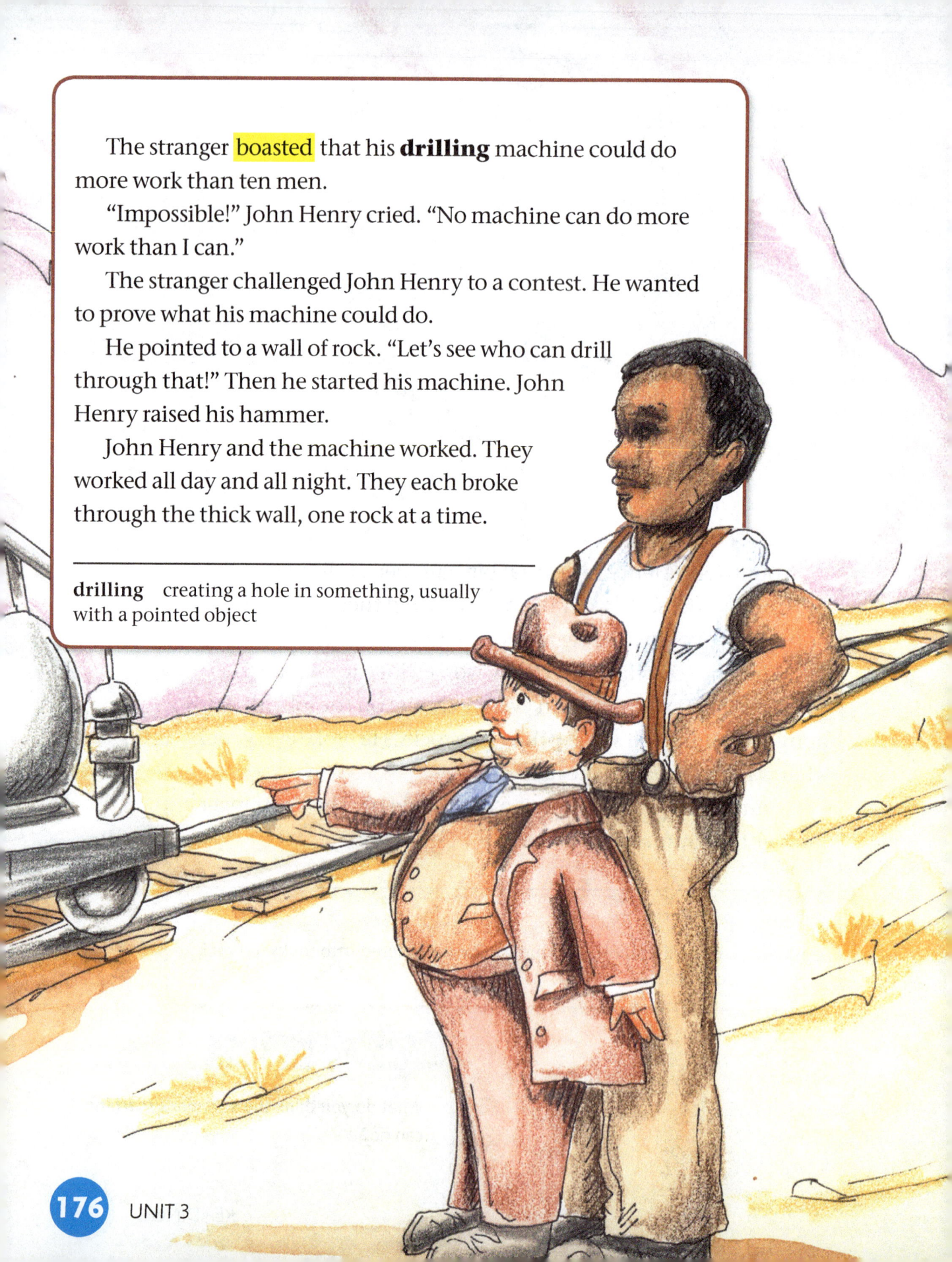

The stranger boasted that his **drilling** machine could do more work than ten men.

"Impossible!" John Henry cried. "No machine can do more work than I can."

The stranger challenged John Henry to a contest. He wanted to prove what his machine could do.

He pointed to a wall of rock. "Let's see who can drill through that!" Then he started his machine. John Henry raised his hammer.

John Henry and the machine worked. They worked all day and all night. They each broke through the thick wall, one rock at a time.

---

drilling creating a hole in something, usually with a pointed object

The next morning, dust and people were everywhere. A crowd had gathered to watch the contest. They came to cheer for John Henry.

By noon, the stranger's machine began to **sputter**. But John Henry was still going strong.

Suddenly, the machine hissed. Then it died. John Henry brought his hammer down for one final blow.

When the dust cleared, everyone saw that John Henry had broken through the rock wall!

"You won the contest!" they cried.

John Henry smiled. "Yes, I did," he said. "Now, I just want to get back to work."

WB 102–104

Reading Strategy

Identify Characters

- Who were the characters in the story?
- Who was the main character? If there was more than one, who were they?
- Who was a minor character? If there was more than one, who were they?

Think It Over

1. **Recall** What was the scenario that led someone to suggest a race?
2. **Analyze** Why did the stranger anticipate that his machine would win?
3. **Comprehend** What feeling in John Henry does the illustration on this page display?

READING 3

A Closer Look at... Tall Tale Characters

▲ Paul Bunyan
Paul Bunyan was a giant lumberjack with some unusual skills. Legend has it that he could cut down an entire forest with one swing of his axe. Stories of Paul Bunyan's adventures almost always include his giant blue ox named Babe.

▲ The Hero of Bremen
Hans was a cobbler, or a shoe repair man. He could move around only by crawling on his knees and knuckles. Bremen, in Germany, the town where Hans lived, was getting very crowded. The people from Bremen wanted to buy more land from a very rich countess. The countess' nephew offered to give the people land for free! He said, I'll give you "all the land that a man can walk around in a day!" But he chose Hans as the walker! Hans crawled on his knees and knuckles across the land that the countess' nephew promised. Roland, Han's favorite knight from the Middle Ages, appeared and helped Hans by stopping time to give Hans more time to cover more land.

▲ Ali, the Honest Man

Ali was a young man from Persia who never told a lie. The king didn't believe this was possible. He tried to trick Ali into lying to the queen. He said, "Ali, I am traveling by horse to see my parents. Please go to the garden and tell the queen." But the king stayed at the castle to trick Ali into a lie. Ali went to the garden and said to the queen, "The king says that he is traveling to see his parents by horse." The king rushed into the garden because he was sure that Ali told a lie. "No," said the queen, "this young man did not lie. He simply told me your exact words."

▲ Sally Ann Thunder

Sally Ann Thunder was the legendary wife of Davy Crockett. She was a fearless woman who scared a grizzly bear out of a cave and tossed an alligator many miles.

Activity to Do

These use pictures and words to tell about famous characters from tall tales.

- Research one of these characters that interests you.
- Create two pages, using pictures and words, to tell about that character.

READING 3

Reading 3

Learning Strategies

Identify Character

Characters are the people or animals in a story or poem. The main characters are the most important ones. The minor characters are less important.

> **Practice**

Make a list of all the characters you can remember from each of these fairy tales. On each list, circle the main character.

1. Cinderella
2. Little Red Riding Hood
3. Goldilocks and the Three Bears
4. Jack and the Beanstalk

Use a Character Web

A Character Web can help you organize information about characters in a story or poem.

Practice
GO 14

Complete this Character Web. Use it to show what you know about John Henry.

- Complete your web with information from the story.
- Share your web with a partner.
- Discuss why it is important to know more about a main character.

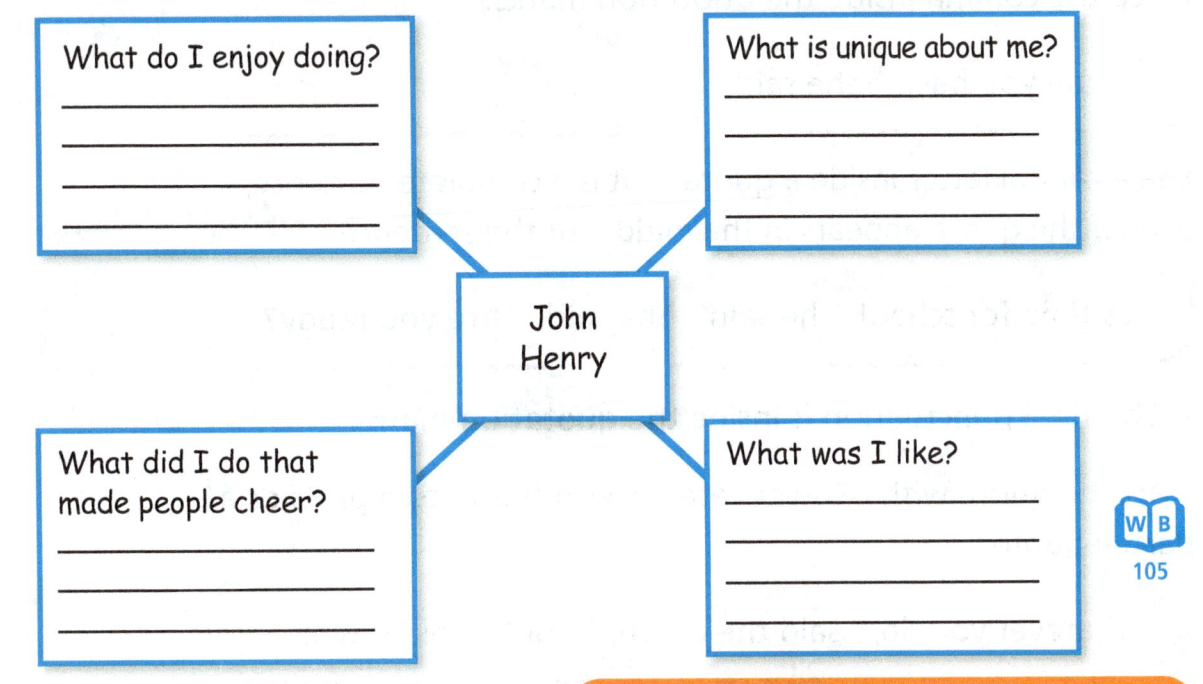

What do I enjoy doing?	What is unique about me?
John Henry	
What did I do that made people cheer?	What was I like?

WB 105

Apply

Retell the story to a partner. You can refer to the pictures as you speak.

Extension

Talk with your partner about another story that has a character who wins a contest. Work together to write and draw a comic strip of the character and the adventure. Share and **display** your comic strip to the class.

READING 3   181

Reading 3

Grammar

Quotations

Quotation marks show the exact words that a person said or wrote. Follow these rules:

Always use quotation marks in pairs (" "). Use an open quotation mark (") at the beginning of quoted material and a close quotation mark (") at the end.

Use a comma if the quote ends in the middle of a sentence. Place the comma inside the quotation marks.

> "I'll call you back," she said.

Use a capital letter inside a quote that is a complete sentence, even if the quote appears in the middle of the sentence.

> "It's time for school," he said.   She said, "Are you ready?"

- The final punctuation is inside the quotation marks.

Start the quote with a lower-case letter if it is in two parts or a partial quote.

> "Whatever you do," said the coach, "don't look down."

Use quotation marks to set off titles of short stories, poems, songs, and articles.

> Have you read the poem "The Raven"?

- Question marks go outside when the title isn't a question.

Practice

Rewrite the sentences using quotation marks. Write the sentences in your notebook.

1. Impossible! John Henry cried.
   "Impossible!" John Henry cried.

2. My drilling machine can do more work than ten men, the stranger **boasted**.

3. The teacher asked, What's the **scenario**?

4. Have you read the short story, The Hidden Treasure?

5. The ant is small but **mighty**, our teacher told us.

6. He said, We don't **anticipate** any trouble.

7. Let's go to a movie, Amelia said, and then we can eat.

Apply

Work with a partner. Ask and answer these questions about "John Henry and the Machine." Write the answers in your notebook. Use quotation marks.

Example: A: What did the stranger say to John Henry while pointing to a wall of rock?

B: The stranger said, "Let's see who can drill through that!"

> **Grammar Check** ✓
> What do quotation marks show?

1. What did John Henry say to the stranger's boast that his machine could work more than ten men?

2. What did the people say after John Henry won?

3. What did John Henry say after he won?

READING 3

Reading 3

Writing

Write a Dialogue between Two Characters

A **dialogue** is a conversation between two people. It tells their exact words. Always use quotation marks to set off what each speaker says.

Writing Prompt

Write a narrative paragraph that includes a dialogue between a character from this unit and his or her make-believe friend. The two characters should talk to each other about the past week. Be sure to use quotation marks correctly.

① Prewrite

Think of a character from this unit. Invent a friend for the character. These two characters will talk to each other about their past week. List the characters' names on the top of a T-chart. Under each name, write a few words or phrases that will be used in the dialogue.

A student named Rob listed his ideas in this T-chart:

John Henry
1. John Henry said he had an unusual week.
2. John Henry explained about the stranger and the machine.
3. John Henry agreed with his friend, Buck.

Buck (John Henry's friend)
1. Buck was very curious.
2. Buck thought the stranger was ridiculous.
3. Buck hoped the stranger learned a lesson.

② Draft

Use your T-chart to help you write a first draft.
- Keep in mind your purpose for writing—to write a dialogue.
- Remember to set off each speaker's exact words in quotation marks.

③ Revise

Read over your draft. Look for places where the dialogue needs improvement. Use the Writing Checklist to help you.

④ Edit

Check your work for errors. Trade papers with a partner to get feedback. Use the Peer Review Checklist on page 402. Edit your final draft in response to feedback from your partner and your teacher.

> **Writing Checklist**
>
> ✓ **Ideas**
> I wrote different dialogue for each character.
> I expressed my ideas clearly.
>
> ✓ **Conventions**
> I used quotation marks correctly.

⑤ Publish

Prepare a clean copy of your final draft. Share your paragraph with the class. Save your work. You will need to refer to it in the Writing Workshop.

Here is Rob's dialogue:

Rob Hudson

A Foolish Stranger

After the big week at work, John Henry had a conversation with his friend, Buck.

"Buck, I had a very unusual week," John Henry said.

This made Buck was very curious. "Unusual?" he said, "What happened exactly?"

John Henry explained, "A stranger came to town with a machine. He said his machine could do more work than me."

"More work than you!" Buck cried, "That's ridiculous."

"It is ridiculous," John Henry agreed, "and I showed him. I won a contest with the machine!"

"I hope that foolish stranger learned a lesson," Buck said.

Put It All Together

Apply and Extend

Link the Readings

Look at the information in the column heads. Put a check (√) if the information is true for the story. Put an X if the information is not true for the story.

	Informational Text	Literature	Animal Characters	People Characters
Why Mosquitoes Buzz in People's Ears				
The Shoemakers and the Elves				
John Henry and the Machine				

Discussion

1. In *Why Mosquitoes Buzz in People's Ears* how do the characters **respond** to each other?

2. How do the shoemakers **react** when they discover the new shoes? What do they do?

3. How do the characters in the first two stories show that they care about each other?

THE BIG QUESTION What do characters in tales have in common?

Listening Skills

If you can't hear someone, you can say, "Could you speak more loudly, please?"

UNIT 3

Projects

Your teacher will help you choose one of these projects.

Written	Oral	Visual/Active
Character Sketch Choose your favorite character from the selections. Describe the character. Tell why the character is your favorite.	**20 Questions** With a partner, play 20 Questions. Choose a character from the unit. Your partner must ask you questions to try to identify the character.	**Book Cover** Make a book cover for one of the selections. Include the title and the main character or characters on your cover.
Mixed-Up Tale Choose one selection. Write your own version of the story. Include a character from one of the other selections.	**Act It Out** Work with a group to perform *The Shoemakers and the Elves* for your classmates. Include props and costumes.	**Character Charades** Play charades with a small group. Act out a character from the unit. Others must guess who your character is.

Put It All Together

Listening and Speaking Workshop
Perform a Play

You are going to write and perform a play. Then you will listen as your classmates perform a play, too.

① Prepare

A. Form a group of four. Choose a short, well-known story or fairy tale.

B. Discuss the story or fairy tale with your group. Plan your play. Include a character for each of you. As you work together, listen to each other's ideas and work cooperatively. Now write your play. Discuss and find props and costumes to use in your play.

Useful Language

🎧 Listen and repeat.

Which story should we choose?

Which character do you want to be?

I'll play the . . .

What props do we need?

We need . . .

The Little Red Hen	
Little Red Hen:	Hello, Duck. Will you help me plant some seeds?
Duck:	No, Hen. I have to go swimming. Ask Dog.
Little Red Hen:	Hello, Dog. Will you help me plant some seeds?
Dog:	Sorry, Hen. I can't. I have to take my nap now. Ask Cat.
Little Red Hen:	Hi, Cat. Will you help me plant some seeds?
Cat:	Oh, no, Hen. Absolutely not. I just cleaned my fur.

② Practice

Practice your play with your props. Perform it in front of your family or friends. Record your play and listen to it. What can you improve? Record it again and try to improve.

3 Present

As you speak, do the following:
- Have fun! Don't be nervous.
- Perform your play—don't read it.
- Pay attention to your group, so you know when to say your lines.

As you listen, do the following:
- Watch the actions of the actors to help you understand.
- Pay close attention. Your teacher will ask you questions after the play.

Speaking Skills
Use informal language in your play. You can speak using simple sentences, conversational words, and even slang.

4 Evaluate

After you speak, answer these questions:
- ✓ Did you perform your play?
- ✓ Did you use props and costumes?

After you listen, answer these questions:
- ✓ Did you understand the play? Summarize it for a partner.
- ✓ Did you watch the actions of the actors?
- ✓ How did the actions help you understand the play?

Listening Skills
Listen carefully for ideas and information that aren't stated directly.

Put It All Together

Writing Workshop
Write a Story

Writing Prompt
Write a group story that explains how or why something in the natural world came to be. Include characters, setting, conflict, and resolution.

① Prewrite

With your group, review the writing you've done in this unit. Then choose a topic. Think about how something in the natural world came to be. What are the setting, characters, conflict, and resolution? List your ideas in a graphic organizer.

A group of students, Alex, Andres, Paula, and Luz, listed their ideas in this chart:

CHARACTERS Beaver, Raccoon	SETTING Time: Long Ago Place: Forest
CONFLICT (STRUGGLE) Beaver and Raccoon want the same branch.	RESOLUTION (SOLUTION) Beaver gets stick so his teeth grow big and strong.

② Draft

Use your graphic organizer to write a draft.

- Keep your purpose in mind—to write a story.
- Include characters, setting, conflict, and resolution.

UNIT 3

3. Revise

Read over your draft. Look for places where the writing needs improvement. Use the Writing Checklist to help you. Then revise your draft.

Here is how the group revised their story:

Six Traits of Writing Checklist

✓ **Ideas**
Did we describe how something developed?

✓ **Organization**
Did the resolution follow the conflict?

✓ **Voice**
Does our tone suit our audience?

✓ **Word Choice**
Did we choose interesting details?

✓ **Sentence Fluency**
Did we vary our sentences?

✓ **Conventions**
Did we use quotation marks correctly?

Group: Alex, Andres, Paula, Luz

How the Beaver Got Strong, Long Teeth

Long, long ago, a beaver had an idea.

"By building a dam across the stream, I can create a pond for my home. But I will need logs and branches," he thought.

Revised to correct error in mechanics.

He used his short, weak teeth to try to cut down a tree. After an hour of hard work, he managed to cut down one branch from the tree. "This is harder than I thought," he ~~thought~~. said to himself.

Revised to use a variety of language.

Just then a raccoon sniffed at the branch. She tried to pull it away. "Find you*r* own branch," the beaver shouted.

Revised to correct spelling.

For two days the raccoon and the beaver tugged and tugged, until they fell asleep with the branch still in their mouths.

When the beaver woke up, the raccoon was gone. Picking up the branch, he realized ~~her~~ *his* teeth were very long and strong.

Revised to correct agreement of pronoun and possessive.

From that day on beavers have used their long, strong teeth to cut down trees.

Put It All Together

④ Edit
Check your work for errors. Trade papers with another group. Use the Peer Review Checklist to give each other feedback.

⑤ Publish
Prepare a clean copy of your final draft. Share your story with the class.

WB 111–112

Peer Review Checklist
- ✓ The story explains a natural event.
- ✓ There are characters, a setting, a conflict, and a resolution.
- ✓ The writing is fun and interesting.

Spelling Tip
Add *-er* to a word to mean *more* and *-est* to mean *most*.
low – lower – lowest
When a word ends in a silent *e*, add *-r* or *-st*.
wide – wider – widest

Put It All Together

Fluency 🎧

Listen to the sentences. Pay attention to the groups of words. Read aloud.

1. Mosquito's gossip causes mischief among the animals, so the lion never lets him talk again.
2. Two elves make shoes in secret to help an elderly couple.
3. Soon after the machine stopped, John Henry broke through the wall.

Work in pairs. Take turns reading aloud for one minute. Count the number of words you read.

One night, two elves are looking into the window of a	11
house where a shoemaker and his wife are inside. The elves	22
are tired and cold. They listen to the shoemakers talk	32
about their worries. The shoemakers have no leather for	41
shoes. They're afraid they'll have to close their shop.	50
The elves decide to sneak into the shop at midnight	60
and make lots of shoes in order to help the shoemakers.	71
Night after night, the elves continue to make shoes. The	81
shoemakers are speechless. They wonder who is helping them.	90
When they find out the truth, they leave clothes and food	101
for the elves. In the end, the shoemakers and the elves are	113
all happy.	115

With your partner, find the words that slowed you down.

- Practice saying each word and then say the sentence each word is in.
- Then take turns reading the text again. Count the number of words you read.

Test Preparation

Taking Tests

You will often take tests that help show what you know. Follow these tips to improve your test-taking skills.

> ### Coaching Corner
>
> **Answering Multiple-Choice Test Questions**
>
> - Many test items will ask you to read a selection and then answer questions about it.
>
> - The selections can be fiction or nonfiction. They can be long or short.
>
> - Before you read the selection, preview the questions and answer choices.
>
> - After reading the selection, first try to answer the question in your head.
>
> - Look for the answer choice that matches the answer in your head.
>
> - Check to make sure the answer you chose is supported by the text.

Practice

Read the selection. Then answer the questions.

1   Once upon a time, Dog and Cat lived together. Dog said, "We need to share the work. I'll go find food, if you will take care of the house." Cat agreed, and Dog went to find food.

2   Cat jumped up to the window, where the warm sunshine poured in. "I think I'll take a little nap before I work."

3   Day after day, it was the same. Cat slept while Dog worked. Every day, Dog came home and said, "What did you do all day, Cat? The house is a mess!" Cat just yawned.

4   Then Dog got an idea. One day she told Cat she was going to work, but she hid under the sink instead. She watched Cat sleep all day. When Cat went to the sink to get a drink of water, Dog jumped out. "Yikes!" Cat screeched. Dog was furious and chased Cat around the room. That's how dogs started to chase cats.

1 What is Cat like?

   A Hungry

   B Lazy

   C Busy

   D Angry

2 Where did Dog hide?

   F Under the sink

   G At work

   H Behind the house

   J Under the bed

3 Why did Dog chase Cat?

   A Cat ate all the food.

   B Cat did not keep her promise.

   C Cat hurt Dog's feelings.

   D Cat screeched at Dog.

Tips

✓ Read the questions and answer choices before you read the selection.

✓ Eliminate choices that don't make sense.

Unit 4
Problem Solvers

You will read about how people—and animals—work to solve problems, from out-of-control plants to people who solve problems with technology.

Reading 1
Photo Essay

The Trouble with Kudzu

Reading 2
Fables

The Fox and the Crow
The Fox and the Goat

Reading 3
Social Studies

Creative Problem Solving

THE BiG QUESTION

How do we solve problems?

Listening and Speaking

You will talk about problems and solutions. In the Listening and Speaking Workshop, you will give a speech.

Writing

You will practice persuasive writing. In the Writing Workshop, you will write a review.

Quick Write

What are some problems in your town? Write about one of them.

View and Respond

Talk about the poster for this unit. Then watch and listen to the video and answer the questions at Pearson English Portal.

Build Unit Vocabulary

What do you know about problem solvers?

Words to Know 🎧

Listen and repeat. Use these words to talk about solving problems.

brainstorm

research

debate

investigate

design

Practice

Work with a partner. Look up these words in a dictionary. Then ask and answer questions using these words and the words above.

| doctor | student | lawyer | scientist |

Example: A: How can a <u>scientist</u> solve problems?

B: A <u>scientist</u> can do <u>research</u> to solve problems.

Write

Read the question. Write your response in your notebook.

What are some things you do to solve problems?

Make Connections

Complete the sentences with the following words and phrases.

politicians

a detective

an architect

inventors

1. _____ often debate concerns or problems in their communities.

2. _____ designs buildings. He or she often has to solve problems in creative ways.

3. _____ brainstorm new ideas together. They think of new things to invent and help each other solve problems that come up.

4. _____ has to investigate in order to solve crimes or mysteries.

What about you?

Talk about problems you have solved. How did you solve them?

Build Unit Background

Kids' Stories from around the World 🎧

Arnoud

I live in Canada. My school has a new program. It teaches students to solve problems without fighting. I learn special skills, such as how to listen to others. I also learn to say what I feel without getting angry.

Marta

My school is in Texas, U.S.A. Every year we have a science fair. This year, I studied what happens if you don't get enough vitamins. Then I showed people my research. This year I won an award.

Suna

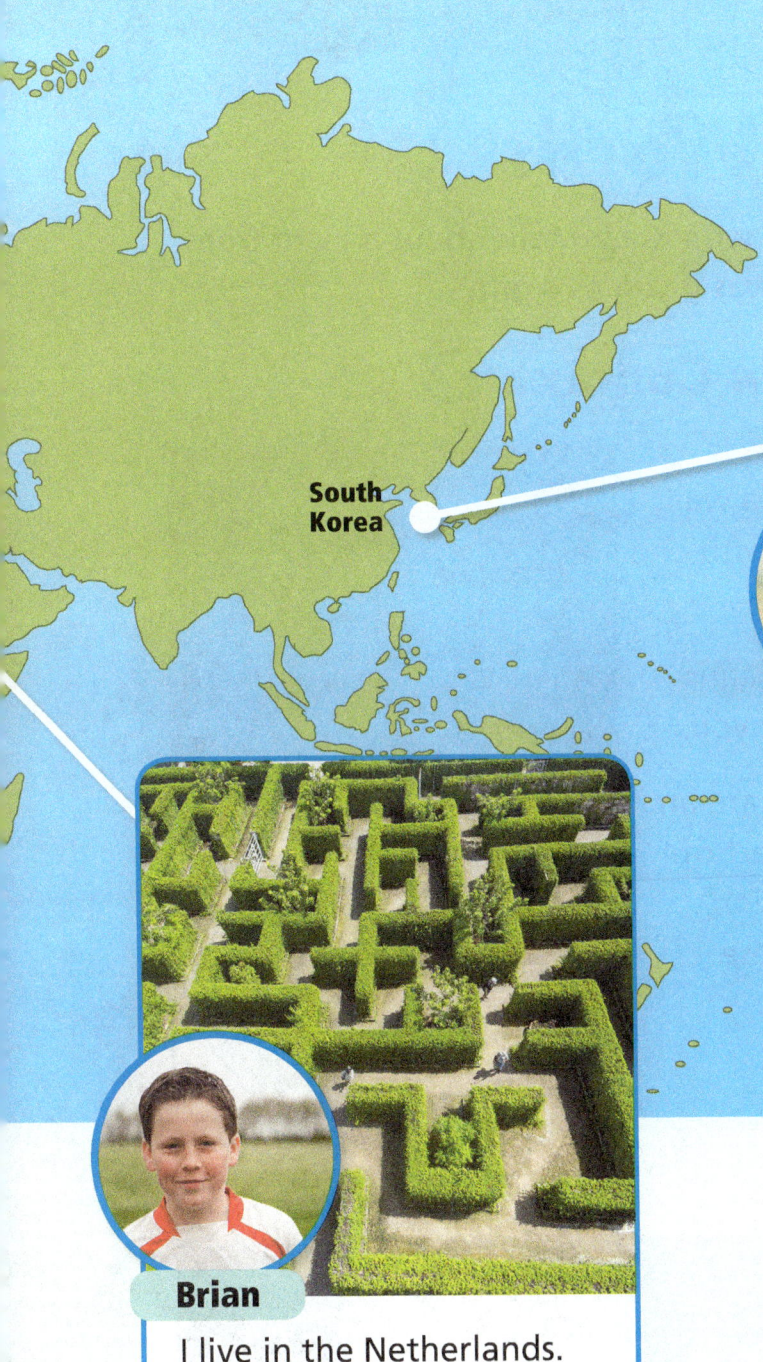

In South Korea people love to play Go. It is an old Chinese board game. You try to circle the other player's stones with your own. It's not easy, but it's fun!

Brian

I live in the Netherlands. Some of our parks have mazes made of hedges. There is only one correct path through the maze. I enter at one end and exit at the other. It's fun to get lost in a maze.

What about you?

1. Think of a problem you had. Did you solve it? How did solving the problem make you feel?
2. Do you know of a problem in your community that was solved? Share your story with the class.

UNIT 4

Reading 1
Prepare to Read

Key Words

The Trouble with Kudzu tells about a plant from Japan that was given as a gift.

Words in Context 🎧

1 The **vine** is climbing up a wall. It is a plant with long stems.

2 Green **beans** are good for you.

3 Parades are an important part of the **celebration** for the Chinese New Year.

What You Will Learn

Reading
- Vocabulary building: Context, phonics
- Reading strategy: Identify main idea and details
- Text type: Informational text (photo essay)

Grammar
Comparative adjectives

Writing
Write a persuasive business letter

These words will help you understand the reading.

Key Words
vine
bean
celebration
gardener
roots

202   UNIT 4

4 The <mark>gardener</mark> plants vegetables and flowers in her backyard.

5 The <mark>roots</mark> are underground and support the tree. They also help the tree get water from underground.

Practice

Make flashcards to help you memorize the words.
- Write a key word on the front.
- On the back, make a drawing of each word.

Make Connections

What do you know about plants and trees? Have you ever planted a seed? Write your response in your notebook using some key words. Then discuss what you know with a partner.

Speaking Skills

When you don't know the right word to use, explain or describe the idea using words you know.

READING 1

Reading 1

These words will help you talk about the reading.

Academic Words

affect
have an influence on

eliminate
remove or get rid of

outcome
final result

Academic Words

Words in Context 🎧

The new classroom rules **affect** all the students.

Having a good plan at the beginning of a project will **eliminate** problems later.

Everyone wanted to know the **outcome** of Ari's science experiment.

Practice

Choose an academic word to complete each sentence.

1. I have to _____ peanut butter from my diet because I am allergic to peanuts.

2. One way to achieve the best _____ on a test is to study very hard.

3. You can _____ how people treat you by being kind and polite.

Apply

Ask and answer with a partner.

1. What good and bad study habits **affect** your grades at school?

2. What can you do to **eliminate** low grades?

3. Think of a project or competition you joined. What was the **outcome**?

Phonics
Soft and Hard c 🎧

Listen to your teacher read each word in the box. Then read each word aloud. Notice the difference between soft c and hard c.

Soft c	Hard c
celebrate	**ca**ke
de**ci**de	dis**cu**ss
fan**cy**	**co**untry

When does c have the same sound as the *s* in **sun**?
When does c have the same sound as the *k* in **kite**?

Rule

The letter c usually has the soft sound when it is followed by *e*, *i*, or *y*. Otherwise, c usually has the hard sound.

Practice

Use a word from the chart to match each clue.

1. It's what you do when you choose something. (soft c)

2. It's another word for *nation*. (hard c)

3. It's a sweet food you eat on your birthday. (hard c)

4. It's what you do for a special time. (soft c)

5. It's another word for *talk*. (hard c)

Reading 1

Informational Text
Photo Essay

More About THE BIG QUESTION

How can an unwanted plant cause problems?

🎧 **Listen to the Audio.**
Listen for the main points and important details.

Reading Strategy

Identify Main Idea and Details

The main idea is the most important idea in the selection. The details give you information about the main idea. As you read ask yourself:

- What is the most important, or main, idea?
- What details help support the main idea?

Listen as your teacher models the reading strategy.

The Trouble with Kudzu

by Laura Sewell

Big, beautiful leaves and sweet-smelling purple flowers made kudzu popular.

206 UNIT 4

This old truck is not going anywhere!

Do you know the story of Jack and the Beanstalk? Jack planted a magic bean. A vine grew from the bean. It grew and grew. Finally, the vine was so high and strong that Jack could climb up it and reach the clouds.

Well, kudzu doesn't come from a magic bean, but it is a member of the bean family. When people saw kudzu for the first time, they must have thought it was magic. Why? Because kudzu grows very fast—much faster than most other plants. In fact, it can grow up to 12 inches in only one day!

Before You Go On

After Jack planted the magic bean, what was the outcome?

Kudzu is a native plant of China and Japan. That means it grew naturally in those countries. Kudzu was brought to the United States from Japan in 1876 as a gift for a special celebration. The United States was celebrating its first 100 years as a **nation**.

Soon, every gardener and farmer wanted to plant kudzu seeds. Gardeners grew kudzu because it looked pretty and smelled good. Farmers grew it to feed their animals.

At first, kudzu was a big success! But it did not stop growing. It **blocked** sunlight that other plants needed. It killed trees and whole forests. Nothing was safe!

---

nation country
blocked stopped

Where have the trees gone? They are all covered with kudzu!

It takes only two or three years for kudzu to cover a house.

Artists use kudzu to make and sell items.

Now, people call kudzu a weed. It is a wild plant that grows where it is not wanted. People cut it down and dig up its **roots**. But **getting rid of** kudzu is not easy.

Over the years, people have learned to use every part of the kudzu plant. Cooks and artists use it to make jelly, paper, clothes, baskets, and chairs. This weed might be useful after all.

---

getting rid of   removing completely

Reading Strategy
Identify Main Idea and Details

- What was the main idea?
- What were some details?
- How did thinking about the main idea help you understand the selection?

Think It Over

1. **Recall** What are some ways that the kudzu plant is used today?
2. **Comprehend** How did kudzu affect the forests? Explain.
3. **Analyze** Why is it difficult to eliminate kudzu?

READING 1   209

Reading 1

Learning Strategies

Main Idea and Details

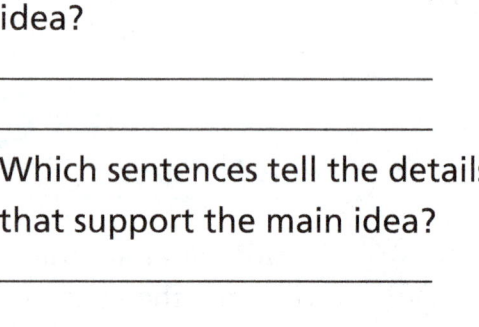

Identifying the **main idea and details** can help you understand what you read. Ask yourself, "What was the reading about?" Your answer is the main idea of the selection.

Practice

Read these sentences.

- Kudzu killed trees and whole forests.
- Kudzu is a wild plant that grows where it is not wanted.
- Gardeners grew kudzu because it looked pretty.
- Artists make baskets with kudzu.
- Kudzu blocked sunlight that other plants and trees needed.

1. Which sentence tells the main idea?
   _____
   _____

2. Which sentences tell the details that support the main idea?
   _____
   _____

Use a Main Idea and Details Chart

This chart can help you figure out the main idea of the selection. You can show the details that support the main idea.

Practice

Fill in the main idea and details.

- Reread the selection. What is the main idea of *The Trouble with Kudzu*?
- Choose three of the most important details that support the main idea.

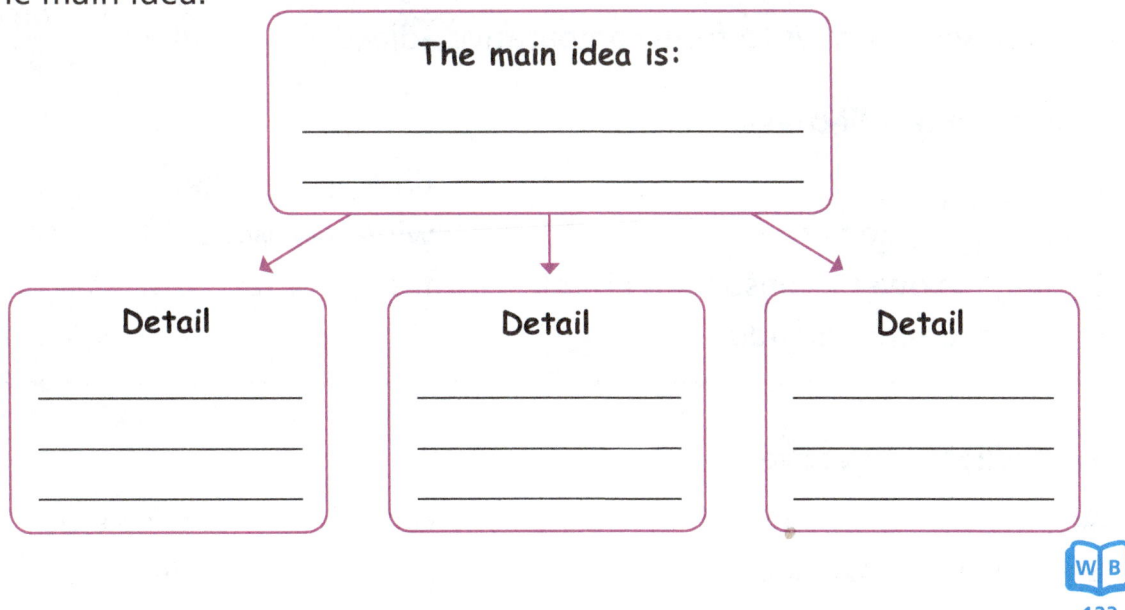

The main idea is:
_____

Detail	Detail	Detail
___	___	___

Apply

Using the photographs, retell the selection to a partner.

Extension

Research and find out how to plant a seed. Write the steps. Explain them to a partner. Ask your partner to follow the steps to show that he or she understands. Then switch roles and follow your partner's directions.

Reading 1

Grammar

Comparative Adjectives

Use the comparative form of an adjective to compare or talk about the difference between two nouns. A comparative adjective is usually followed by *than*.

> The red car is **fast**.   The red car is **faster than** the blue car.
> A lion is **beautiful**.   A cheetah is **more beautiful than** a lion.

There are several ways to form comparative adjectives:

One-syllable adjectives

Add *-er*	dark → dark**er**
Ending in *-e*, add *-r*	wide → wide**r**
Ending in vowel + consonant, double the consonant and add *-er*	fat → fa**tter**

Two-syllable adjectives

Add *more*	careful → **more** careful
Ending in *-le*, *-ow*, add *-(e)r*	gent**le** → gentle**r**
Ending in *-y*, change *-y* to *-i* and add *-er*	happy → happ**ier**

Three- or more syllable adjectives

Add *more*	likable → **more** likable

Irregular comparatives

good → **better**   far → **farther**   bad → **worse**   fun → **more** fun

Practice A

Complete the sentences with the comparative form + *than*.

1. Kudzu grows __faster than__ other plants. (fast)

2. It is _____ to eliminate kudzu _____ other weeds. (difficult)

3. The year's celebration is _____ last year's. (big)

4. My mom is _____ this week _____ last week. (busy)

5. Today is _____ yesterday! (bad)

Practice B

Write sentences comparing these:

1. baseball and basketball (exciting)
   Baseball is more exciting than basketball.

2. watching a sports game and playing a sports game (fun)

3. Restaurant A and Restaurant B (bad)

> **Grammar Check ✔**
> What are two ways to form a comparative?

Apply

Work with a partner. Choose a topic from the box. Think of two things for that topic to compare. Tell your partner which one is better or worse.

Example: A: Cats are more interesting than dogs.
B: Oh, really? I think dogs are more interesting.

animals   sports   foods   school subjects

READING 1

Reading 1

Writing

Write a Persuasive Business Letter

In a persuasive business letter a writer tries to persuade someone to think or act in a certain way. Always include facts to support your ideas. Be sure to include all the parts of a business letter.

Writing Prompt

Write a persuasive business letter to someone in your community. Try to persuade that person to help solve a community problem. Be sure to use comparatives correctly.

① Prewrite

Choose someone to write to about a community problem. Find the person's address. List your ideas in a graphic organizer.

A student named Tony listed his ideas like this:

```
Date
Address of recipient
Greeting
Body
    • Ask Ms. Hughes to donate art supplies.
    • Include facts to support my ideas.
    • End letter by thanking Ms. Hughes.
Closing
Signature
```

② Draft

Use your graphic organizer to help you write a first draft.
- Keep in mind your purpose for writing—to persuade.
- Include only the most important information.

③ Revise

Read over your draft. Look for places where the writing needs improvement. Use the Writing Checklist to help you revise your draft.

④ Edit

Check your work for errors. Use the Peer Review Checklist on page 402.

⑤ Publish

Prepare a clean copy of your final draft. Share your paragraph with the class.

> **Writing Checklist**
>
> ✓ **Ideas**
> I included persuasive facts.
>
> ✓ **Organize**
> I included all the parts of a business letter.
>
> ✓ **Conventions**
> I used comparatives correctly.

Here is Tony's business letter:

March 26, 2019

Ms. Kim Hughes
Hughes Arts Supply Store
Toronto, Ontario M1B 5K7

Dear Ms. Hughes,
We have a favor to ask you. The students at Webster School love their art classes. Art is fun! Also, art skills are more important today than ever before.

The problem is we need art supplies. Can you donate any supplies to our school? We would be very happy and thankful. Thank you for your help.

Sincerely,
Tony Liu

Reading 2
Prepare to Read

Key Words

These fables are about a tricky fox.

Words in Context

1 My sister tried to **flatter** my brother to get him to help her with her chores.

You're the best brother in the world!

2 My father gave me **praise** for the quality of my work. I received an A in math class.

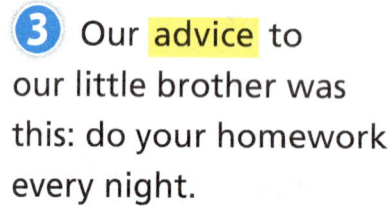

3 Our **advice** to our little brother was this: do your homework every night.

What You Will Learn

Reading
- Vocabulary building: *Context, word study*
- Reading strategy: *Compare and contrast*
- Text type: *Literature (fables)*

Grammar
Superlatives

Writing
Write an advertisement

These words will help you understand the reading.

Key Words

flatter
praise
advice
guzzled
scampered

④ After playing outside, the thirsty horse eagerly **guzzled** water from the river.

⑤ The squirrel ran past us and quickly **scampered** up into the tree as we walked by.

Practice

Add a page to your vocabulary notebook.
- Divide your page into three columns: the new words, their definitions, and drawings of the words when possible.
- Test yourself by covering one of the columns.

Make Connections

Have you ever been tricked? What happened? How might you have stopped it from happening? Explain.

Reading 2

These words will help you talk about the reading.

Academic Words

evaluate
judge how good something is

resourceful
good at finding ways to deal with problems effectively

scheme
tricky plan

Academic Words

Words in Context 🎧

The doctor will **evaluate** your health during the examination.

We have to be creative and **resourceful** to get a good grade on our project.

The thief had a clever **scheme** to steal money from the company.

Practice

Choose an academic word to complete each sentence.

1. The pirates thought of a good _____ to steal the treasure.

2. If the teachers _____ your work and like what they see, you will get good grades.

3. Carlos showed how _____ he was by getting his whole family to help him with his homework.

Apply

Ask and answer with a partner.

1. How do teachers **evaluate** your work?

2. Who do you know that's very **resourceful**?

3. Why does a villain's **scheme** make a story interesting?

Word Study

Thesaurus

A **dictionary** tells the meaning of a word. A **thesaurus** lists synonyms, or words with similar meanings, for a word.

Read this sentence.

> The fox escaped from the trap because he was very **smart**.

If you wanted to know the meaning of the word *smart*, you would look up the word in a dictionary. If you wanted to find a synonym for *smart*, a thesaurus would help you choose the best word. *Clever* is a synonym for the word *smart* and would be a good fit in this sentence.

Practice

Work with a partner.

- Read the sentence and the thesaurus entry that follows.
- Circle the synonym that could go in that sentence.

> "This is **bad** news," said the unlucky goat.

  bad *adj.* **1.** terrible. **2.** wrong. **3.** harmful. **4.** sick.

Reading 2

Literature
Fables

More About THE BIG QUESTION

Why do some characters use tricks to solve their problems?

🎧 **Listen to the Audio.**
Listen for the main points and important details.

Reading Strategy
Compare and Contrast

When you compare you see how things are similar. When you contrast you see how things are different. As you read the two stories think about how they are alike and different.

- Who are the characters in each story?
- How does Fox act in each story?
- What is the lesson each story teaches?

Listen as your teacher models the reading strategy.

The Fox and the Crow

an Aesop's fable retold by Lee Martin

One sunny, fall day, Mr. Fox went walking through the forest. "This would be a perfect afternoon," he said to himself, "except for my empty tummy." Echoing his thoughts, his stomach rumbled loudly.

Just then, Mr. Fox heard wings flapping overhead and he looked up to see a crow with a large piece of cheese in its beak. The crow landed in a tree nearby and Mr. Fox thought to himself, *That cheese looks very tasty. I must find a way to get it.* Being a clever fellow, he soon came up with an idea.

"Hello, Ms. Crow. Your feathers look especially **glossy** today and your eyes are as bright as glass beads."

---

glossy   shiny

As Ms. Crow **cocked** her head, Mr. Fox knew he had her attention. He continued, "Your voice must be even more beautiful than the lovely picture you make sitting in that tree. I am sure if I could hear you sing, I would call you the Queen of All Birds!"

Pleased with Mr. Fox's praise, Ms. Crow took a deep breath and opened her beak to **caw**. Out fell the cheese, straight to the ground. Mr. Fox snapped it up.

"Yum! That is just what I needed, Ms. Crow. Let me offer you some advice: Do not trust someone whose words are meant only to flatter."

---

cocked   tilted

caw   make a sharp, scratchy call, from a crow

Before You Go On

What was Mr. Fox's scheme for getting Ms. Crow to drop her cheese?

The Fox and the Goat

an Aesop's fable retold by Lee Martin

Mr. Fox fell into a **well** one day and could not find a way to get out. But just as he was about to give up hope, Mr. Goat looked over the edge of the well.

"Oh, I am so thirsty, Fox," he said. "Is the water good? And by the way, what are you doing in the well?"

Right away, Mr. Fox saw his chance to escape, so he said, "I am enjoying the water, of course! You should jump in and have a drink."

Without thinking, Mr. Goat jumped right into the well and guzzled the water noisily. After he had finished drinking, he looked at the smooth, steep walls of the well. "How will we get out of here?" he asked.

---

well   a deep hole that contains water and is often lined with stones

"Ahh," said Mr. Fox, "that is the problem, but I think I have an idea. If you put your front hooves on the wall, I will run up your back and out of the well. Then I will return to help you."

Mr. Goat did as Mr. Fox asked, and Mr. Fox <mark>scampered</mark> up his back and away as quickly as he could. He called back over his shoulder, "Goat, next time, you should look before you **leap**!"

---

leap   jump

Reading Strategy
Compare and Contrast

- Who are the characters in each story?
- How does Fox act in each story?
- **Evaluate** the lessons each story teaches. How are they similar? How are they different?

Think It Over

1. **Recall** Who did Mr. Fox fool in each story?
2. **Comprehend** How was Mr. Fox resourceful in solving his problems?
3. **Analyze** Why was Mr. Fox successful in tricking others?

Reading 2

Learning Strategies

Compare and Contrast

To understand what you read, compare and contrast ideas.

- When you **compare**, you tell how two or more things are alike.
- When you **contrast**, you tell how two or more things are different.

Practice

Compare and contrast the items listed. Tell two ways they are alike. Then tell two ways they are different.

1. a fishbowl and a swimming pool
2. a duck and a swan
3. a football and a basketball

Use a T-Chart

You can use a T-Chart to compare and contrast events, characters, or objects in a story or a non-fiction selection.

Practice

Compare and contrast the stories.

1. Write about how *The Fox and the Crow* and *The Fox and the Goat* are the same. Use the pictures and the words in the selections.
2. Then write about how they are different.
3. Compare your completed T-Chart with a partner's.

How Are They Alike?	How Are They Different?

Apply

Reread the story and take notes. Then close your book and retell the story to a partner. Use the key words as you speak.

Extension

Think about amusement park rides. Compare and contrast two rides. You can write descriptions, draw them, or act them out. Show your class how they are alike and how they are different.

READING 2

Reading 2

Grammar

Superlatives

Use the superlative form of adjectives to show that something or someone is at the top of a group. Use **the** before a superlative adjective. Study these rules for forming superlatives.

One-syllable adjectives

Add -*est*	smart → **the** smart**est**
Ending in -*e*, add -*st*	nice → **the** nice**st**
Ending in vowel + consonant, double the consonant and add -*est*	fit → **the** fit**test**

Two-syllable adjectives

Add *most*	pleasant → **the most** pleasant
Ending in -*le*, -*ow*, add -(*e*)*st*	simple → **the** simple**st**
Ending in -*y*, change -*y* to -*i*, add -*est*	shiny → **the** shin**iest**

Three or more syllable adjectives

Add *most*	exciting → **the most** exciting

Irregular comparatives and superlatives

good → better → **the best**   bad → worse → **the worst**

The superlative adjective is often used with expressions that begin with *in* or *of* such as *in the world*, *of all*.

A crow is **the smartest** bird **of all**. It may be **the most resourceful** animal **in the world**.

226   UNIT 4

Practice A

Work with a partner. Take turns giving the superlative form of these adjectives.

1. loud *the loudest*
2. intelligent
3. good
4. heavy
5. tall
6. kind

Practice B

Change each adjective to a superlative.

1. Ms. Crow's feathers were _____*the shiniest*_____ (shiny) of all.

2. The desert is _____ (hot) place on Earth.

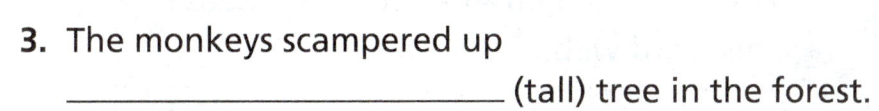

3. The monkeys scampered up _____ (tall) tree in the forest.

4. Her new scheme is _____ (dangerous) of all.

5. What was _____ (bad) trick Mr. Fox played?

Apply

Work with a partner. Read the sentences below and make statements. Use superlative adjectives.

Example: Juan is the tallest.

- Juan is taller than Rob. Rob is shorter than Paul.
- Stella is wise. Maria is wiser than Stella.
- The forest is a more peaceful place than the beach. It is a more peaceful place than the mountains.

Grammar Check ✔

When do we use superlative adjectives?

READING 2

Reading 2

Writing

Write an Advertisement

Advertisements persuade people to buy products. Short sentences include important details and facts that will appeal to buyers. These details describe the most important features of the product.

Writing Prompt

Write an advertisement about a real or imaginary product you can use in your home or school. Include important details and facts to persuade people to buy the products. Be sure to use superlatives correctly.

① Prewrite GO 13

Choose a product to write about. Think about the words you will use to describe the most important features of this product. List your ideas in a word web.

A student named Ana listed her ideas in this word web:

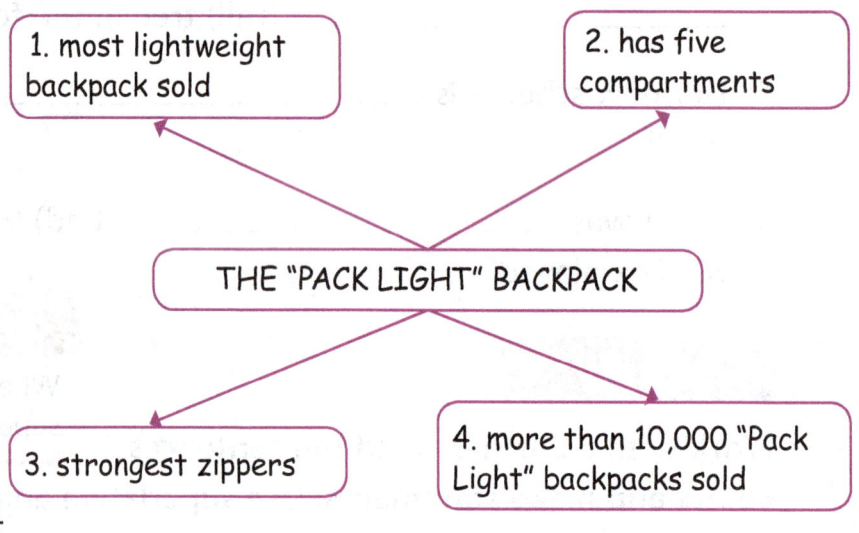

- THE "PACK LIGHT" BACKPACK
  1. most lightweight backpack sold
  2. has five compartments
  3. strongest zippers
  4. more than 10,000 "Pack Light" backpacks sold

② Draft

Use your word web to help you write a first draft.

- Keep in mind your purpose for writing—to create an interesting ad.
- Include details that describe the features of the product.

228 UNIT 4

3 Revise

Read over your draft. Look for places where the sentences are too long or the details are not interesting. Use the Writing Checklist to help you identify problems. Then revise your draft.

4 Edit

Check your work for errors. Trade papers with a partner to get feedback. Use the Peer Review Checklist on page 402. Edit your final draft in response to feedback from your partner and your teacher.

5 Publish

Prepare a clean copy of your final draft. Share your paragraph with the class. Save your work.

Here is Ana's ad for a backpack:

> **Writing Checklist**
>
> ✓ **Ideas**
> I included interesting details to appeal to buyers.
> I wrote short sentences to clearly explain my ideas.
>
> ✓ **Conventions**
> I used superlatives correctly.

Ana Yang

The "Pack Light" is today's newest backpack!
- It's the most lightweight backpack sold!
- It has five different compartments!
- It's easy to pack and unpack!
- Its zippers are the strongest!
- More than 10,000 "Pack Lights" sold!

Carrying a "Pack Light" makes a difference. Be the coolest kid in class. Buy one today.

Reading 3
Prepare to Read

What You Will Learn

Reading
- Vocabulary building: *Context, phonics*
- Reading strategy: *Identify cause and effect*
- Text type: *Informational text (social studies)*

Grammar
Adverbs of frequency and intensity

Writing
Write a persuasive brochure

These words will help you understand the reading.

Key Words

solve
communities
purpose
concerned
waste

Key Words

Creative Problem Solving is about solving problems in new and interesting ways.

Words in Context

1 Brainstorming is a good way to try and **solve** problems.

2 Many **communities** have lots of businesses and services, such as shopping centers and restaurants.

3 The **purpose** of the food drive was to fill the food pantry shelves and help feed hungry people.

230 UNIT 4

4 My mother was **concerned** about my brother when he was sick and had a fever.

5 It's important not to **waste** food. Some people don't have enough to eat.

Practice

Make flashcards for the words.
- Write a key word on the front.
- On the back, write a sentence, but leave a blank where the key word should be.
- Use the cards to quiz yourself.

Make Connections

Can you think of a problem that you solved? What was the problem and how did you solve it? How did you think of the solution? Write your answers in your notebook.

Reading 3

These words will help you talk about the reading.

Academic Words

creative
new and interesting

restore
repair something to make it seem new again

objective
goal

Academic Words

Words in Context

She always has very **creative** and different ideas.

The watchmakers fix and **restore** old, broken watches.

The cook's **objective** was to create a healthy and tasty meal.

Practice

Choose an academic word to complete each sentence.

1. Sue's _____ was to win the race.

2. The students found some _____ solutions to stopping food waste in the school cafeteria.

3. We couldn't _____ the old boat; it had too many holes in it.

Apply

Ask and answer with a partner.

1. Why is it a good idea to write your **objective** before starting a task?

2. Do you own something old that you want to **restore**?

3. Tell about the last time you did something **creative**. What was it?

232 UNIT 4

Phonics

Digraph: ow 🎧

Sometimes the letters *ow* make one sound. Listen. Sound out the words in the box.

Words with digraph *ow*	
gr**ow**	c**ow**
own	d**ow**n
yell**ow**	t**ow**er

What two vowel sounds do the letters *ow* have? Say the words in the box aloud.

Rule

The letters *ow* can have the long *o* sound you hear in **grow** or the vowel sound you hear in **how**. Some words, such as **bow**, have two meanings and can be pronounced either way.

Practice

Read the sentences with a partner. Look for words with *ow*.

Before you can solve a problem, you have to know what it is.
How did you think of that solution?
Their objective is to grow new forests.
Now communities are trying to solve problems creatively.

1. Circle the words in which *ow* has the long *o* sound heard in **show**.
2. Underline the words in which *ow* has the *o* sound heard in **cow**.

WB 139

READING 3   233

Reading 3

Informational Text
Social Studies

More About THE BIG QUESTION

What problems can we solve by using technology?

🎧 **Listen to the Audio.**
Listen for the main points and important details.

Reading Strategy
Identify Cause and Effect

What makes an event happen is a cause. The result of a cause is an effect.

- Think about what caused the three problems in the text.
- Identify some effects of the problems.

Listen as your teacher models the reading strategy.

Creative Problem Solving

We all know that problems are a part of life. What's interesting is how we deal with problems. Today we'll look at three problems and three companies trying to solve them.

Deforestation, the removal of forests, is a problem all over the world. And deforestation has effects. Plant and animal species lose their habitats. The air becomes more polluted. If we don't **restore** the forests, there will be more **climate change**.

---

climate change — the warming of the Earth's climate

People plant new trees to restore the forest.

234 UNIT 4

One company working to counter deforestation is *Tree Planet*, a company in South Korea. They developed a **mobile** game about trees. Their objective is to plant trees in the real world. Players plant trees online and then *Tree Planet* plants trees in the ground. They have planted hundreds of thousands of trees in many different countries.

Another problem that requires creative problem solving is lack of access to electricity in some places. Electricity powers many things that help us. Think about refrigerators, washing machines, and lights. But some communities don't always have electricity. Life can be very difficult with no electricity.

Maya Pedal is a business in Guatemala. They **recycle** old bicycles into power machines. People **pedal** the bicycles to power everything from a water pump to a kitchen blender! *Maya Pedal* is nonprofit. Their purpose is not to make money. They are concerned with helping people.

---

mobile relating to mobile phones
recycle to use something again for a new purpose
pedal to push on bike pedals to make the wheels move

Maya Pedal recycles bicycles that people can use to power machines.

Before You Go On

How might people creatively solve the problem of food waste?

READING 3 **235**

Zéro-Gâchis has stands in many supermarkets in France.

For-profit companies can help, too. Supermarkets can't sell some food after a **sell-by date**, or expiration date. They often throw away a lot of food. *Zéro-Gâchis* is a company in France. They help supermarkets to sell more food and waste less. The company communicates with **customers** online. Customers learn where they can go to buy cheaper food close to the sell-by date. It's a **win-win**! Customers pay lower prices and supermarkets sell more food. Supermarkets that work with *Zéro-Gâchis* have reduced food waste by 50%.

---

sell-by date the latest date a food product should be sold
customers people who buy something
win-win a situation where everyone is a winner

Customers can use the Zéro-Gâchis website to find cheaper food.

These three companies are good examples of creative problem solving. They saw a problem and thought of a way to help solve it creatively. Creative thinking can usually solve most problems!

Which of these companies do you think is the most creative? Why? Can you think of some other examples of creative problem solving in your community? Talk about it with your class.

> People use wind turbines to harness wind power and make electricity. This is an example of creative problem solving.

Reading Strategy

Identify Cause and Effect

As you read this selection, you looked for causes and effects.

- What examples of causes and effects did you identify?
- Did looking for causes and effects help you to understand the selection?

Think It Over

1. **Recall** What is one of the effects of deforestation?
2. **Comprehend** What are the objectives of nonprofit companies?
3. **Analyze** How are the solutions to the problems in the text creative?

Reading 3

Learning Strategies

Cause and Effect

Finding cause and effect relationships can help you to understand what you read.

- The **cause** is what makes something happen.
- The **effect** is the result of the cause.

To find an effect in a story, ask yourself: "What happened?"
To find the cause, ask yourself: "Why did this happen?"

Practice

Read the sentences below with a partner.

- Make a chart with two columns. Write "Cause" in one column. Write "Effect" in the other column.
- List each cause and each effect in the correct column.

1. The water started to boil. Katie heated the tea kettle.

2. Stan studies every day. Stan does well on quizzes.

3. The baseball broke the window. Tom hit the baseball.

4. Plants grew in the field. The farmer planted the seeds.

Use a Cause and Effect Chart

You can use a Cause and Effect Chart to help you understand cause and effect relationships in a story.

Practice

Complete this Cause and Effect Chart for *Creative Problem Solving*. Then compare your completed chart with a partner's.

Cause	Effect
Deforestation, the removal of forests, is a problem all over the world.	
	Life can be very difficult with no electricity.
Supermarkets can't sell some food after a sell-by, or expiration, date.	

Apply

Take notes on the selection. Share them with a partner.

Extension

Are people in your community solving problems in **creative** ways? How? What is one problem that you would like to see solved? Tell your class about it.

READING 3

Reading 3

Grammar

Adverbs of Frequency and Intensity

Adverbs of frequency answer the question **How often?**

> **How often** do you see your grandparents?
> I **always** see my grandparents on holidays.

Study the positions of frequency adverbs:

Positions of adverbs	Examples
After the *be* verb Before other verbs	She is **never** late. We **always** study after school.
Positions of *usually* In the middle of a sentence After *be*	We **usually** go to the beach. We are **usually** at home on weekends.
Positions of *sometimes* At the beginning of a sentence In the middle of a sentence At the end of a sentence	**Sometimes** I eat early. I **sometimes** eat early. I eat early **sometimes**.

In questions: Adverbs come directly after the subject

> Is she **always** here?   Do you **always** bring your lunch?

Adverbs of intensity come before the adjective they modify or before another adverb.

> I ran **very** fast.   You are **too** funny!   She is **really** smart.

Practice A

Reorder the words to make sentences. Write the sentences in your notebook. More than one answer is possible.

1. He / home / sometimes / comes / late   He sometimes comes home late.
2. She / busy / on weekend / always / is
3. They / the movies / rarely / to / go
4. We / late / never / stay out
5. Does / him / visit / his grandmother / often / ?

Practice B

Ask and answer questions with your partner using adverbs of intensity. Use the questions below or create your own.

Example: A: How well do you speak English?

B: I speak English very well.

How well can you swim?
How easy is your English class?
How far is your house from school?

Grammar Check ✔

What do adverbs of frequency tell us? What do adverbs of intensity tell us?

Apply

Work with a partner. Make statements about your schedule and things you do. Use adverbs of frequency and intensity in your statements.

Example: A: I always eat breakfast at home. Sometimes I bring my lunch to school.

B: I never eat breakfast. I'm not very hungry in the morning. I usually bring my lunch.

WB 144

READING 3

Reading 3

Writing

Write a Persuasive Brochure

A brochure is a small book about a topic. A persuasive brochure convinces someone to act or think in a certain way. Clear details present information that will persuade the reader.

Writing Prompt

Write a persuasive brochure to encourage people to attend an event in your community. Include all the necessary information about the event. Use clear, interesting details to present the information in a persuasive way. Be sure to use adverbs of frequency and intensity correctly.

① Prewrite

Choose an event to write about. Think about the information that will persuade readers to attend. List the information in a graphic organizer.

A student named Sam listed his ideas like this:

Page 1
- Community Clean Up Our Park day. Show you care!
- All plastic, metal, and glass will be recycled.
- Free barbeque after the work is completed.
- Games with prizes!

Page 2
- Date + Time: Friday, September 10 at 9 A.M.
- Place: Downtown Park – meet at the kids' playground.

② Draft

Use your storyboard to help you write a first draft.
- Keep in mind your purpose for writing—to persuade.
- Show interesting details to appeal to your readers.

3 Revise

Read over your draft. Look for places where the writing needs improvement. Use the Writing Checklist to help you identify problems. Then revise your draft.

4 Edit

Check your work for errors. Trade papers with a partner to get feedback. Use the Peer Review Checklist on page 402.

5 Publish

Prepare a clean copy of your final draft. Share your paragraph with the class. Save your work.

> **Writing Checklist**
>
> ✓ **Ideas**
> I included information about the event.
> I used interesting details to persuade the reader.
>
> ✓ **Conventions**
> I used adverbs of frequency and intensity correctly.

Here is Sam's brochure:

Please come to the Community Clean Up Our Park Day! Downtown Park is the most popular park in our town, but it needs a cleanup.
- We will separate the trash into recycling bins.
- There will be a delicious barbeque for all volunteers. And it's free!
- We will play some fun games and prizes will be awarded.

Please mark the date on your calendar.
- Friday, September 10 at 9 A.M.
- Downtown Park - we will meet at the kids' playground.

We are looking forward to seeing you there! Show some community spirit!

Put It All Together

Apply and Extend

Link the Readings

Read the words in the top row.
Then follow these steps:

- For *The Trouble with Kudzu*, put an X under the words that remind you of the text.

- Repeat the same activity for *The Fox and the Crow* and *The Fox and the Goat* and *Creative Problem Solving*.

	Informational text	Literature	Solution helps one character	Solution helps many
The Trouble with Kudzu				
The Fox and the Crow, The Fox and the Goat				
Creative Problem Solving				

Discussion

1. The title of the story is *The Trouble with Kudzu*. Does kudzu still cause trouble? Why or why not?

2. How did Mr. Fox's actions **affect** the other characters in the stories? How does *Maya Pedal* **affect** people's lives?

3. How does **restoring** forests solve problems?

THE BIG QUESTION

How do we solve problems?

Projects

Your teacher will help you choose one of these projects.

Written	Oral	Visual/Active
Skit Choose one of the selections. Write a skit about the problem and how it was solved. Make sure the problem and solution are clear.	**Fable** Many fables are about solving a problem. The way a character solves a problem leads to a lesson. Write a fable about someone who must solve a problem.	**Flowchart of Steps** Think of a problem you read about and how it was solved. Identify the problem. Tell what steps were taken to solve it. Then explain the solution.
News Article Write a newspaper article about a problem that you heard about. Tell how people solved it. Answer the 5 W questions in your article.	**Interview** Interview someone who has solved a problem. Find out what the problem was. Tell how the person solved it. Record your interview.	**Comic Strip** Create a comic strip about a problem and how it is solved. Use a problem you read about, or think of your own problem.

Put It All Together

Listening and Speaking Workshop
Give a Speech 🎧

You are going to write and give a speech. Then you will listen as your classmates give a speech.

① Prepare

A. Choose a problem that has been solved. It can be from your school, your community, or somewhere else in the world. Research it and give a speech based on your research.

B. Think about what you want to tell your classmates. You will need to describe the problem, tell about the person who solved it, and explain how the person solved the problem. Find photos, posters, or other props to show during your speech.

> **Useful Language**
>
> 🎧 Listen and repeat.
>
> I'm going to talk about . . .
>
> We had a problem in our city for a long time. The problem was . . .
>
> People were worried about . . . Luckily, some of us had a great solution!

We had a problem at the most popular park in our town. So many people used the park and it was very dirty. The town didn't always keep it clean. We wanted to do something. We organized a cleanup day for the park. We asked people to volunteer. We offered a free barbeque and games with prizes. So many people came! The park was very clean and looked really beautiful. And everyone had so much fun! Now we're going to have a park cleanup day every month!

② Practice

Practice your speech with your props. Practice in front of your family or friends. If possible, record your speech. Then listen to yourself. How do you sound? Record yourself again and try to improve.

③ Present

As you speak, do the following:
- Face your audience and relax.
- Speak clearly and take your time.
- Show your props and other visuals.

As you listen, do the following:
- Listen for the general meaning, main point, and any details.
- Pay close attention. Your teacher will ask you questions about the speech.

Speaking Skills
Formal language is used in speeches. Remember to use correct grammar and complete sentences of different lengths and types.

Listening Skills
Listen carefully for ideas and information that aren't stated directly.

④ Evaluate

After you speak, answer these questions:
- ✓ Did you describe the problem clearly?
- ✓ Did you explain who solved it and how?

After you listen, answer these questions:
- ✓ Did you know anything about the problem before the speech?
- ✓ Did the speaker use formal or informal language?
- ✓ Think about the general meaning of the speech. Can you think of a title for it? Tell your idea to the class.

UNIT 4

Put It All Together

Writing Workshop
Write a Review

Writing Prompt
Write a review of a book, movie, or play. Clearly express your opinion of the work and include reasons that support your view.

① Prewrite

Review your writing for this unit. Then think of a movie, play, or book that you liked or disliked. Why did you feel as you did? List your ideas in a graphic organizer.

A student named Rob listed his ideas in this chart:

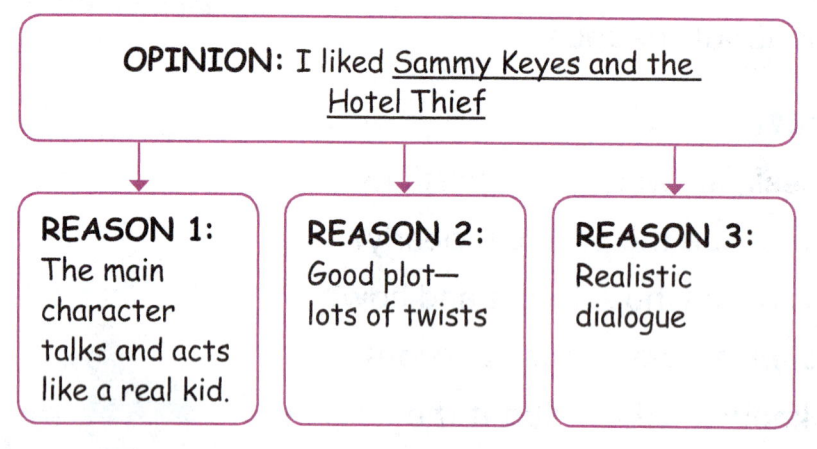

OPINION: I liked <u>Sammy Keyes and the Hotel Thief</u>

REASON 1:	REASON 2:	REASON 3:
The main character talks and acts like a real kid.	Good plot—lots of twists	Realistic dialogue

② Draft

Use your graphic organizer to write a draft.

- Keep your purpose in mind—to write a review.
- Support your opinion with reasons.

3 Revise

Read over your draft. Look for places where the writing needs improvement. Use the Writing Checklist to help you. Then revise your draft.

Here is how Rob revised his review:

Six Traits of Writing Checklist

✓ **Ideas**
Did I clearly express my opinion?

✓ **Organization**
Did I give reasons for my opinion?

✓ **Voice**
Does my writing sound like me?

✓ **Word Choice**
Did I choose specific words?

✓ **Sentence Fluency**
Did I use different kinds of sentences?

✓ **Conventions**
Did I begin and end sentences correctly?

Rob Park

I enjoyed reading *Sammy Keyes and the Hotel Thief* by Wendelin Van Draanen. This mystery begins, when 13-year-old Sammy sees a thief in one of the hotel rooms across the street from her grandmother's house. She watches until the thief sees her staring. Sammy realizes that she has to help the police or ~~they~~ *she and her grandmother* might be in danger. By the end of the book, Sammy cracks the case and catches (an ice cream vendor,) the thief. She also learns that taking risks is sometimes necessary.

Sammy talks and acts like a real kid does. The plot was exciting, with enough twists to keep me ~~involved~~ *guessing*. The dialogue is sharp. As you read, you feel that Sammy, the narrator, is talking directly to you.

Sammy is a funny, smart person I liked knowing. I think you will, too.

Revised to correct mechanics.

Revised to clarify meaning.

Revised to make writing smoother.

Revised to make more vivid.

UNIT 4

Put It All Together

④ Edit
Check your work for errors. Trade papers with a partner. Use the Peer Review Checklist to give each other feedback.

⑤ Publish
Prepare a clean copy of your final draft. Share your essay with the class.

WB 149–150

Peer Review Checklist

✓ The opinion is clearly stated.
✓ The opinion is supported by reasons.
✓ The writing is clear and interesting.

Spelling Tip

The *k* sound can be spelled with the letter *c*, *k*, or *ck*.

boo**k** **c**ave tra**ck**

Use a dictionary to check the spelling of words with the *k* sound.

250 UNIT 4

Put It All Together

Fluency 🎧

Listen to the sentences. Pay attention to the groups of words. Read aloud.

1. Kudzu doesn't come from a magic bean, but it is a member of the bean family.
2. One sunny, fall day, Mr. Fox went walking through the forest.
3. Players plant trees online and then *Tree Planet* plants trees in the ground.

Work in pairs. Take turns reading the passage below aloud for one minute. Count the number of words you read.

Kudzu is a native plant of China and Japan. That	10
means it grew naturally in those countries. Kudzu was	19
brought to the United States from Japan in 1876 as a	30
gift for a special celebration. The United States was	39
celebrating its first 100 years as a nation.	47
Soon, every gardener and farmer wanted to plant kudzu	56
seeds. Gardeners grew kudzu because it looked pretty and	65
smelled good. Farmers grew it to feed their animals.	74
At first, kudzu was a big success! But it did not stop	86
growing. It blocked sunlight that other plants needed. It	95
killed trees and whole forests. Nothing was safe!	103
Now, people call kudzu a weed. It is a wild plant	114
that grows where it is not wanted.	121

With your partner, find the words that slowed you down.

- Practice saying each word and then say the sentence each word is in.
- Then take turns reading the text again. Count the number of words you read.

WB 151

UNIT 4

Test Preparation

Taking Tests

You will often take tests that help show what you know. Follow these tips to improve your test-taking skills.

Coaching Corner

Answering Test Items for Revising and Editing

- Revising and Editing Tests often ask you to look for corrections and improvements that a writer should make.

- Before you read the written selection, preview the questions and answer choices.

- Read the whole selection carefully.

- After reading the selection, go back and carefully reread the sentences mentioned in the questions. Do you notice any mistakes in grammar or punctuation?

- Read each of the answer choices to yourself to see if one of them sounds better than the sentence in the selection. Choose the answer that does the most to improve the whole sentence.

- Remember that sometimes the sentence will not need any corrections.

Practice

Read the following test sample. Study the tips in the box. Answer the questions that follow.

(1) At tonight's town meeting, the City Council will announce its decision to make skateboarding on the sidewalk against the law. (2) Too many skateboarders have run into people and cars. (3) These accidents are making people verry angry. (4) But responsible skateboarders are angry, too. (5) Parents of skateboarders may be angryier than the kids. (6) They will have to pay fines if their kids are caught skateboarding on the sidewalk. (7) Mr. Ikeda has offered to give the town a plot of land to build a skateboard park. (8) It's a great offer, but we need money to build it. (9) Come to the town meeting and share your ideas!

1 What change should be made in sentence 3?

  A Change *accidents* to **accident**
  B Change *are* to **is**
  C Change *These* to **Thi**
  D Change *verry* to **very**

2 Which change, if any, is needed in sentence 5?

  F Change *Parents* to **Parents'**
  G Change *are* to **is**
  H Change *angryier* to **angrier**
  J Make no change

3 What change, if any, should be made in sentence 9?

  A Change *share* to **say**
  B Change *Come* to **Came**
  C Delete **meeting**
  D Make no change

> **Tips**
> ✓ Think about what you have learned about adverbs of intensity.
> ✓ Review what you know about forming comparatives.

UNIT 4

Unit 5
Where We Live

You will learn about different types of homes and the people who live in them.

Reading 1
Article

The Underground City

Reading 2
Letters

A House of Grass

Reading 3
Informational Text/Social Studies

A Cold Autumn Morning

THE BIG QUESTION

What is it like to live in an unusual home?

Listening and Speaking

You will talk about places to live. In the Listening and Speaking Workshop, you will present a TV talk show.

Writing

You will practice expository writing. In the Writing Workshop, you will write a magazine or newspaper article.

Quick Write

Where do you live? What is your home like? Describe it.

View and Respond

Talk about the poster for this unit. Then watch and listen to the video and answer the questions at Pearson English Portal.

Build Unit Vocabulary

What do you know about places to live?

Words to Know 🎧

Listen and repeat. Use these words to talk about places to live.

- townhouse
- apartment 
- treehouse 
- houseboat 
- retirement home 
- single-family home 

Practice

Work with a partner. Ask questions using the words above. Answer them using words from the box or your own ideas.

| cousin | friend | uncle | aunt | grandparents |

Example: A: Do you know anyone who lives in a <u>retirement home</u>?

B: Yes, my <u>grandparents</u> live in a <u>retirement home</u>.

Write

Read the questions. Write your response in your notebook.

Where do you live? Who do you live with?

Make Connections

Complete the sentences with the following phrases.

play on the swings

swim in the water

ride an elevator

eat dinner

1. My uncle lives on a houseboat. We like to _____ when we visit him.

2. My grandparents live in a retirement home. They _____ in a dining hall with many friends.

3. My friend Ava lives in a single-family home. In the backyard we like to _____ .

4. My parents and I live in an apartment. We live on the fifth floor, so every day we _____ .

What about you?

Talk with a partner. Talk about your home.

UNIT 5

Background

Kids' Stories from around the World

Carlito

I live in the town of Niagara Falls in Ontario, Canada. People come from far away to see the "Upside Down House" in my town. Everything inside the house is upside down! I think it would be fun to live in this house.

Jemma

I live in Scotland near a very interesting house. It's called "the Pineapple." It was built in 1761. Its stone top looks like a giant pineapple. Today, people rent the house for vacations. I want to stay there. Then I can say I slept in a pineapple.

China

Papua New Guinea

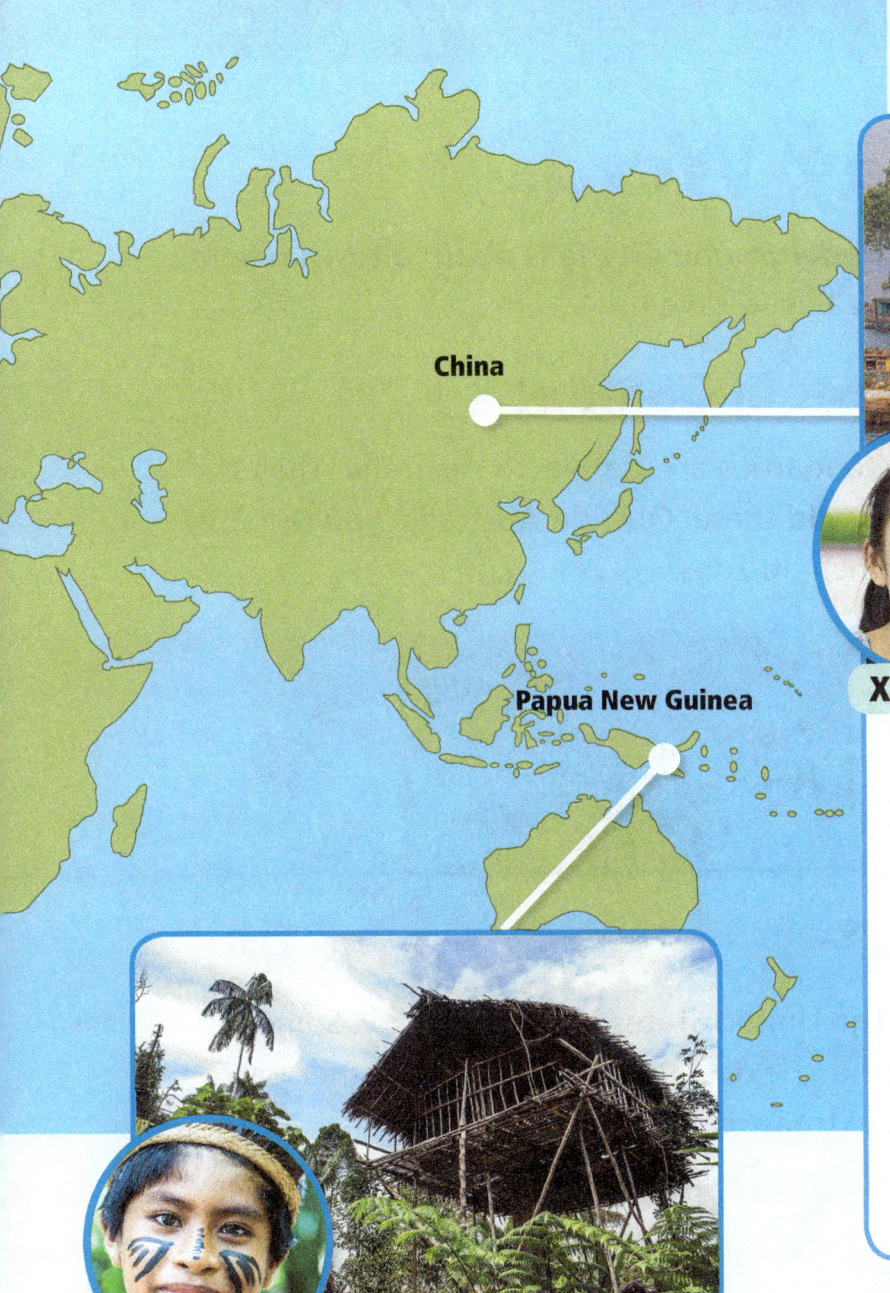

Xiao Hong

I live in China. Many families here live on boats. My family has a houseboat. We have a fishing business. My father and my brother take the boat into the ocean. They catch fish. Then they return to the harbor. I eat the fish they bring home.

Rabbie

I live in Papua New Guinea. In my country, some people live in treehouses. Some families live in trees that are 80 feet high! I live in a house on the ground. But I hope to live in a treehouse one day.

What about you?

1. Which house would you like to live in? Explain why.
2. Do you have a story about an unusual home? Share your story.

UNIT 5

Reading 1
Prepare to Read

What You Will Learn

Reading
- Vocabulary building: *Context, word study*
- Reading strategy: *Identify fact and opinion*
- Text type: *Informational text (magazine article)*

Grammar
Capitalizing proper nouns

Writing
Write to classify

These words will help you understand the reading.

Key Words
native
extreme
architecture
underground
mining
efficient

Key Words

The Underground City tells about a town where people live in caves.

Words in Context

1 Kangaroos are **native** to Australia. They live in the wild there. Outside Australia, you can only find them in zoos.

2 The United States is a big country. Some parts have **extreme**, or great, heat. Other parts have extreme cold.

260 UNIT 5

3 Styles of **architecture** change with time. Look at these two museums. Which one is an older style? How do you know?

4 Coal and gold are found **underground**. They are deep under Earth's surface. We get them by **mining**. Workers dig down to where the coal or gold is. Then they bring it up to the surface.

5 Being **efficient** means working quickly and well. When you are efficient, you do not waste time.

Practice

Add a page to your vocabulary notebook.
- Divide your page into three columns: the new words, their definitions, and drawings of the words when possible.
- Test yourself by covering one of the columns.

Speaking Skills

If you don't know the exact English word, use a synonym.

Make Connections

Have you ever been in a cave? Describe how it feels. Was it warm or cold? Was it damp or dry? Why do you think some people like living in caves?

Reading 1

These words will help you talk about the reading.

Academic Words

adapt
change to fit a new situation

environment
world of land, sea, and air that you live in; your surroundings

located
be in a particular place

Academic Words

Words in Context 🎧

Wolves **adapt** to cold weather by growing a thick coat.

Recycling paper and plastic is good for the **environment**.

The park is **located** near the school.

Practice

Choose an academic word to complete each sentence.

1. Rio de Janeiro is _____ in Brazil.

2. After we moved to a new town, it took some time to _____ to it.

3. Trees, water, and air are all part of our _____ .

Apply

Ask and answer with a partner.

1. Think of a time when you visited a new place. How did you **adapt** to it?

2. Where was the new place **located**?

3. How was the **environment** there different from the one at home?

Word Study

Homophones

How are the words in purple alike?
How are they different?

> Do the stores **sell** opals?
> Is there a jail **cell** in town?

The words *sell* and *cell* sound the same, but they have different spellings and different meanings. They are **homophones**.
- In the first sentence, *sell* means "to exchange for money."
- In the second sentence, *cell* means "a small room in a jail."

Practice

Choose a homophone to complete each sentence.

1. I _____ like to visit Australia. (wood, would)

2. I want to meet the people who live _____. (their, there)

3. We will _____ the miners at work. (sea, see)

4. She might _____ an opal. (buy, by)

5. I can hardly _____ him. (hear, here)

6. _____ coming to the party aren't you? (Your, You're)

Reading 1

Informational Text
Magazine Article

More About THE BIG QUESTION

Why is it important that people and animals **adapt** their homes to their **environment**?

🎧 **Listen to the Audio.**
Listen for the main points and important details.

Reading Strategy
Identify Fact and Opinion

- A fact is something that is true. You can prove something is a fact.
- An opinion is something that someone thinks is true but cannot be proven.
- As you read, think about what is a fact and what is an opinion.

Listen as your teacher models the reading strategy.

The Underground City
by Claudio Ponti

Have you ever seen a house that is under the ground? Come visit a town called Coober Pedy!

The town of Coober Pedy is in southern Australia.

264 UNIT 5

Friends play a game in an underground home.

About 3,500 people live in Coober Pedy, Australia. From the street, you might see only dirt and some trees. But under the ground, there are homes! More than half of the people in the town live in **underground** houses. These are regular houses that look a lot like yours!

The summer heat in Coober Pedy is **extreme**. But the underground homes are **efficient**. They stay cool during the hot months. That means people don't spend money on air conditioning. In the winter, the homes stay warm. That means people pay less for heat.

The underground houses look just like regular homes.

Before You Go On

How did the people of Coober Pedy **adapt** to the extreme heat?

READING 1

Opals are beautiful gems that are used for jewelry.

Reading Skills

Ask your teacher or classmates if you don't understand a word, phrase, or a language structure.

Opals are **native** to Coober Pedy. Most of the people who live there work in the opal **business**. They dig up opals from under the ground. Then they sell the opals to people all over the world.

The first opal was found in Coober Pedy in 1915. Soon, **mining** became popular there. The miners noticed how cool the air was inside the mines. These men had slept in **trenches** in World War I, so they knew that living under the ground was cooler than living in the **desert** heat. That's how the underground homes began.

---

business   buying or selling of goods and services
trenches   long, narrow holes dug into the ground
desert   large area of land that is very dry and usually very hot

Soldiers in World War I lived in trenches below the ground.

266   UNIT 5

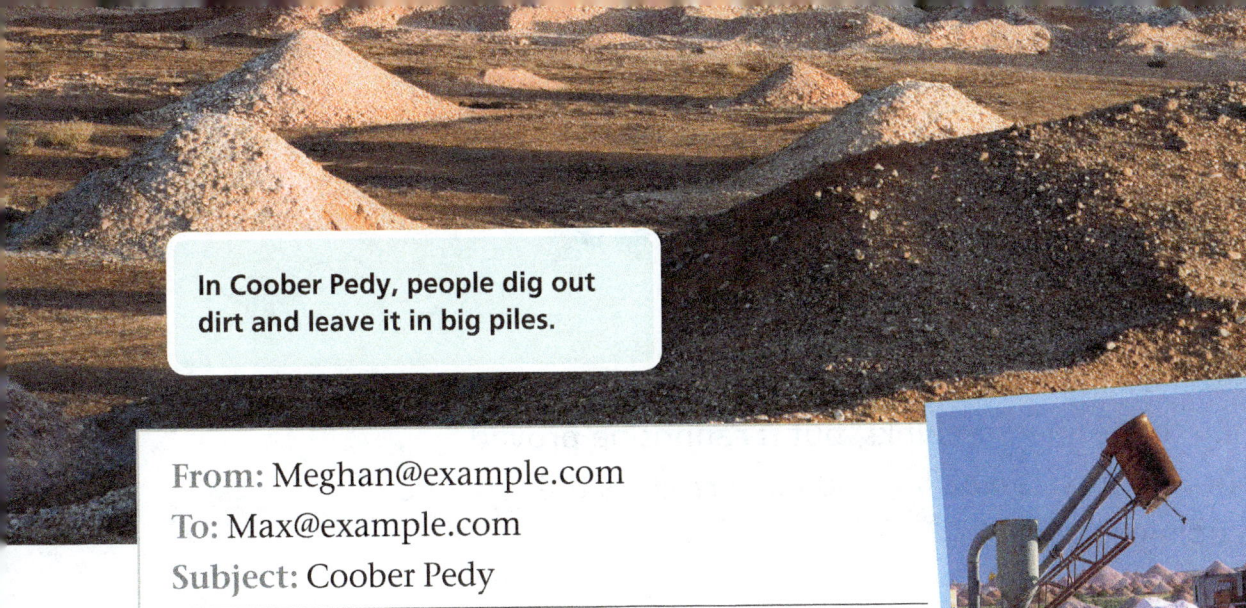

In Coober Pedy, people dig out dirt and leave it in big piles.

From: Meghan@example.com
To: Max@example.com
Subject: Coober Pedy

Hello Max,

I am in Coober Pedy. It is a special town in Australia. Many **visitors** come to see the underground architecture. The people who live in Coober Pedy work hard in the heat all day. They spend many hours drilling for opals. At the end of the day, they go to their nice, cool homes. They live in underground caves!

I'll see you soon!

Meghan

I saw workers use large machines to dig opals out of the ground.

visitors   people who come to see a place or a person

Reading Strategy
Identify Fact and Opinion

- What is one fact about Coober Pedy?
- What is one opinion of Coober Pedy?
- Did looking for facts and opinions help you understand the selection? How?

Think It Over

1. **Recall** Where is Coober Pedy located?
2. **Comprehend** How do the people who live in Coober Pedy adapt to the heat?
3. **Analyze** How is the environment of Coober Pedy different from the environment where you live?

Reading 1

Learning Strategies

Fact and Opinion

A **fact** is something that can be proved. An **opinion** is something that someone thinks, but it cannot be proved. Words such as *great, amazing,* and *bad* are clues that you are reading opinions.

Practice

Tell whether each sentence states a fact or an opinion. If it is a fact, tell where you can find the proof.

1. The town of Coober Pedy is **located** in Australia.
2. It is hard to live underground.
3. About 3,500 people live in Coober Pedy.
4. People who live underground are friendly.
5. The temperature of underground homes is under 23 degrees Celsius in the summer.

Use a Fact and Opinion Chart

A Fact and Opinion Chart can help you tell facts from opinions.

Practice

Sort the list of facts and opinions from the previous page. Explain your choice in the third column. Then answer the questions below.

Fact	Opinion	Why?
The town of Coober Pedy is located in Australia.		You can prove it by looking on a map of Australia.
	It is hard to live underground.	The word "hard" is a clue that this is an opinion.

1. Which sentence would you add to the Fact column?
   a. Opals are beautiful gems.
   b. The first opal was found in Coober Pedy in 1915.
   c. People who live underground are friendly.
   d. Coober Pedy is a special town.

2. How could you prove the fact that you chose?
   a. Ask a friend.
   b. Look it up on a website that you trust.
   c. Read about it in a newspaper.
   d. Buy an opal.

Extension

Would you like to live underground? Make a drawing that shows what your house would look like. Share your drawing with the class.

Apply

Summarize the selection for a partner. Use the key words as you speak.

Reading 1

Grammar

Capitalizing Proper Nouns

Proper nouns name a specific person, place, or thing. They begin with a capital letter.

Use proper nouns to talk about:

Names and titles of specific people
> **M**ax, **M**r. **S**mith, **P**resident **W**ashington

Names of specific places
> **S**outh **K**orea, **S**hanghai, **S**ydney **O**pera **H**ouse

Names of specific things
> **M**anchester **U**nited, **R**ed **S**tone **B**akery

Days of the week and months (except seasons)
> **M**onday, **T**uesday, **J**anuary, **F**ebruary, **s**pring

Historical events and documents
> the **H**arvest **M**oon **F**estival, the **C**onstitution

Titles of books, stories, and essays (only important words)
> *Alice's Adventures in Wonderland*, "**T**he **B**eaches of **C**olombia"

Languages and nationalities
> **S**panish language, **T**hai people, **M**exican

Practice A

Look for proper nouns on pages 254–267. Write them in your notebook.

Practice B

**Rewrite the sentences in your notebook.
Use correct capitalization.**

1. Opals are native to coober pedy. *Opals are native to Coober Pedy.*

2. dr. and mrs. robinson were late on friday.

3. steven hasn't read *a wrinkle in time*.

4. diamond mining has become popular in canada.

5. tracy is studying about greek architecture in school.

6. A goal in yellowstone national park is to protect the environment.

Apply

Work with a partner. Ask and answer the questions in your notebook. Write the answers using correct capitalization. Then compare them with your partner.

Example: A: What is your favorite book?

B: My favorite book is <u>My Side of the Mountain</u>.

- What is your favorite book?
- Who is your favorite singer?
- Who is your favorite movie actor?
- What is your favorite month?
- What town were you born in?
- What place would you like to visit?
- What language would you like to learn?
- What country would you like to visit?

Grammar Check ✓

List some proper nouns for people, places, and things that are near you now.

Reading 1

Writing

Write to Classify

When you classify, you group different kinds of information about a subject into categories. In each paragraph, discuss one category of information at a time.

Writing Prompt

Write two paragraphs that classify information about an animal. Think about how to organize information into categories. Capitalize proper nouns correctly.

① Prewrite

Choose an animal. Think about categories you will use to classify, or group, information about the animal. Then list the information from each category in a Three-Column Chart.

A student named Joyce listed her information in this chart:

Features	Flying Birds	Flightless Birds
Wings	Longer wings	Shorter wings
Number of feathers	Fewer feathers	More feathers
Shape of feathers	Different shapes	Same shapes
Examples	Owls	Ostriches

② Draft

Use your Three-Column Chart to help you write a first draft.
- Keep in mind your purpose for writing—to classify.
- Group each category of information in one paragraph.

272   UNIT 5

3 Revise

Read over your draft. Look for places where the information categories are not clear or your sentences are too long. Use the Writing Checklist to help you identify problems. Then revise your draft.

4 Edit

Check your work for errors. Trade papers with a partner to get feedback. Use the Peer Review Checklist on page 402. Edit your final draft in response to feedback from your partner and your teacher.

> **Writing Checklist**
>
> ✓ **Ideas**
> I clearly grouped the different kinds of information.
>
> ✓ **Word Choice**
> I used interesting vocabulary in my paragraph.
>
> ✓ **Conventions**
> I capitalized proper nouns correctly.

5 Publish

Prepare a clean copy of your final draft. Share your paragraph with the class. Save your work. You will need to refer to it in the Writing Workshop.

Here are Joyce's paragraphs:

Joyce Lopez

　While most birds fly, some birds can't fly. Flying birds have longer wings but fewer feathers. An owl is a flying bird that eats meat and hunts at night. Owls are found in North America and rainforests in South America.

　Flightless birds first developed on islands. There they had few enemies to fly away from. These birds have shorter wings. They have more feathers all over their bodies. An ostrich is a fast-running, flightless bird that lives in Africa. These are the largest and heaviest of all birds.

Reading 2
Prepare to Read

What You Will Learn

Reading
- Vocabulary building: *Context, phonics*
- Reading strategy: *Identify author's purpose*
- Text type: *Literature (letters)*

Grammar
Prepositions and prepositional phrases

Writing
Organize ideas by problem and solution

These words will help you understand the reading.

Key Words

prairie
sod
climate
harsh
record

Key Words

In *A House of Grass*, two cousins communicate through letters. One girl lives on the prairie. The other lives in a city.

Words in Context

1 The **prairie**, a wide open area of grasslands, is full of flowers and tall grasses.

2 Some people scatter grass seed and wait for the grass to grow. Others buy rolls of **sod** and have lawns right away.

274 UNIT 5

3 The climate in this desert is harsh. It is always very dry. During the day, the desert gets very hot. At night, it gets very cold.

4 Our coach keeps a record of how many times we hit the ball.

Practice

Make flashcards to help you memorize the words.
- Write a key word on the front.
- On the back, write a sentence, but leave a blank where the key word should be.

Make Connections

Long ago, friends wrote letters to each other. How do friends communicate today? Which way do you like best? Why? Write your opinion in your notebook. Then explain it to a partner.

Reading 2

These words will help you talk about the reading.

Academic Words

correspond
write and receive messages with someone

previously
before

reside
live somewhere

Academic Words

Words in Context 🎧

I **correspond** with my pen pal. He lives in Mexico.

Mr. Monroe **previously** worked in a bank. Now he is a famous writer.

All of my cousins **reside** in Phoenix.

Practice

Choose an academic word to complete each sentence.

1. Two friends might _____ in different cities, but they can still be good friends.

2. Now you can send messages through the phone. _____, this was not possible.

3. People can _____ using letters they send in the mail, or they can email.

Apply

Ask and answer with a partner.

1. How would you **correspond** with friends who moved to a different city?

2. What is your favorite movie now? What was it **previously**?

3. How many people **reside** in your home?

WB 166

276 UNIT 5

Phonics

Y as a Vowel 🎧

Sometimes the letter *y* acts as a vowel. Each word in the chart below has the letter *y* at the end. Sound out the words.

- When does the letter *y* have the long *i* sound?
- When does the letter *y* have the long *e* sound?

Long *i*	Long *e*
by	city
dry	dirty
my	worry

Rule

- The letter *y* usually has the long *i* sound when it comes after a consonant at the end of a one-syllable word.
- The letter *y* usually has the long *e* sound when it comes after a consonant at the end of a word with more than one syllable.

Practice

Read the sentences with a partner. Take turns.

- Molly lives in the city.
- My new home is in Tianjin.
- It was not easy to move.
- We share many stories.

1. List the words in which *y* has the long *i* sound.

2. List the words in which *y* has the long *e* sound.

Reading 2

Literature
Letters

A House of Grass
by Kathy Furgang

More About THE BIG QUESTION

In this selection, a young girl moves to a new home. Why does she **correspond** with her cousin back home?

🎧 **Listen to the Audio.**
Listen for the main points and important details.

Reading Strategy
Identify Author's Purpose

Before you read, think about the author's purpose. Is the author writing:

- to entertain?
- to tell about something?
- to persuade you to do or think something?

As you read, think about why Sarah and Molly wrote their letters.

Listen as your teacher models the reading strategy.

278 UNIT 5

Dear Cousin Molly,

I often think of you, your nice home, and our beautiful Boston! The trip to Kansas has been long and hard. I look out the back of the wagon as the miles pass and I see only grass and more grass.

I have seen some funny houses on the prairie. They look like they are made of dirt. Ma says the prairie grass, or sod, is thick as a **mat**. She jokes that Pa will build us a sod house, too. It would be strange to live in a house made of dirt! How would we keep it clean?

Affectionately,
Sarah

---

mat   thick piece of material used to cover a floor
affectionately   way to end a letter, showing love or caring

Before You Go On

Where did Sarah previously live?

READING 2   279

Dear Cousin Sarah,

I was happy to **receive** your letter. I hope you now have a nice new home. Please **assure** me it is not made of dirt! Mother said sod houses are hard to live in. They are tiny, their roofs leak, and the dirt walls are filled with bugs!

Will you ever return to Boston? The prairie must be a difficult place to live. Life is easier here.

I hope you keep a **diary**. If you keep a record of your adventures, one day your children can learn about your new life and experiences.

Love,
Molly

---

receive   get from someone
assure   tell or promise
diary   book in which you write things that happen each day

Reading Skills

If you don't understand something, ask your classmates or your teacher, "What does this mean?" If you are not sure, ask, "Does this mean…?"

Dear Molly,

I have funny news! We live in a sod house! It is dark and **damp**, but do not worry. It will protect us from the climate. It is an excellent shelter!

There are few trees on the prairie. The land looks like a sea of grass.

People here have little money, but they are **clever**. Since many can't buy wood, stone, or bricks, they build with sod. They cut the sod into pieces and then they **stack** the pieces like bricks to make things.

That is how Pa made our new house!

Love,
Sarah

---

damp   moist or a little bit wet
clever   creative and quick to learn
stack   form a neat pile of things, one on top of the other

Before You Go On

Why do people on the prairie reside in sod homes?

READING 2

Dear Sarah,

   I would love to live near you again, but I would not like to live on the **frontier**! I prefer my life in Boston.

   When I look out my window, I see churches, museums, and stores. These are strong buildings that were built to last forever. But even rain could hurt your buildings. Your house could turn to mud.

   A sod house does not **appeal** to me. I **certainly** do not like grass or dirt. I do not want to live with bugs!

   I enjoy your letters. They help me learn about your new life.

Love,
Molly

---

frontier   area beyond places people know well

appeal   seem interesting or fun

certainly   without any doubt

Dear Molly,

  Do not worry about me and my little sod house. I agree that sometimes the climate is harsh. But our house is cool in summer and warm in winter.

  I love my new life on the prairie. I know that someday more people will move to the frontier and build towns and cities. Then we will have all the **comforts** of Boston!

Your loving cousin,
Sarah

---

comforts   things that make life nicer

Reading Strategy

Identify Author's Purpose

- Molly and Sarah had different reasons for corresponding. What were they?
- Did thinking about the author's purpose help you to understand the selection? How?

Think It Over

1. **Recall** Why should Sarah keep a record of her adventures?
2. **Comprehend** Where does Molly prefer to reside? Why?
3. **Analyze** Would you like to live in a sod house? Why or why not?

Reading 2

Learning Strategies

Author's Purpose

Authors have different purposes for writing. An author writes to entertain, persuade, or inform. Knowing the author's purpose will help you understand what you read.

Practice

Read the sentences. Tell if the author's purpose is to entertain, persuade, or inform. Explain your answers.

1. Sod houses are made of dirt. Today's houses are made of brick or wood.
2. You will love our sod house. When it rains, the roof leaks. Then mud falls on your head!
3. Sod houses and today's houses protect you from harsh weather.
4. Sod houses are the best houses. They are cool in the summer and warm in the winter. You must build a sod house.

Use a Compare and Contrast Chart

A compare and contrast chart can help you compare and contrast the information you are reading.
- When you compare, you tell how two or more things are alike.
- When you contrast, you tell how two or more things are different.

Practice

Copy and complete this chart. Use the questions below to help you.

1. What other information from the selection can you put in the Alike box?
2. What other information from the selection can you put in the Different box?
3. What information from your own experiences can you put in the Alike box?
4. What information from your own experiences can you put in the Different box?

```
        Sod Houses
            and
       Today's Houses
        /          \
    Alike         Different
protect from     Sod: dirt
bad weather      Today: brick
                 or wood
```

WB 171

Apply

Retell the selection to a partner. Use academic and key words as you speak.

Extension

Write a letter to Molly or Sarah. Describe where you live. Include a drawing that shows some of what you are describing. Share your drawing with the class.

Reading 2

Grammar

Prepositions and Prepositional Phrases

A **preposition** is a word that shows location, time, or direction, or provides details. Here are some prepositions.

above	below	for	on	through
after	by	from	out	to
at	down	in	over	under

A preposition + a noun or pronoun is called a **prepositional phrase**.

The horse *jumped* **over the fence.**

A prepositional phrase can describe a noun.

I see the *house* **with the big windows.**

Prepositions can describe relationships with time.

We will eat cake **after school.**

Practice A

Circle the prepositions; underline the prepositional phrases.

1. We're going ⓣⓞ Grandma's house.

2. This book is by Jane Austen.

3. My backpack is under the table.

286 UNIT 5

4. We always eat breakfast before class.

5. Our soccer practice starts at 3:30.

Practice B

Complete each sentence with a preposition.

1. It was a harsh life on the prairie.

2. Do you live _____ an apartment or a house?

3. Are you _____ Canada?

4. Hector **resides** in the house _____ the tile roof.

5. The baby crawled _____ the table.

6. **Previously**, he went _____ a private school.

Apply

Work with a partner. Discuss your hobbies and activities that you usually do on the weekend. Use prepositions and prepositional phrases.

Example: A: What do you like to do on the weekend?
B: I like to play with my dog in my yard.

- What do you like to do on the weekend?
- What time do you get up?
- Where do you like to go?
- How long have you liked this activity?
- Who goes with you?

Grammar Check ✓

Which prepositional phrases above:

- tell where something happens?
- tell when something happens?
- describe a noun?

Reading 2

Writing

Organize Ideas by Problem and Solution

You can organize the ideas in your writing by describing problems and solutions. A problem is a difficulty that people face. A solution is the way to solve or fix the problem. First, describe the problem. Then, describe the solution.

Writing Prompt

Write a paragraph that describes a problem in your school or community. Then write a paragraph that explains how you solved it. Be sure to use prepositions correctly.

① Prewrite

Choose a problem to write about. Think about how you solved the problem. Then list the information in a problem and solution chart.

A student named Billy listed his ideas in this graphic organizer:

PROBLEM	SOLUTION
Trash, bottles, and boxes filled the lot.	Students and teachers cleared out the lot.
No dirt to plant flowers and grass.	We carried bags of dirt and planted flowers and grass.
There were no lights or benches.	People gave money to buy lights and benches.

② Draft

Use your problem and solution chart to help you write a first draft.

- Keep in mind your purpose for writing— to identify a problem and solution.
- Show clearly that each part of the problem has a solution.

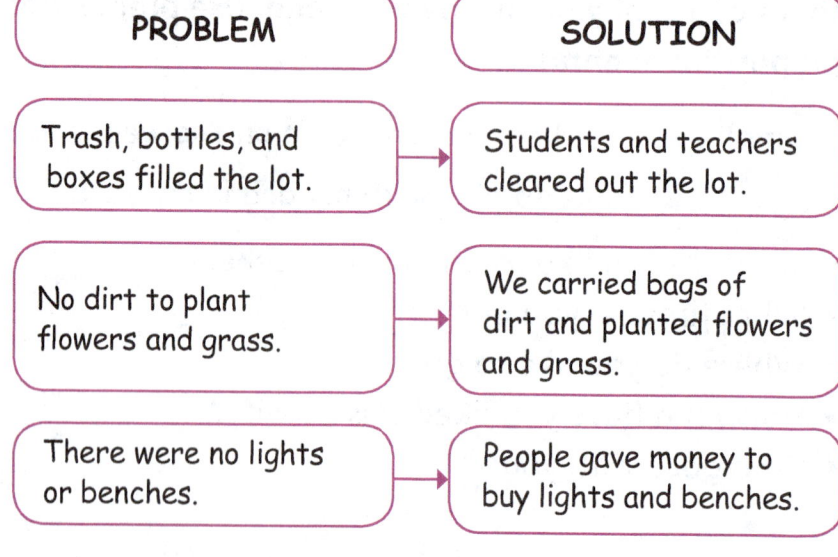

3 Revise

Read over your draft. Look for places where the writing is not well organized. Use the Writing Checklist to help you identify problems. Then revise your draft.

4 Edit

Check your work for errors. Trade papers with a partner to get feedback. Use the Peer Review Checklist on page 402. Edit your final draft in response to feedback from your partner and your teacher.

5 Publish

Prepare a clean copy of your final draft. Share your paragraph with the class. Save your work.

Here are Billy's paragraphs:

> **Writing Checklist**
>
> ✓ **Ideas**
> I clearly identified each problem and solution.
>
> ✓ **Organize**
> I first wrote about the problems and then wrote the solutions.
>
> ✓ **Conventions**
> I used prepositions correctly.

Billy Martin

I wanted to turn an empty lot near our school into a small community park. But the lot was filled trash, bottles, and boxes. There was no dirt to plant flowers and grass. There were no lights or benches, either. Without help, I wasn't sure how to make my dream come true.

My teacher, Ms. Han, told our school about the problem. Students and teachers worked together to clear out the lot. We planted flowers and grass. People gave us money. We used it to buy lights and benches. By working together we turned an empty lot into a beautiful park.

Reading 3
Prepare to Read

What You Will Learn

Reading
- Vocabulary building: *Context, phonics*
- Reading strategy: *Visualize*
- Text type: *Informational text (social studies)*

Grammar
Present perfect

Writing
Write to compare and contrast

These words will help you understand the reading.

Key Words
- reindeer
- seal
- shelter
- igloo
- sled

Key Words
Words in Context

1 The Inuit made many things from **reindeer** skin, like blankets and boots.

2 **Seal** skins were used to make the walls of tents.

3 A tent is a kind of **shelter**; it protects you from the weather.

UNIT 5

4 An **igloo** is a house for the winter made of large blocks of hard snow.

5 A **sled** is something you can ride on to travel over snow or ice.

Practice

Draw a picture of a home that might be found in a very cold climate. Label the picture with sentences using key words.

Make Connections

What stories have you heard about Inuit people? Do you think you would have liked living as an Inuit in the 1800s? Write your opinion in your notebook. Then explain it to a partner.

READING 3

Reading 3

These words will help you talk about the reading.

Academic Words

considerable
large enough to be important

labor
hard work

undertake
take on as a responsibility

Academic Words

Words in Context

Ramona did a **considerable** amount of work on the group project.

Cleaning up the park involved a lot of physical **labor**.

The boys agreed to **undertake** the job of cleaning the garage.

Practice

Choose an academic word to complete each sentence.

1. Kenji chose to _____ the job of washing the dishes tonight.

2. Nina could not go to out to play because she had a _____ amount of homework.

3. Tony did not mind the _____ involved in raking leaves. He liked to work outside.

Apply

Ask and answer with a partner.

1. When did you have to **undertake** a tough job?

2. What kind of **labor** did you do?

3. Did the job take a **considerable** amount of time?

Phonics

R-Controlled Vowels: *ar, or, ore* 🎧

Listen. Then read each pair of words. Notice how the letter *r* changes the vowel sound.

am	ton	toe
arm	t**or**n	t**ore**

Here are more words with an *r* that follows a vowel. Sound out the words in the box.

art	f**or**
h**ar**d	st**or**y
g**ar**den	m**ore**

Rule

The letters *ar* usually have the vowel sound heard in **art**. The letters *or* and *ore* usually have the vowel sound in **torn** and **tore**.

Practice

Read each pair of words with a partner. Tell whether the words have the same vowel sound.

1. bark, yard
2. port, park
3. part, pat
4. hose, horse

READING 3

Reading 3

Informational Text
Social Studies

More About THE BIG QUESTION

What is it like to live in a tent?

🎧 **Listen to the Audio.**
Listen for the main points and important details.

Reading Strategy
Visualize

Readers often try to visualize, or see in their minds, what they are reading about.

- As you read, look for words that describe people, places, and things.
- Use the descriptions in the selection and the photos to help you create pictures in your mind.

Listen as your teacher models the reading strategy.

A Cold Autumn Morning

It's a November morning in 1895, near the **coast** of Hudson Bay, in Canada. Wrapped in several blankets made from reindeer skins, a young Inuit girl named Meeka opens her eyes and feels a **chill** on her face from the cold autumn air. Inside the tent made of seal skins, a fire is burning in a stone lamp. The lamp provides light and heat for the family inside the tent, and it also heats water for cooking food.

---

coast   the land near a large body of water
chill   a feeling of cold

Meeka's mother is quietly singing a song to Meeka's baby brother, Koomanah, as she prepares breakfast. Meeka's father has already gone out for the day with other men from their village. In the fall, when the ice becomes thick, the Inuit men cut small holes in the ice. They sit there for many hours, waiting for seals to **poke** their noses out of the holes in the ice to get some air. Then they catch the seals. Animals provide everything for the Inuit: food, clothing, tools, lamp oil, shelter, and many other things. If they do not catch enough animals, their lives will become difficult.

---

poke push out

Reading Skills

If you don't understand a word, look at the context to try to guess the meaning.

Before You Go On

Why do the Inuit men undertake the long wait on the ice?

READING 3   295

Meeka sits down near the lamp and rubs her hands together by the fire. Meeka's mother gives her a piece of dried fish for breakfast and a cup of hot water made from melted snow. Meeka drinks the water and takes a bite of the fish. It has a salty taste and is a little hard to chew, but it is one of her favorite meals.

After breakfast, Meeka puts on her coat and pulls the **hood** up, so that only her eyes, nose, and mouth can be seen. It is still mostly dark outside. Outside the tent, she **inhales** deeply, feeling the cold air enter her nose and throat. The snow is deep and covers the land around their tent. She can see little streams of smoke from lamps rising up from the holes in the top of her neighbors' tents.

---

hood   part of a coat that covers the head

inhales   breathes air in

Meeka knows that her family will soon have to build a snow house, or **igloo**, to live in through the winter. The first snow of the season is not good for building an igloo. They have to wait a few more weeks for *illusaq*. This Inuit word means "hard snow that is good for building houses." Building igloos is an important event in Meeka's village. All of the men get together and cut large blocks of snow, using long, sharp knives. The first blocks of snow are stacked in a circle on the ground. More blocks of snow are stacked on top. This continues until the igloo is finished. The women use soft snow to fill in the spaces between the blocks of snow. It is very hard, but everyone works together to do the job.

However, today is not igloo day. Today, Meeka will play with her friends. She and her friends like to ride on **sleds** that are made of ice. Sometimes they **race** each other on the sleds. After a few hours of play, the sun has already started to go down, and it's snowing hard. Meeka wonders if her father has brought home a seal today. She lifts her reindeer skin boots as she walks through the soft, deep snow, looking forward to the warmth of her tent.

---

race   compete against others to be the fastest

Reading Strategy
Visualize

- What did you visualize as you read about Meeka's home?
- What did you visualize as you read about the land surrounding Meeka's village?
- Did visualizing help you understand the selection? How?

Think It Over

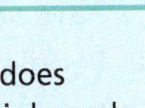

1. **Recall** What does Meeka eat, drink, and wear in the story?
2. **Comprehend** What are some **considerable** hardships that the Inuit people faced?
3. **Analyze** What types of **labor** might Meeka have done as part of her daily chores?

Reading 3

Learning Strategies

Visualize

When you read, try to **visualize**, or picture in your mind, what the author is describing. Authors use words to help readers create mind pictures.

Practice

What picture do you visualize when you read each sentence? Choose one sentence and draw what you visualize.

1. People can make treehouses in backyards. They must secure wooden boards to strong tree branches.
2. Some people build treehouses high in the jungle.
3. Some treehouses have many rooms. They even have staircases.
4. People who live in treehouses nest high in the sky with the birds.

Use an Organizational Chart

An organizational chart helps you put your thoughts in order. Suppose you want a friend to picture the different places that Meeka sees during her day. The chart will help you think of ways to describe the different scenes.

Practice

Copy and complete this chart. Then answer the questions.

Scenes	Object Described	Detail 1	Detail 2
Meeka waking up in the morning	inside of tent	cold autumn air	tent made of seal skins

1. Describe to a partner the scenes from the selection you added to your chart. Use a **considerable** amount of detail in your description.
2. How did the organizational chart help you describe the scene?
3. What did Meeka do before she went outside that day?
4. Would you have wanted to live in an Inuit village during this period? Why or why not?

WB 181

Apply

Using the pictures, summarize the story for a partner.

Extension

Describe a similar morning for you at home. Draw or describe it. Share your description with your class.

Reading 3

Grammar

Present Perfect

The **present perfect** is used to talk about a past event that might happen again in the future. The **simple past** is used to talk about something that happened at a certain time in the past and is finished.

Simple past
I **saw** a horror movie last night.
She **went** to a concert yesterday.

Present perfect
I**'ve seen** horror movies before.
She**'s been** to concerts before.

have → **'ve**
has → **'s**

The present perfect form is this: **have** or **has** + the past participle. For most regular verbs, add -*ed* to the form the past participle.

start → started   stop → stopped   study → studied

For irregular verbs, learn the past participle form.

be → been	go → gone	see → seen
eat → eaten	meet → met	spend → spent
get → gotten	ride → ridden	write → written

Use the present perfect + *ever* to ask people about their experiences. Use non-specific time phrases, such as **once, ever, never, before**, or **a few times**, to answer.

Have you **ever eaten** sushi?   Yes, I **have**. I**'ve eaten** sushi a **few times**.
No, I **haven't**. I**'ve never eaten** sushi.

300   UNIT 5

Practice A

Complete the sentences. Use the present perfect form of the verb in parentheses.

1. We ___have been___ to Cairo. (be)

2. She _____ a book about Inuit people. (write)

3. I _____ a **considerable** amount of time on my homework. (spend)

4. The students _____ to a quiet room to work. (go)

5. My family _____ many countries. (visit)

Practice B

Complete the conversation with the present perfect form of *be*.

1. Have your parents ever _____ to Florida?

2. No, they haven't. They've never _____ to the U.S. Have you ever _____ to the U.S.?

3. No, I haven't. But my sister has _____ to the U.S. before. She's _____ to New York a few times.

Apply

Work with a partner. Use the prompts below to ask and answer questions. Try to use the present perfect form.

Grammar Check ✔

Circle examples of the present perfect in the reading on pages 294–297.

Example: A: Have you ever been to London?

B: Yes, I have. I have been there a few times.

- been to London?
- ridden a horse?
- met a famous person?
- visited a national park?
- eaten sushi?
- gotten a very bad present?

READING 3

Reading 3

Writing

Write to Compare and Contrast

When you compare two things you explain how they are alike. When you contrast two things you explain how they are different. Use details to show how the things are alike and different.

Writing Prompt

Write a paragraph to compare and contrast two sports or hobbies. Use details to show how they are alike and different. Be sure to use present perfect verbs correctly.

① Prewrite

Choose two sports or hobbies to compare and contrast. Think about how they are alike and different. Then list your ideas in a Venn Diagram.

A student named Julie listed her ideas like this:

Baseball
- Players use a glove and a bat.
- Players take turns.
- Sometimes, players must wait a long time.

Both
sports are fun.

Soccer
- You kick the ball with your feet.
- Players run all the time.
- There's lots of activity for every player.

② Draft

Use your Venn Diagram to help you write a first draft.
- Keep in mind your purpose for writing—to compare and contrast.
- Include details that show how the sports are alike and different.

③ Revise

Read over your draft. Look for places where the writing is unclear. Use the Writing Checklist to help you identify problems. Then revise your draft.

④ Edit

Check your work for errors. Trade papers with a partner to get feedback. Use the Peer Review Checklist on page 402. Edit your final draft in response to feedback from your partner.

> **Writing Checklist**
>
> ✓ **Ideas**
> I showed how the subjects are alike and different.
>
> ✓ **Word Choice**
> I used details to compare and contrast.
> I used action verbs correctly.

⑤ Publish

Prepare a clean copy of your final draft. Share your paragraph with the class. Save your work.

Here is Julie's compare and contrast paragraph:

Julie Fernandez

Baseball and soccer are both fun sports to play, but they are very different. In baseball, you catch a ball with a glove and hit it with a bat. In soccer, you kick the ball with your feet. You can use your head, too, but not your hands. In baseball, players take turns batting and running to the bases. Sometimes they wait a long time. In soccer, players run all the time. I have played soccer for two years, while my brother has played baseball. I like soccer better because there is more activity for every player.

Put It All Together

Apply and Extend

Link the Readings

Read the words in the top row of the chart. Then follow these steps:

- For *The Underground City*, put an X under the words that remind you of the text.
- Repeat the same activity for *A House of Grass* and *A Cold Autumn Morning*.

	Informational text	Literature	Hard Times	Harsh Climate
The Underground City				
A House of Grass				
A Cold Autumn Morning				

Discussion

1. Why are the people of Coober Pedy happy about where they **reside**?
2. How does Sarah think life on the prairie will change in the future?
3. The people in *A House of Grass* and *A Cold Autumn Morning* build some unusual homes. How are the homes similar?

THE BIG QUESTION What is it like to live in an unusual home?

> **Listening Skills**
>
> If you don't understand something a speaker says, you can say, "I don't understand. Can you explain it, please?"

Projects

Your teacher will help you choose one of these projects.

Written ✎	Oral 💬	Visual/Active 👏
Journal Entry Imagine you live in one of the houses you read about. Write a journal entry describing a day in your life. Include specific details and descriptions.	**Description** Describe one of the houses you read about. Give details, but do not identify the house. Have listeners guess which house you are describing.	**Illustration** Choose one of the houses you read about. Create your own illustration of that house. Use the illustrations in the book as a guide.
Building Proposal Think of a new kind of house. Write a proposal for building that house. Tell why your house would be special. Include details.	**Interview** Interview someone who lives in a different kind of house than you. Ask about the good and bad parts of living in that house. Record your interview.	**Charades** Choose a house you read about. Act out a daily activity in that house. Have other students guess which house you are living in. Act out living in other houses.

For more projects, visit Pearson English Portal.

WB 185–186

UNIT 5 305

Put It All Together

Listening and Speaking Workshop
Present a TV Talk Show 🎧

You are going to write and present a TV talk show. Then you will listen as your classmates present a TV talk show, too.

① **Prepare**

A. Find two partners. One will be the host, and the other two will be the guests. Your group will present a TV talk show about where people live. Your classmates (the audience) will ask the guests questions at the end of the show.

B. Choose two interesting places where people live. Do some research for facts, details, and examples. Share the information and work cooperatively. Then write your TV talk show. Find photos or simple props to show during the talk show.

> **Useful Language**
>
> 🎧 Listen and repeat.
>
> Welcome to the show.
>
> Thanks for joining us. Tell us about …
>
> Thanks for watching. See you next time.

Host:	Welcome to our show today. We have two special guests. Maria and Tobias. Let's have each of you tell our audience where you live. Maria?
Maria:	I live in a cave.
Host:	And, Tobias, what about you?
Tobias:	I live on a boat.
Host:	Two very different places, two very different homes. Maria, where is your cave. . . I mean home?

② Practice

Practice your TV talk show with your props in front of your family or friends. If possible, record your talk show. Then listen to it. Record it again and try to improve.

Speaking Skills

Choose your words based on who is listening. A TV talk show is informal. Use simple, conversational language.

③ Present

As you speak, do the following:
- Speak loudly and face your audience.
- Use hand and body movements to make a point.
- Answer your audience's questions.

As you listen, do the following:
- Think about what you already know about the subject.
- Think of questions to ask at the end of the talk show.

Listening Skills

Listen carefully for specific facts and observations to predict what you don't already know.

Listen carefully for ideas and information that aren't stated directly.

④ Evaluate

After you speak, answer these questions:
- ✓ Did you speak loudly and face your audience?
- ✓ Did you give interesting facts, details, and examples in your answers?

After you listen, answer these questions:
- ✓ Did you understand the questions and answers?
- ✓ Did you ask a question?
- ✓ Did you enjoy the talk show?

Put It All Together

Writing Workshop
Write a Magazine or Newspaper Article

Writing Prompt
Write a magazine or newspaper article about something that happened in your school or community. Answer each of the 5W questions: Who? What? Where? When? and Why?

① Prewrite

Review your previous work in this unit. Then choose a topic. Think about something that happened recently in your school or community. Research information about the event that answers the 5W questions. List your ideas in a graphic organizer.

A student named Rosie listed her ideas on this chart:

WHO? Ms. Irene Gomez	WHAT? Hampton Community Center opened
WHERE? three blocks from our school	WHEN? October 1

WHY? offers many services, including classes, for our community

② Draft

Use your graphic organizer to write a draft.

- Keep your purpose in mind—to write a magazine or newspaper article.
- Research information to answer the 5W questions.

3 Revise

Read over your draft. Look for places where the writing needs improvement. Use the Writing Checklist to help you. Then revise your draft.

Here is how Rosie revised her newspaper article:

Six Traits of Writing Checklist

✓ **Ideas**
Did I write about something in my school or community?

✓ **Organization**
Do I answer the 5W questions?

✓ **Voice**
Is my tone serious?

✓ **Word Choice**
Did I choose precise words?

✓ **Sentence Fluency**
Did I use different sentence types?

✓ **Conventions**
Did I spell homophones correctly?

Rosie Humphrey

Hampton Community Center Opens

Philadelphia, PA, October 10

  The Hampton Community Center opened October 1, just three blocks from our school. Last week Ms. Irene Gomez, the director, gave me a guided tour.

Revised to correct mechanical error.

  The center offers many services, including classes, for members of our community. Currently, there are eight classrooms for adults and children. The courses range from cooking and welding to drawing and job training. and resume writing classes help prepare adults and teens to find work.

Revised to create a sentence.

  Ms. Gomez said a new indoor pool will be ready by next summer. Free swimming classes will be offered every morning of the week. To enroll, you must fill out an application form by June 1.

Revised to correct spelling error.

  Future plans for the center include movie nights, concerts, and art events festivals. Ms. Gomez believes the community center will help all of us. She encourages everyone in our school to visit soon.

Revised to make meaning clearer.

UNIT 5

Put It All Together

④ Edit
Check your work for errors. Trade papers with a partner. Use the Peer Review Checklist to give each other feedback.

⑤ Publish
Prepare a clean copy of your final draft. Share your essay with the class.

WB 187–188

Peer Review Checklist
- ✓ The article answers all 5W questions.
- ✓ The writing is informative.
- ✓ The main ideas and details are clearly organized.

Spelling Tip
Homophones are words that sound alike, but are spelled differently and have different meanings.

Example: patients/patience

Use a dictionary to check the spelling of homophones.

Fluency 🎧

Listen to the sentences. Pay attention to the groups of words. Read aloud.

1. Many visitors come to see the underground architecture in Coober Pedy, Australia.
2. Molly's letters to her cousin Sarah describe life in a sod house on the Kansas prairie.
3. Meeka was a young Inuit girl who lived with her family in the harsh climate of northern Canada.

Work in pairs. Take turns reading the passage aloud for one minute. Count the number of words you read.

Have you ever seen an underground house? Come visit	9
a town called Coober Pedy!	14
About 3,500 people live in Coober Pedy, Australia.	22
From the street, you might see only dirt and some	32
trees. But underground, there are homes! More	39
than half of the people in the town live in	49
underground houses. These are regular houses that	56
look a lot like yours!	61
The summer heat in Coober Pedy is extreme, but the	71
underground homes are efficient. They stay cool	78
during the hot months. That means people don't spend	87
money on air conditioning. In the winter, the homes	96
stay warm, and that means people pay less for heat.	106
When opal mining became popular in Coober Pedy,	114
miners noticed the cool air in the mines. That's how	124
the underground homes began.	128

With your partner, find the words that slowed you down.

- Practice saying each word and then say the sentence each word is in.
- Then take turns reading the text again. Count the number of words you read.

Put It All Together

WB 189–190

Test Preparation

Taking Tests

You will often take tests that help show what you know. Follow these tips to improve your test-taking skills.

> ### Coaching Corner
>
> **Answering Questions about a Selection**
>
> - Many test questions have you answer questions about a selection.
>
> - The selection can be fiction or nonfiction.
>
> - Before you read the selection, preview the questions and answer choices.
>
> - Look for words like *best, least, main, most, most likely, not,* and *probably*.
>
> - After reading the selection, first try to answer each question in your head.
>
> - Choose the answer that comes closest to the answer in your head.
>
> - Make sure your answer choice is supported by the text.

WB 191–192

Practice

Read the selection. Then answer the questions.

Prairie Dogs

1   A prairie dog is a rodent that is about the size of a rabbit. Prairie dogs are native to the grasslands of North America. They are very social animals. Many species live together underground in large networks of burrows called towns. The towns can cover one half of a square mile and house hundreds of animals. The towns have special rooms where prairie dogs store food and raise their young.

2   Prairie dogs may share their burrows with other animals such as snakes, burrowing owls, and ferrets. They feed on grass during the day. They guard the entrances to their towns. If a predator comes, the guard prairie dog barks to warn the others.

1 Where are many prairie dogs most likely to live?

  A in underground burrows
  B on hilltops
  C with rabbits
  D in Arctic towns

2 In paragraph 1, what does <u>social</u> mean?

  A liking to be with others
  B living in tiny burrows
  C a friendly gathering
  D predatory

3 What is one way in which prairie dogs protect one another?

  A They store food and raise their young.
  B They gather grass for all of them to eat.
  C They share their homes with rabbits.
  D They guard the entrances to their towns.

Tips

✓ Read the question and answer choices before you read the selection.

✓ Sometimes you can infer something to help you answer test questions. What can you infer from the last two sentences?

UNIT 5

Unit 6
Links to Our Past

Do you ever think about the past? Stories about the past can help you learn about life long ago.

Reading 1
Short Story

The Moon Tree

Reading 2
Short Story

Following Grandpa's Footsteps

Reading 3
Social Studies

The History of Money

THE BiG QUESTION

What was life like in the past and why should we learn about it?

Listening and Speaking
You will talk about something in the past. In the Listening and Speaking Workshop, you will give an oral report.

Writing
You will practice skills needed to write a research report. In the Writing Workshop, you will write a research report.

Quick Write
Does your family tell stories from the past? Describe an interesting or exciting event from your family's past.

View and Respond
Talk about the poster for this unit. Then watch and listen to the video and answer the questions at Pearson English Portal.

Build Unit Vocabulary

What do you know about the past?

Words to Know 🎧

Listen and repeat. Use these words to talk about studying the past.

- photographs
- journals 
- museums 
- cave paintings 
- fossils 

Practice

Work with a partner. Ask and answer questions using the words above, from the box, or your own ideas.

| read | study | visit | look at |

Example: A: How can you learn about the past?

B: I can <u>study</u> pictures of <u>cave paintings</u>.

Write

Read the questions. Write your responses in your notebook.

What are some events in your life that you would like to remember in the future? What could you do to remember them?

Make Connections

Complete the sentences with the following phrases.

what people wore

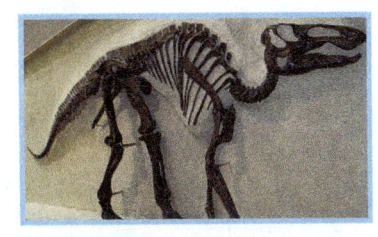

prehistoric animals

prehistoric people

what people did

1. We can learn a lot by studying cave paintings. One way _____ communicated was through art.

2. Carlos and his brothers like to look at the fossils of _____ when they visit museums.

3. By reading journals from long ago you could find out what games people played and _____ to have fun.

4. I love to look at my grandparents' photo albums to see what people looked like and _____ when they were my age.

What about you?

Talk with a partner. How do you save special memories?

UNIT 6 317

Build Unit Background

Kids' Stories from around the World 🎧

Jacob

I live in Washington, D.C. That is the capital of the United States. My mom works for the United States Mint. That is where American money is printed. Mom says we can learn a lot about a country's past by looking at its money. George Washington's picture is on our dollar bill. He was our first president.

Alicia

I live in Mexico. Did you know that there are many pyramids in Mexico? The Mayan people built these pyramids. One of the most famous pyramids in Mexico is El Castillo, also known as the Temple of Kukulcan. El Castillo has four sides. Each side has 91 steps. If you add the steps on the four sides and the top platform, you'll get 365 steps!

France

India

Marie-Paule

I live in France. I like to visit caves where people lived long ago. You can see tools and clothing that prehistoric people used. Many of the caves have paintings on the walls. Ancient people painted objects and animals that were important to them.

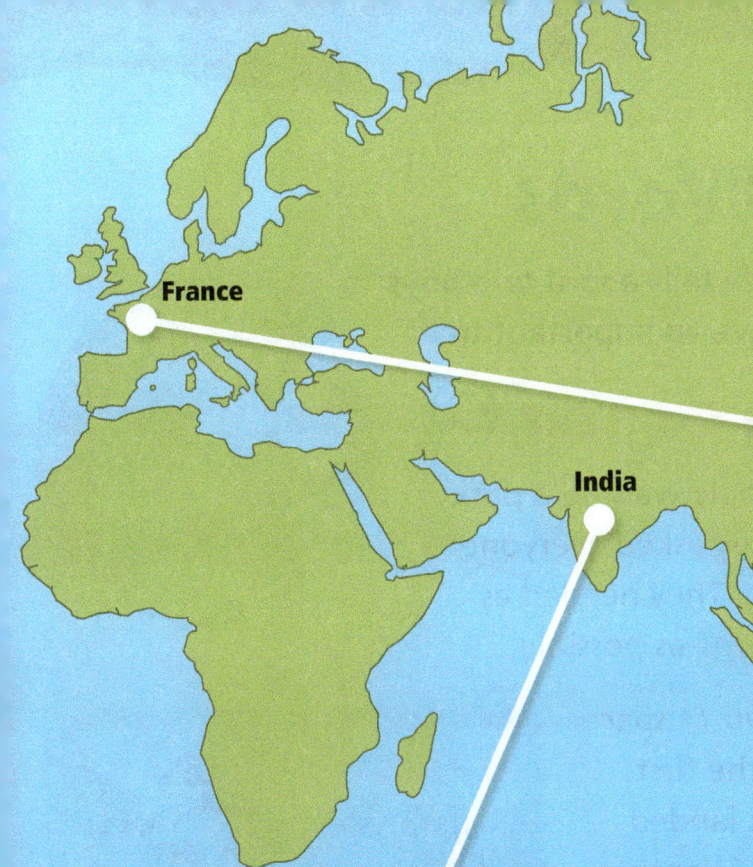

Rajan

I live in India. There are many weavers in my country. They use colorful wool yarns to make beautiful fabric. Many of the patterns are hundreds of years old. They have been passed down through generations.

What about you?

1. What object would you like to save to help you remember your past? Why?
2. What are some ways that your family celebrates the past? Describe them. Share your story.

Reading 1
Prepare to Read

Key Words

The Moon Tree tells about two boys who try to save an important tree.

Words in Context

1 Some people wanted a park in the city. They asked everyone to sign a form. They needed as many **signatures** as possible.

2 The *Apollo 11* space **mission** was the first time a human landed on the moon. Scientists worked for many years to make the mission a success.

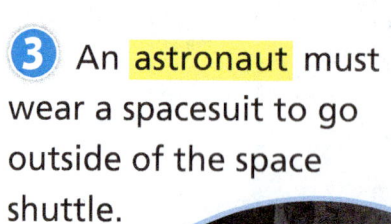

3 An **astronaut** must wear a spacesuit to go outside of the space shuttle.

What You Will Learn

Reading
- Vocabulary building: *Context, phonics*
- Reading strategy: *Identify problem and solution*
- Text type: *Literature (short story)*

Grammar
Compound sentences: *and, but, or*

Writing
Plan a research report

These words will help you understand the reading.

Key Words

signatures
mission
astronaut
plaque
explorer
surrounded

320 UNIT 6

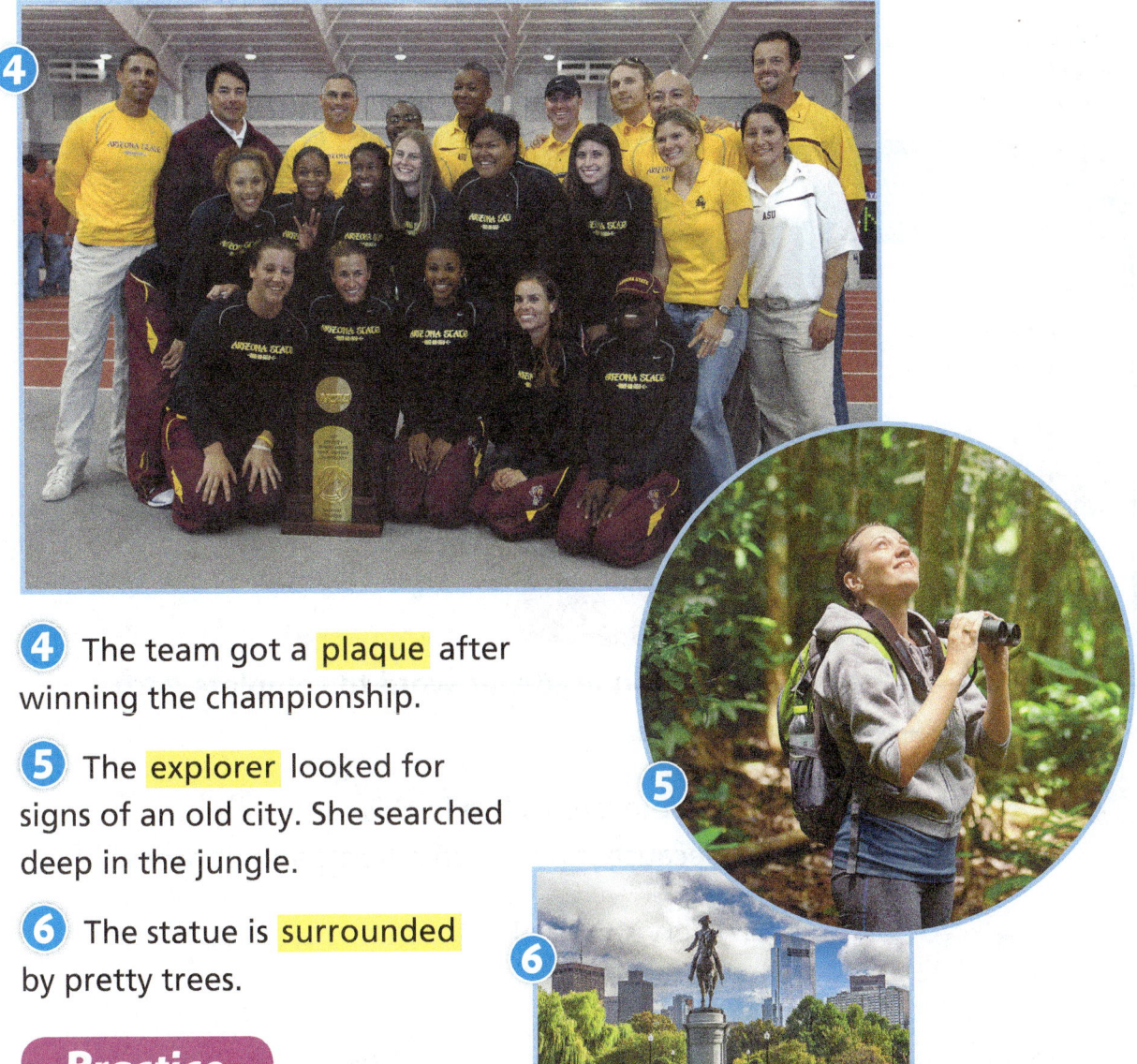

④ The team got a **plaque** after winning the championship.

⑤ The **explorer** looked for signs of an old city. She searched deep in the jungle.

⑥ The statue is **surrounded** by pretty trees.

Practice

Make flashcards to help you memorize the words.
- Write a key word on the front.
- On the back, write the meaning.

Make Connections

Some buildings have plaques telling about a famous person who lived there. Imagine a plaque on the place where you live. What would it say about you? After discussing this question, write your response in your notebook using the key words.

Reading 1

These words will help you talk about the reading.

Academic Words

achieve
succeed in doing something

community
group of people who live in the same area

unique
special, one of a kind

Academic Words

Words in Context

With hard work and practice, Tom was able to **achieve** his goal of learning to play the guitar.

Our **community** all worked together to get more books for our town library.

Your presentation was **unique** because no one else in the class did that.

Practice

Choose an academic word to complete each sentence.

1. People like to live in this _____ because it has good schools and libraries.

2. Every snowflake is _____; no two are alike.

3. To _____ success in school you need to work hard and do your homework.

Apply

Ask and answer with a partner.

1. What would you like to **achieve** by next year?

2. What makes a good **community**?

3. What makes you **unique**?

Phonics

Diphthongs: ow, ou 🎧

Listen as your teacher reads the words. Notice the vowel sounds in these words. Then read the words aloud.

how   loud   low

Which words have the same letters?
Which words have the same vowel sound?

Rule

The letters *ow* and *ou* can have the vowel sound you hear in *how* and *loud*. The letters *ow* can also have the long *o* sound you hear in *low*. The words *how* and *low* have the same *ow* spelling, but different sounds.

Practice

Read the words below with a partner.

around   cow   show
down   know   south
flower   out   tomorrow

- Circle the words in which *ow* has the long *o* sound in *low*.
- Underline the words in which *ow* or *ou* has the vowel sound in *how*.

Reading 1

Literature
Short Story

More About THE BIG QUESTION

Why is it important for people to save things from the past?

🎧 **Listen to the Audio.**
First, listen for the main points. Then listen again for the important details. Take notes as you listen. Retell the story to a partner.

Reading Strategy
Identify Problem and Solution

- As you read, think about the problems the characters face.
- Keep reading to find the solutions to the problems.
- Ask your teacher or classmates if you don't understand.

Listen as your teacher models the reading strategy.

The Moon Tree

by Dan Ahearn
illustrated by Lee White

324 UNIT 6

The ball flew like a rocket into the woods. Hector found the ball next to a strange, flat stone that was dirty and scratched. It rested against a tall **sycamore** tree. On the stone was a brass plaque. It said:

*The seed of this tree was a explorer.
It went to the moon
with the **crew** of the **Apollo 14**.
The seed was planted here on July 4, 1976.*

Hector ran to get his friend Stuart. He didn't notice the red flags that circled the tree.

---

sycamore   North American tree with broad leaves

crew   people who work together

Apollo 14   third spaceship to land on the moon

Before You Go On

What did Hector find when he was looking for a ball?

READING 1

Hector and Stuart ran to the library, and they read about the moon trees. The boys learned that 500 seeds went on the space **mission**. The seeds didn't land on the moon. They stayed in **orbit** with **astronaut** Stuart Roosa. It had been his idea to bring the seeds.

Back on Earth, the seeds grew into normal trees. Space travel had not changed them. People planted hundreds of moon tree **seedlings**, and the trees grew all over the world.

The boys told the librarian, Mrs. Wu, about the moon tree.

---

orbit   a path in space made when one thing moves around a larger thing

seedlings   young plants grown from seeds

"I forgot about our moon tree," said Mrs. Wu. "But I have bad news." She explained that most of the woods would be gone soon. **Stakes** with red flags surrounded each tree that would be cut down.

"Why?" cried Hector.

"To make room for the new shopping mall," said Mrs. Wu.

"That's not right," said Stuart. "There must be something we can do!"

Mrs. Wu said they needed a plan. She and the boys talked all day about how to save the moon tree. By the time the library closed, they had a plan.

---

stakes   pointed objects stuck in the ground to mark places

Before You Go On

What problem did the boys discover?

The boys met with their friends. They told their friends the plan to save the moon tree.

Hector held up a paper. "This is a **petition**," he said. "It says, 'The moon tree is an important part of history. It is too valuable to lose. Please **spare** our moon tree.' We need everybody in town to sign this petition."

"Signatures will show that people care," Stuart said. "We need a lot of signatures. Then the builders might not cut down the moon tree."

Hector said, "Ask everybody to sign the petition! Save the moon tree!"

---

petition   written request signed by a lot of people

spare   save or not damage

They called themselves the Moon Tree Crew. Then Stuart named the tree. He said, "Our moon tree needs a name. People will care more about a tree called . . . Apollo."

Stuart knew about these things. His father worked in the **advertising** business.

Mrs. Wu made posters. Each poster had a **slogan**, "Save Apollo, the moon tree."

The boys and their friends were busy. Some went to stores, others walked down Main Street. They told people the moon tree's story. The whole town wanted to help so the Moon Tree Crew got hundreds of signatures.

---

advertising   business that tells people about a product

slogan   short phrase that is easy to remember

Before You Go On

How did the community become involved?

Hector and Stuart took the petition to Mr. Bowman. He built shopping malls **for a living**.

"Boys, you've made this tree famous," he said. "How did you do it?"

"My father told me how," said Stuart. "He works in advertising."

Mr. Bowman laughed. "When I was your age, I saw the first **lunar** landing on TV. But has this tree really been to the moon?"

"Yes, but it was only a seed then," said Hector.

"It never actually landed on the moon," Stuart added. "It only **orbited** the moon."

Mr. Bowman was silent for a moment. "That's close enough for me," he said.

---

for a living   way to earn money

lunar   about the moon

orbited   traveled in a circle in space around a larger thing

Mr. Bowman did build a shopping mall, but he saved Apollo, the moon tree. He had the old plaque cleaned and shined. Under the old plaque, he added a new one. It said:

The Moon Tree Crew saved this tree.

"Thank you!" said Hector and Stuart.

"No, thank you," said Mr. Bowman. "This tree brings all of us closer to the moon."

Reading Strategy
Identify Problem and Solution

- What problems did the boys in the story have?
- How did they solve the problems?
- Did thinking about the problems and solutions help you understand this story? How?

Think It Over

1. **Recall** What was **unique** about the moon tree?
2. **Comprehend** Why was the moon tree in danger? Explain.
3. **Analyze** How did the boys **achieve** their goal?

Reading 1

Learning Strategies

Problem and Solution

Problems and solutions make a story more interesting. A **problem** is a conflict that characters have. The **solution** is how characters solve, or fix, the problem. There can be more than one problem and solution in a story.

As you read, ask yourself:
- "What is the main, or most important, conflict?"
- "What does the main character want?"

Practice

Write the solution to each problem. The first one is done for you.

PROBLEM	SOLUTION
1. Hector and Stuart wanted to learn about moon trees.	1. Hector and Stuart went to the library to read about moon trees.
2. Hector, Stuart, and Mrs. Wu wanted to save the *unique* tree.	2.
3. Hector, Stuart, and Mrs. Wu wanted the *community* to know about their plan.	3.
4. Mr. Bowman wanted to build a new shopping mall.	4.

Use a Problem and Solution Chart

A Problem and Solution Chart can help you record problems and solutions in a story.

Practice

Copy this chart. Then reread *The Moon Tree*. Write about the main problem and its solution.

Problem
Who? _____
What? _____
Why? _____

Solution
Who? _____
What? _____
Why? _____

Results
_____
_____
_____

Apply

Outline the events in the story. Then narrate the story using key words.

Extension

Work with a small group. Write a short skit about the story. Present your skit to the class.

READING 1

Reading 1

Grammar

Compound Sentences: *and*, *but*, *or*

A **simple sentence** has a subject and a verb. It expresses a complete thought.

> Hector found a moon tree.
> He ran to get his friend Stuart.

Two simple sentences can be joined to form a **compound sentence** using connecting words such as *and*, *but*, and *or*.

Compound sentence with *and*

To combine two similar sentences together, use *and*.

> Hector found a moon tree**, and** he ran to get his friend.

Compound sentence with *but*

To combine two contrasting sentences, use *but*.

> Tim wants to be a pilot. He is afraid of heights.
> Tim wants to be a pilot**, but** he is afraid of heights.

Compound sentence with *or*

To offer a choice, use *or* to combine two simple sentences.

> They can go out to eat. They can cook dinner at home.
> They can go out to eat**, or** they can cook dinner at home.

- Remember to always use a comma before the connecting word in a compound sentence.

Practice A

Use connecting words *and*, *but*, or *or* to complete the compound sentence.

1. It was difficult, _____but_____ the astronauts completed the mission.

2. You could stay at my house tonight, _____ you could stay at a hotel.

3. We had a party for Mom, _____ she had a lot of fun.

4. We got seeds, _____ we forgot to plant them!

Practice B

Use connecting words *and*, *but*, or *or* to combine the sentences. Write the sentences in your notebook.

1. Many seeds went to space. The seeds didn't land on the moon.
   Many seeds went to space, but the seeds didn't land on the moon.

2. The painting could be an original. It could be a fake.

3. The signatures were collected. Then they turned in the petition.

4. The community voted for the law. No one obeyed it.

Apply

Work with a partner. One student says the first part of a compound sentence with *and*, *but*, or *or*. The other completes the sentence.

Grammar Check ✓

What connectors can you use to make compound sentences?

Example: A: The moon tree grew in the woods, but . . .

B: . . . it would soon be cut down.

- Hector and Stuart wrote a petition, and . . . .
- The mall developer could ignore the petition, or . . . .

Reading 1

Writing

Plan a Research Report

In a research report, you explain a topic that you have studied fully. You include information that you have gathered from different sources.

Choose a Topic

Before you can write a research report, you need to choose a topic. You can begin by thinking of a broad topic. Then ask yourself questions about this topic and do a little research. Your findings can give you ideas for a more specific topic. Then think of an open-ended question, which is a question that needs more than a one- or two-word response. This will be the topic of your report.

Task 1

Think about topic ideas, and ask yourself some questions. What interests you? What would you like to learn more about? List your ideas, questions, and answers in a graphic organizer.

A student named Jamie listed his ideas in this chart:

BROAD TOPIC:	The Olympic Games
QUESTION:	How did the Olympic games start?
ANSWER:	The Greeks loved sports. Every four years, thousands watched and participated in sports activities.
QUESTION:	When did the Olympic games begin?
ANSWER:	The Olympic Games started in Greece more than 2,700 years ago.

The answers Jamie found to his questions helped him decide to write about the history of the Olympic Games.

Write a Research Question

Jamie still needed to write a question to direct his research. Here is Jamie's research question.

1. What is the history of the Olympic Games?

Task 2

Once you've chosen a topic and written a research question, begin to organize your ideas and look for reliable sources of information.

Make a Research Plan

To create a research plan, Jamie made a list of things he wanted to know about his topic. He listed them in a T-chart.

What do I want to know?	Where can I find it?
1. What is the history of the ancient Olympic Games?	https://www.olympic.org/ancient-olympic-games/history-old
2. How did the Games begin again?	https://www.olympic.org/athens-1896
3. What are the modern Olympics like?	a print or online encyclopedia

Task 3

Finally, create a research plan. Make a list of what you want to learn and where to look for it. Use a T-chart like the one above.

READING 1

Reading 2
Prepare to Read

What You Will Learn

Reading
- Vocabulary building: *Context, phonics*
- Reading strategy: *Identify plot and setting*
- Text type: *Literature (short story)*

Grammar
Past progressive

Writing
Paraphrasing a source

These words will help you understand the reading.

Key Words
- thrive
- hiking
- trails
- thrilling
- valley
- ledge

Key Words

Following Grandpa's Footsteps is a story about a girl who visits a valley that her grandfather loved.

Words in Context

1 Plants need water to grow and **thrive**. Which plant do you think gets more water?

2 **Hiking** is a lot of fun. You don't need a bike or a car. You just walk on **trails** that go up a mountain.

338 UNIT 6

③ The rides at the fair are ==thrilling==! They are scary and fun at the same time.

④ The ==valley== was deep and wide, with a river running through it.

⑤ The hiker stopped to look over the ==ledge== of the mountain.

Practice

Add a page to your vocabulary notebook.
- Divide your page into three columns: the new words, their definitions, and a sentence using the new word.
- Test yourself by covering one of the columns.

Make Connections

Have you ever been on a hike? Where did you go? If you have not been on a hike, where would you like to go? Why? Be sure to use key words as you speak.

Reading 2

These words will help you talk about the reading.

Academic Words

equipped
provided with things that are needed to do something

motivated
determined or eager to do something

route
way from one place to another

Academic Words

Words in Context 🎧

When you go hiking, it is important to be **equipped** with good hiking boots.

Emily was **motivated** to finish her homework quickly because she wanted to go outside and play.

The map shows the best **route** to school.

Practice

Choose an academic word to complete each sentence.

1. The _____ I take to my friend's house goes through the park.

2. I was _____ with water and a hat for my hike.

3. I was _____ to read a lot of books so that I could win the award.

Apply

Ask and answer with a partner.

1. What does a well-**equipped** student need?

2. What subject in school are you **motivated** to do well in?

3. What is the best **route** from your house to school?

Phonics

Variant Vowel: *oo* 🎧

Listen as your teacher reads the words in the chart. Identify the two sounds of the letters *oo*. Then read the words aloud.

Words with Letters *oo*

b**oo**k	t**oo**
w**oo**d	pr**oo**f
f**oo**t	r**oo**m

Rule

Sometimes the letters *oo* have the sound you hear in ***took***.
Sometimes the letters *oo* have the sound you hear in ***soon***.

Practice

Read the sentences with a partner. Take turns.

- Come look at my scrapbook.
- It has pictures of the trip we took.
- We spent the afternoon walking in the woods.
- There's a pool near the waterfall, too!

1. List the words in which *oo* has the vowel sound in *took*.

   took _____ _____ _____

2. List the words in which *oo* has the vowel sound in *soon*.

   _____ _____ _____

READING 2

Reading 2

Literature
Short Story

More About THE BIG QUESTION

How do some places help people think about the past?

🎧 **Listen to the Audio.**
First, listen for the main points. Then listen again for the important details. Take notes as you listen. Retell the story to a partner.

Reading Strategy
Identify Plot and Setting

- The plot is what happens in a story.
- The setting is where a story takes place.
- Picture the plot and the setting in your mind as you read.

Listen as your teacher models the reading strategy.

Following Grandpa's Footsteps

Last winter my parents took me **hiking** in a deep, wide **valley** near our home. We all love being outside in **nature**, and my father said this was one of my grandfather's favorite places. I don't remember my grandfather very well, so I was very excited. I wanted to learn more about my Grandpa and see why he loved this place so much.

---

nature everything in the natural world including landscapes, animals, and plants

My father gave me a picture of my grandfather standing on a frozen lake. He was next to a hole in the ice, holding a big fish he had caught. He looked really **proud**. And there was a young boy in the picture too. It looked like the boy was helping my Grandpa. "Who's that boy in the picture?" I asked. "Hmm, I really don't know, Sophia," my father said. "But maybe we can find out who it is on our visit." Now I was really excited. There's nothing I love more than a good **mystery**. I might even become a **detective** one day!

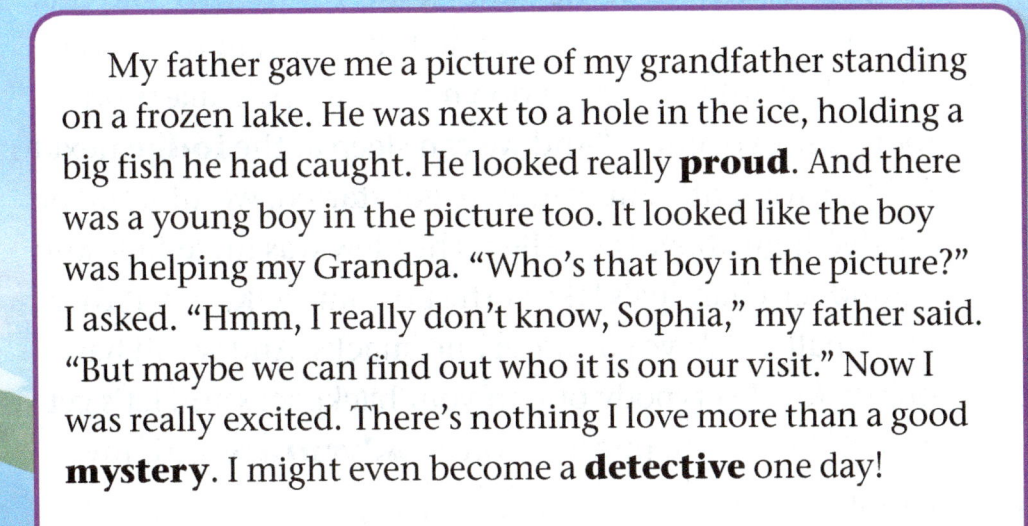

proud feeling good about something you did or own
mystery something that can't be explained or understood
detective someone whose job is to discover information

Before You Go On

What makes the girl think about becoming a detective?

READING 2

After we arrived at the valley trail, my mother said that we had to leave our car there and hike down to the frozen lake. "The only way to get down to Grandpa's lake is on foot," she explained. "And we can sleep at the **lodge** next to the lake tonight." But before we got started, we all stood on a ledge high above the valley. The view was incredible and I could see Grandpa's lake at the bottom. "OK," my father said finally. "We've got water and snacks. And we all have our skates. Everybody put on your backpacks and let's get going." I was so happy to be on an **adventure** with my parents!

---

lodge hotel, often in nature

adventure an exciting, sometimes dangerous, experience

About halfway down, we stopped for a rest. We sat on rocks and had some cookies and hot chocolate. Mom surprised us! There were so many birds and small animals all around us. And somebody made a snowman! "It's so beautiful here," I said. "It is," my mother agreed. "Even in winter, birds and animals **thrive** in this valley."

"And the frozen lake has lots of fish under the ice," my father added. "Your grandfather loved to go ice fishing in that lake." "Can we skate on the lake, Mom and Dad?" I asked. "Yes, of course," they said. "But first we have to get down this trail!"

Before You Go On

What do they need to do before they can go skating?

After a long hike, we finally made it to the bottom. I was tired, and my parents knew it. "Well, just wait till we have to climb back up the trail, and I'm not carrying your backpack!" my father laughed. "Gee, I hadn't thought of that," I said. Then Mom said, "Let's check in at the lodge and get our room. Then we can go skating on the lake before dinner." I could already feel myself skating across the ice. "And I have to figure out who that boy is in the picture," I remembered.

The lodge was very natural and really nice. Everything was made of wood, and there was a big fire burning. We could even see the lake from our room! I asked the woman at the front desk if she knew the boy in the picture, but she had no idea. Then we all went skating! My Dad held my hand and spun me in a circle. It was so much fun! We could see some people ice fishing too. That night, after a delicious dinner, we were all very tired. "Today was a great day," my Mom said. "Now let's all get some sleep." As I started to fall asleep, I was still thinking about the boy in the picture with my Grandpa. Who was he?

Before You Go On

What **motivated** the girl to speak with the woman at the front desk?

READING 2

The next morning, we were eating our breakfast when a man came up to our table. "Good morning, everyone. I hope you're enjoying your visit to the lodge. My name is Rick and I am the owner." My parents thanked him and said how **lovely** everything was. And then I thought to myself, maybe he would know the boy in the picture. "Excuse me, sir," I said. "My name is Sophia. I have an old picture of my grandfather ice fishing on the lake and …" As I handed him the picture he looked at me, smiled, and said, "I remember your grandfather very well. That's me in the picture with him. He used to take me fishing with him when my parents were running the lodge. He was such a nice man."

---

lovely nice

It was **thrilling**. I had solved the mystery of the picture. The man was very kind and told me many stories about my Grandpa. I felt more **connected** to my grandfather than ever before. I was in a place that he loved, and I was talking with someone who he spent time with. I really felt like I was **walking in** my Grandpa's **footsteps**.

---

connected have a link with

walking in (someone's) footsteps taking the path that someone took before

Reading Strategy
Identify Plot and Setting

- What is the plot of this story?
- What is the setting of this story?
- Did thinking about the plot and setting help you understand this story? How?

Think It Over

1. **Recall** How were they equipped for the hike?
2. **Comprehend** What was the mystery that the girl wanted to solve?
3. **Analyze** Why was it not possible to drive the route to the lodge?

Reading 2

Learning Strategies

Plot and Setting

The **plot** is what happens in a story or play.
The **setting** is the time and place the story happens.

- As you read, look for details that tell you where and when the events happen.

Practice

Read the paragraph. Answer the questions about the plot and setting. Write your responses in your notebook.

Last winter, we went hiking in a valley that my grandfather loved. I tried to solve the mystery of an unknown boy in a photograph with my grandfather. We hiked down a trail to the lodge below. We skated on the lake where my grandfather went ice fishing. I met the owner of the lodge. He was the boy in the photograph!

PLOT	SETTING
1. What happens first?	2. Where does this scene occur?
3. What happens next?	4. When does this scene occur?
5. What happens last?	

Use a Sequence of Events Chart

A Sequence of Events Chart can help you record the main events of a story's plot.

Practice
GO 4

Write the major events that occur in *Following Grandpa's Footsteps*. Then write about the setting of each event.

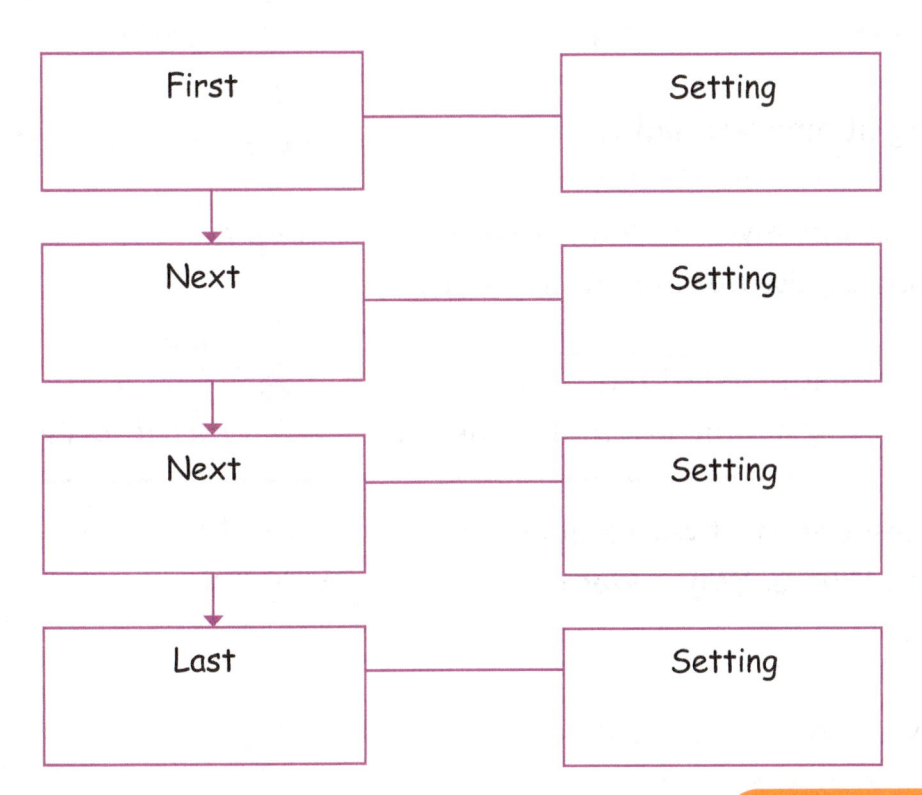

First	→	Setting
Next	→	Setting
Next	→	Setting
Last	→	Setting

WB 209

Apply

**Reread the story and take notes.
Retell the story to a partner.**

Extension

Would the plot of the story change if the setting were different? Choose a new setting. Draw the scene. List plot changes. Present your new story to the class.

READING 2 351

Reading 2

Grammar

Past Progressive

Use the **past progressive** to show an ongoing activity that occurred at a specific time in the past.

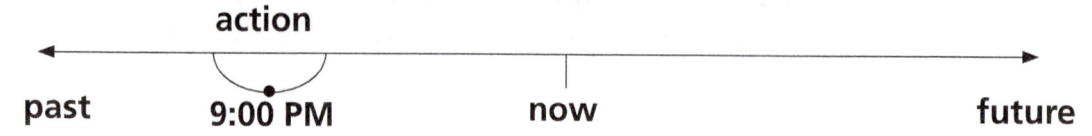

```
              action
    ←———————⌒————————————————————→
    past    9:00 PM         now              future
```

> I **was studying** at nine last night.

To form the past progressive, use **was** or **were** + **verb -ing** in affirmative sentences. Use **not** in negative sentences.

> She **was studying** at nine last night. She **was not watching** TV.
> They **were studying** at nine last night. They **were not watching** TV.

To make **Wh-** questions, start with a question word **Who, What, Where, Why** + **was** or **were** + the subject.

| was not → **wasn't** |
| were not → **weren't** |

> **Where were** you **going** this morning?

Use the past progressive with **when** and **while** to show an ongoing action in the past that was interrupted by another action. Use the simple past for the other action.

> **While** we **were studying**, Dad arrived. OR Dad arrived **while** we **were studying**.
> **When** I **was taking** a walk, it started to rain. OR It started to rain **when** I **was taking** a walk.

Practice A

Complete the sentences with the correct form of the verb in parentheses.

1. During the hike, Sophia _____was wearing_____ a hat. (wear)

2. Her mom _____ a backpack. (carry)

3. Her dad _____ a hat. (not wear)

4. They _____ pictures. (not take)

5. They _____ the view. (admire)

Practice B

Complete the sentences with *when* or *while*.

1. <u>While</u> her parents were resting, the girl explored the lodge.

2. She was walking around _____ she heard a voice.

3. A little boy approached her _____ she was walking.

4. They were walking together _____ the boy's mom arrived.

5. _____ she was talking with the mom, her dad called.

Apply

Work with a partner. Take turns asking and answering questions about what you were doing at these times.

Example: A: What were you doing last Saturday at ten?

B: I was watching television.

- Saturday 10AM
- Monday 5PM
- yesterday 7AM

Grammar Check ✓

What kind of actions does the past progressive describe?

WB 210

READING 2

Reading 2

Writing

Paraphrasing a Source

When you put an author's ideas into your own words, you are paraphrasing. In this lesson, you will learn how to paraphrase information and ideas from the sources you use in your research.

How to Paraphrase

Follow these steps to paraphrase ideas or information from a source:

1. Read the information in the reference source several times, so the important facts are clear in your mind.

2. Put the source away, and write what you learned in your own words.

3. Look at your source again to make sure all the facts in your paraphrase are correct.

4. Finally, make a note of who wrote the book or article, as well as when it was published and who published it. If the information comes from a website, look for an author's name on the site, or copy down the URL, or web address. This information is called a citation.

Task

Begin to research the topic you chose in the last lesson. This will become the research report you will write in the workshop at the end of the unit. To practice paraphrasing, choose a paragraph from one of your sources. Express the ideas in your own words. List the text from the original source, your paraphrase, and the citation in the graphic organizer.

A student named Jamie listed his ideas in this chart:

Text from Source	Paraphrase	Citation
"The 1896 Summer Olympics, officially known as the Games of the I Olympiad, was the first international Olympic Games held in modern history. Organized by the International Olympic Committee (IOC), which had been created by Pierre de Coubertin, it was held in Athens, Greece, from 6 to 15 April 1896."	The 1896 Summer Olympics was the first modern international Olympic Games. It was organized by the International Olympic Committee (IOC), created by Pierre de Coubertin. The Games were held in Athens, Greece, from April 6 to 15, 1896.	First modern Olympics is held https://www.olympicsinhistory8791.com/first-modern-olympics.html

Here is part of Jamie's research report that includes a paraphrase of the information he found on a website. He will use this paraphrase as part of his final research report. He included a description of the source he used for the information.

Jamie Martinez

Imagine you were there at the first modern Olympic Games. What would you see?

The 1896 Summer Olympics was the first modern international Olympic Games. It was organized by the International Olympic Committee (IOC), created by Pierre de Coubertin. The Games were held in Athens, Greece, from April 6 to 15, 1896.

Works Consulted

First modern Olympics is held: https://www.olympicsinhistory8791.com/first-modern-olympics.html

READING 2

Reading 3
Prepare to Read

What You Will Learn

Reading
- Vocabulary building: *Context, word study*
- Reading strategy: *Summarize*
- Text type: *Informational text (social studies)*

Grammar
Complex sentences: *because, so*

Writing
Quoting a source

These words will help you understand the reading.

Key Words
worth
trade
bartered
currency
rulers

Key Words

The History of Money tells about the history of how trading animals slowly changed into the use of coins and paper money.

Words in Context

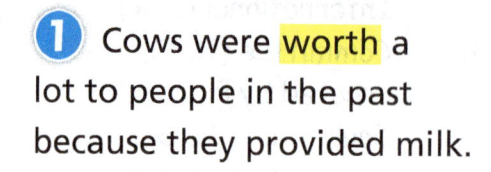

1 Cows were **worth** a lot to people in the past because they provided milk.

2 In the past, people would **trade** many chickens for one cow.

3 The students in the lunchroom **bartered** their lunches with each other.

356 UNIT 6

④ Sea shells were a form of currency that people used to buy goods.

⑤ The rulers of countries often have their faces stamped on coins.

Practice

Add a page to your vocabulary notebook.
- Write a sentence but leave a blank where the key word should be.
- Then exchange notebooks with a partner and fill in the missing key words.

Make Connections

Have you ever made a trade to get something you wanted instead of using money? Maybe you have traded work, like washing the dishes?

213

READING 3 357

Reading 3

These words will help you talk about the reading.

Academic Words

cooperate
work together with someone else

initial
happening at the beginning

tradition
something that people have done for a long time and continue to do

Academic Words

Words in Context

Some of the players refused to **cooperate** with the rest of the team.

The **initial** step is to write down your ideas. Then you can start to write your first draft.

Street festivals are a fun and colorful **tradition** in many countries.

Practice

Choose an academic word to complete each sentence.

1. Many families have at least one _____ that they pass down.

2. His _____ report didn't have enough details, but then he added more.

3. Everyone wanted to _____ so that the project would be done well.

Apply

Ask and answer with a partner.

1. Why should you **cooperate** with your classmates?

2. What was your **initial** response when you got your first A in English?

3. What is your favorite family **tradition**?

WB 214

358 UNIT 6

Word Study

Greek and Latin Roots

Many English words come from Greek or Latin. For example, the word *annual* means *yearly*. It comes from the Latin root *anno*, meaning *year*.

Rule

Look for this pattern in English: words that have Greek and Latin roots within them.

The Greek or Latin root in each word is in purple.

location   **init**ial
biologist   **aqua**rium

Reading Skill

Looking for patterns in English will make you a better reader.

Practice

Complete each statement.

1. The root *init* means "beginning." The **initial** class was the _____.
    a. last   b. second   c. first

2. The root *loc* means "place." **Location** is _____ something occurs.
    a. when   b. where   c. why

3. The root *aqua* means "water." In an **aquarium** there are _____.
    a. fish   b. birds   c. mice

4. The root *bio* means "life." A **biologist** studies _____.
    a. rocks   b. stars   c. animals

Reading 3

Informational Text
Social Studies

More About THE BIG QUESTION

How does the history of money tell us about the past?

🎧 **Listen to the Audio.**
First, listen for the main points. Then listen again for the important details. Take notes as you listen. Retell the selection to a partner.

Reading Strategy
Summarize

To summarize a reading selection, you retell the selection's main ideas and important details in your own words. To help you summarize, ask yourself *Who*, *What*, *Where*, *When*, and *Why* questions as you read.

Listen as your teacher models the reading strategy.

THE HISTORY OF MONEY

by Mbeke Tsango

What is money? The answer might surprise you. Money is what people agree it is. People agree that a pen is worth a dollar, or that an apple is worth an orange.

Did you ever trade an apple for an orange at lunch? If you did, you used your fruit like money. Before money was made for the first time, people bartered, or traded for things they wanted. They traded one thing for another.

Cows, goats, and sheep were the first currency. Later, farmers traded the things they grew.

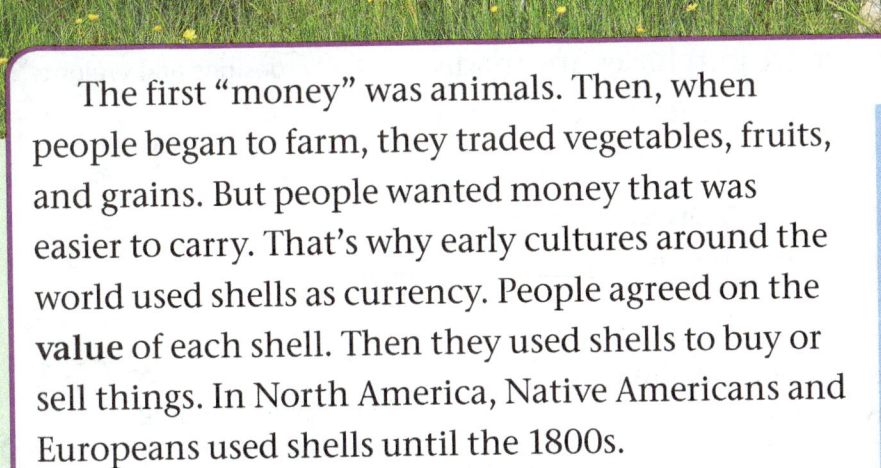

The first "money" was animals. Then, when people began to farm, they traded vegetables, fruits, and grains. But people wanted money that was easier to carry. That's why early cultures around the world used shells as currency. People agreed on the **value** of each shell. Then they used shells to buy or sell things. In North America, Native Americans and Europeans used shells until the 1800s.

About 3,000 years ago, people in China began using metals to make shells. Then they made coins. Slowly, metal currency spread to other countries. People made coins from gold, silver, or bronze. The coins were **stamped** with art or images, such as rulers' faces.

---

value the worth or importance of something
stamped marked or impressed with a design

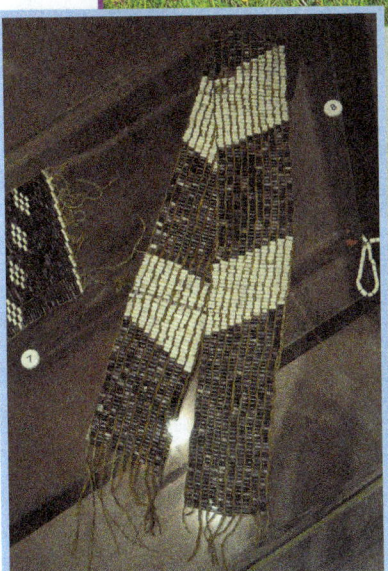

People around the world once used shell money. This belt of shells was very valuable.

Before You Go On

Why did people use shells as currency?

READING 3 **361**

At first, people weighed coins to learn their values. Later, each kind of coin got the same size, weight, and decoration.

Paper money was first made in China around 900. People in Europe did not use paper money until about 1650. Soon, paper money became as common as coins.

People still use paper and metal currency. But technology is changing the way we use money. Now we get money from machines. We use plastic **credit cards** and **debit cards** to buy things in stores and on the internet.

Nowadays, more and more purchases are made digitally, using a computer, smartphone, or even your fingerprint! Can you imagine some other ways that we could pay for something using modern technology? Will we still use bills and coins in the future?

Coins of different values have different designs and weights.

credit cards	cards that let you buy something now and pay for it later
debit cards	cards that let you pay for something directly from your bank account

Technology is changing the way we use money.

Currency Timeline

9000 B.C.E.	animals
6000 B.C.E.	fruits and vegetables
1200 B.C.E.	shells
1100 B.C.E.	metal coins
900	paper money in Europe
1700	shells in North America
Today	credit cards, debit cards, digital purchases
Future	no bills or coins?

Reading Strategy

Summarize

Summarize the selection. Use these questions to help you.

- *What* is money?
- *Why* is money important?
- *Where* did people first start making metal "shells" for money?
- *When* were metal coins invented?
- *Whose* faces were stamped on early coins?
- *How* could people **cooperate** with each other instead of using money?

Think It Over

1. **Recall** What was the initial form of money?
2. **Comprehend** Why did people start using shells for money?
3. **Analyze** How do you think it became a tradition to stamp rulers' faces on early coins?

READING 3

Reading 3

Learning Strategies

Summarize

When you **summarize**, you retell the main ideas and details of a story. The main idea and the details are the most important parts of a story.

- Ask yourself **who**, **what**, **where**, **when**, and **why** questions to find the main idea of a story.
- Look for details that support the main idea.

Practice

Reread *The History of Money*. Look at the pictures. Then answer the questions to complete the Details column.

Questions About the Main Idea	Details
1. Who invented metal coins?	1. the Chinese
2. What types of metal were the coins made of?	2.
3. How did people first determine how much a coin was worth?	3.
4. How has technology changed the way we use money?	4.

When the students traded a banana for an apple, they bartered.

Use a Main Idea and Details Chart

A Main Idea and Details Chart helps you record the main idea and the most important details as you read.

Practice

Use the chart on the previous page to help you.

- Find the main idea of the selection.
- Then list three details that support that idea.

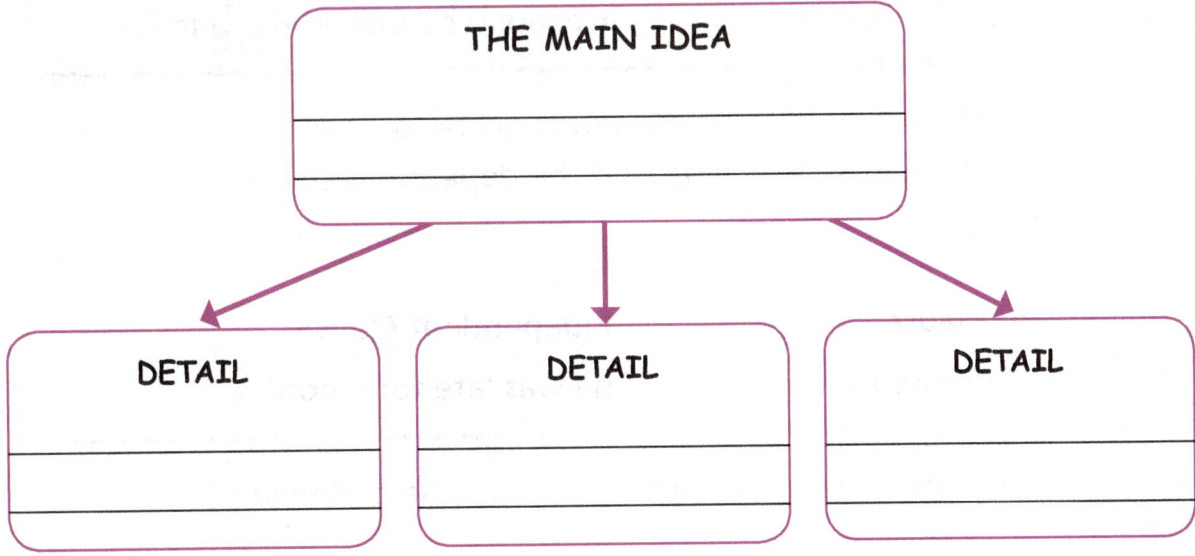

THE MAIN IDEA

DETAIL | **DETAIL** | **DETAIL**

Apply

Summarize the story to a partner. Use the key words as you speak.

Extension

Your country was selected as the happiest country on Earth. Design a celebration coin. What will you put on the coin? Discuss your ideas with a partner. Present your ideas to the class. Use images in your presentation.

READING 3

Reading 3

Grammar

Complex Sentences: *because, so, so that*

A **complex sentence** consists of an independent clause, a connecting word, and a dependent clause.
Use the connecting word **because** to give a reason.

Independent Clause	Dependent Clause
He was late for school	**because** he missed the bus.

The dependent clause with **because** can come before the independent clause. Use a comma (**,**) if the dependent clause comes first.

Dependent Clause	Independent Clause
Because he missed the bus**,**	he was late for school.

Use the connecting word *so* to express a result. Use a comma (**,**) before *so*.

Independent Clause	Dependent Clause
Today people don't want to carry cash when traveling**,**	**so** they use credit cards.

Use *so that* to express purpose or goal. Don't use a comma with *so that*.

Independent Clause	Dependent Clause
They sat with the new student	**so that** he wouldn't eat alone.

Practice A

Complete the sentences with *because*, *so*, and *so that*.

1. <u>Because</u> shells were easy to carry, people used them as currency.

2. Apples and oranges can be traded _____ they are worth the same amount.

3. Many people use credit cards _____ they don't have to carry money.

4. People wanted something easy to carry, _____ money was invented.

Practice B

Combine these sentences with *so*, *because*, and *so that*.

1. She tutored him. He could pass his exam. She tutored him so that he could pass his exam.

2. I miss my cousin. I called her.

3. We formed a study group. We like to work together.

4. Dad studied languages. He could work at the UN.

Apply

Work with a partner. Write two questions each about "The History of Money." Then take turns asking and answering the questions. Use compound sentences in your answers.

Grammar Check ✓

What does a complex sentence consist of?

Example: A: Why did ancient people trade animals?

B: Ancient people traded animals because they didn't have money.

WB 220

READING 3 367

Reading 3

Writing

Quoting a Source

Including quotations from a source in a research report can be an excellent way of supporting your own ideas. In this lesson you will learn how to use quotations in this way.

How to Include Quotations

Follow these steps to quote information directly from a source:

1. Read the text you would like to quote. Think about why you wish to include it in your report. Does it support an idea in a way that you wouldn't be able to do in your own words?

2. Write down the information word-for-word. It may be a sentence or an entire paragraph.

3. Look at your original source again. Make sure you have copied the words correctly.

4. Finally, make a note of who wrote the book or article, when it was published, and who published it. If the information comes from a website, look for an author's name or copy down the URL. This information is for the citation.

5. When you write your report, surround the quoted text in quotation marks. Include your citation.

Task

Continue the research for your report. To practice including quotations, look for information that supports a key point or idea in your report. Copy the text word-for-word. List the idea you want to support, the quotation, and the citation in a graphic organizer.

A student named Jamie listed his ideas in this chart:

Information Search	Direct Quote	Citation
Looking for information about the modern Olympic Games.	"To the delight of the hometown crowd, Greek runner Spyridon Louis won the marathon."	https://www.olympicsinhistory8791.com/first-modern-olympics.html

Here is a paragraph from Jamie's research report. The paragraph includes a quotation from Jamie's source. Jamie also included the URL at the end of his report.

Jamie Martinez

On April 6, 1896, the first modern Olympics began in Athens, Greece. There were 241 athletes from 14 countries competing in 43 events. Greek runner Spyridon Louis won the marathon and thrilled the crowd. The Games ended on April 15, 1896.

Work Consulted

https://www.olympicsinhistory8791.com/first-modern-olympics.html

Spyridon Louis, winner of the marathon in Athens, Greece, 1896, was a guest of honor during the Olympic Games in Berlin.

Put It All Together

Apply and Extend

Link the Readings

Read the words in the top row of the chart. Then follow these steps:

- For each reading, put an X under the words that remind you of the text.

	Informational Text	Literature	Community Working Together	Family Working Together
The Moon Tree				
Following Grandpa's Footsteps				
The History of Money				

Discussion

1. In what way do the characters in "The Moon Tree" and "Following Grandpa's Footsteps" **achieve** similar goals? Explain.

2. All three readings relate to the idea of **cooperating** with others. Give examples from each reading.

3. How can learning about the history of money teach us how people lived in earlier times?

THE BIG QUESTION What was life like in the past and why should we learn about it?

Projects

Your teacher will help you choose one of these projects.

Written ✏️	Oral 💬	Visual/Active 👋
Song Find a song that talks about remembering or living in the past. Play the song in class. How did you feel after listening to the song?	**Oral Report** Choose one of the three selections that you just read. Give an oral report about what you learned from that selection.	**Pantomime** Reread one of the stories. Act out a part of one story. Ask classmates to guess which story you are acting out.
History Article Choose an individual or event from history. Research and write a short article. Ask and answer the 5W questions in your article.	**Tall Tale** A tall tale stretches the facts about a person or an event. Make up a tall tale about a person or an event from the past.	**Park Design** Design a historical park or public place for your town. Think about what kinds of buildings and exhibits you would include. Create a map or model for the park.

Put It All Together

Listening and Speaking Workshop
Give an Oral Report 🎧

You are going to write and give an oral report. Then you will listen as your classmates give an oral report.

① Prepare

A. Think about a historical event that happened in your community, this country, or another country.

B. Choose an event and research it. Organize the facts, details, and examples. You will need to describe the event and explain why it is important. Write your main points and details on note cards. Find photos, posters, or other visuals to show during your oral report.

Note Card 1
Main Point – the *Apollo* 11 space mission
Detail – launched on July 16, 1969
Detail – astronauts first landed on the moon

Note Card 2
Main Point – very important for NASA and for the world
Detail – for NASA, first successful space walk
Detail – for the world, greatest scientific achievement

② Practice

Practice your oral presentation in front of your family or friends with props. Record your oral presentation and then listen. Record yourself again and try to improve.

Useful Language

🎧 Listen and repeat.

My report today is about . . .

This event is important because . . .

Scientists did it so that . . .

This photo shows . . .

③ Present

As you speak, do the following:
- Speak clearly and confidently.
- Look at your audience. Glance at your note cards occasionally.
- Use your props and other visuals.

As you listen, do the following:
- Take notes on important points.
- Watch for gestures and pay attention to visuals. Your teacher will ask you questions about the presentation.

④ Evaluate

After you speak, answer these questions:
- ✓ Did you speak clearly and with confidence?
- ✓ Did you support your main points with facts, examples, and details?

After you listen, answer these questions:
- ✓ Did you hear the speaker easily?
- ✓ Did you understand the general meaning, main points, and details? Retell it to a partner.
- ✓ Did you take good notes?

Speaking Skills
An oral presentation is a formal situation. Use complete sentences and vocabulary that suits the occasion and audience.

Listening Skills
Listen carefully for clearly stated information. It can be used to infer ideas that aren't stated directly.

UNIT 6

Put It All Together

Writing Workshop
Write a Research Report

Writing Prompt
Write a research report that you began earlier in this unit. Present a main idea, and include facts and details to support it. Gather information from a variety of sources such as books, magazines, or online websites.

① Prewrite

Review the lessons in this unit. You have chosen and narrowed a topic. You have created a research plan. You have learned to paraphrase and quote directly from your sources.

A. Taking Notes

Now it is time to do your research. As you do so, you will take notes on your findings. One of the most important things you need to do as you research is to keep track of your sources.

A good way to do this is to use note cards. Use one note card for each idea. Write a label for the idea at the top of the card. Then write your paraphrase or your quotation in the body of the card. Finally, write the source, author, publisher, and page number at the bottom of the card.

You will use your cards when you plan your outline and write your report. You can also use them to put your sources in alphabetical order for your Works Consulted list.

Here is an example of a note card:

> **FIRST MODERN OLYMPICS HELD IN ATHENS, GREECE**
>
> The 1896 Summer Olympics was the first modern international Olympic Games. It was organized by the International Olympic Committee (IOC), created by Pierre de Coubertin. The Games were held in Athens, Greece, from April 6 to 15, 1896.
>
> Source: https://www.olympicsinhistory8791.com/first-modern-olympics.html

B. Making an Outline

Use the labels on your note cards to sort the cards by ideas. Decide what order you would like to present the ideas in your report. Discard any note cards that you decide not to use. Once you are satisfied with the arrangement of your ideas, create an outline.

> **The Modern Olympics**
>
> A. Introduction: The modern Olympic Games
>   1. Winter and summer Games
>   2. Held every four years, but separated only by two years
> B. History: Greek Olympics
>   1. Began in 776 BC
>   2. Held every four years at Olympia, Greece
> C. History: Modern Olympic Games
>   1. Began in 1896 in Athens, Greece
>   2. Winter/summer Olympics held every four years in many different countries
> D. Conclusion: Modern Olympic Games were inspired by ancient Greek Olympics

Put It All Together

② Draft

Use your outline to help you write a first draft.

- Begin with a paragraph that clearly presents your topic.
- Use transition words to keep your ideas flowing smoothly.

> **Six Traits of Writing Checklist**
>
> ✓ **Ideas**
> Does my first paragraph present the topic clearly?
>
> ✓ **Organization**
> Are my ideas presented in a logical order?
>
> ✓ **Voice**
> Is my tone appropriate?
>
> ✓ **Word Choice**
> Do my words express my meaning clearly?
>
> ✓ **Sentence Fluency**
> Are the sentence patterns varied?
>
> ✓ **Conventions**
> Did I capitalize proper nouns correctly?

- Include citations for paraphrases and quotations.

Citing Sources Use the following examples as models:

Book

Pearson, Anne. <u>Ancient Greece</u>. New York: Dorling Kindersley, 2007.

Magazine Article

Fitzgerald, Terrence. "March of the Caterpillars." <u>Natural History</u> September 2008: 28–33.

Internet Website

"Greeks Cheer On Spyridon Louis." <u>Olympics in History</u> 12 March 2019. <http://www.olympcsinhistory8701.com/articles/303867/Article1.asp>

Encyclopedia Article

Lawson, Wendy. "Antarctica." <u>World Book Encyclopedia</u>. 2010 ed.

---

③ Revise

Read your draft. Look for places where the writing needs improvement. Use the Writing Checklist to help you identify problems. Then revise your draft.

Here is how Jamie revised his research report:

The History of the Olympic Games

People all over the world love to watch the Olympic Games. It's a great example of international cooperation ^and a way for countries to compete peacefully. And how many young people are inspired to dream about becoming Olympic athletes one day themselves?

Revised to insert missing word.

But how did the modern Olympic Games come to be? It all began with the Greek Olympics in the year 776 BC. Every four years, male ~~g~~Greek athletes would gather at Olympia, Greece, to compete in different sporting events. Many of the athletes were soldiers.

Revised to correct error in capitalization

Then, in the year 392, the Roman Emperor Theodosius banned the Greek Olympics to maintain control over Greece. It would be 1,500 years before the world saw Olympic Games again. The Frenchman Pierre de Coubertin was largely responsible for restarting the Games. This time, the Games would be international. *The setting for the first modern Olympic Games in 1896 was Athens, Greece.* ~~Athens, Greece held the first modern Olympics in 1896.~~ King Georgios of Greece and tens of thousands of spectators watched athletes from 14 different countries compete in sporting events. The Greek people were thrilled when Greek runner Spyridon Louis won the marathon.

Revised to make meaning clearer.

Today we all look forward to the next Olympic Games. The winter and summer Games are each held every four years but are only separated by two years. Countries around the world apply with the International Olympic Committee (IOC) to have the honor of hosting the Games. We love to watch the intense competition and cheer athletes from our home countries, but it's important to remember ~~thousands of years ago~~ where it all started, in Olympia^*, thousands of years ago*.

Revised to make meaning clearer.

UNIT 6 377

Put It All Together

WORKS CONSULTED LIST
Joe Fullman. <u>The Olympics: Ancient to Modern.</u> Wayland Books, 2017.
https://www.britannica.com/sports/Olympic-Games
https://www.history.com/topics/olympic-games
https://www.olympic.org/ancient-olympic-games/history-old

④ Edit

Check your work for errors. Trade papers with a partner. Use the Peer Review Checklist to give each other feedback.

⑤ Publish

Prepare a clean copy of your final draft. Share your essay with the class.

Peer Review Checklist

✓ The main ideas and details are clear.

✓ The writing is interesting.

✓ All the information is related to the topic.

Put It All Together

Fluency 🎧

Listen to the sentences. Pay attention to the groups of words. Read aloud.

1. Hector discovers and saves a tree whose seeds went on a space mission.

2. A young girl visits a winter valley and thinks about her grandfather when he was there.

3. Learning about the history of money is an interesting way to see how people shopped in the past.

Work in pairs. Take turns reading aloud for one minute. Count the number of words you read.

Last winter my parents took me hiking in a deep,	10
wide valley near our home. We all love being outside in	21
nature, and my father said this was one of my grandfather's	32
favorite places. I don't remember my grandfather very well,	41
so I was very excited. I wanted to learn more about my Grandpa	54
and see why he loved this place so much.	63
My father gave me a picture of my grandfather standing on	74
a frozen lake. He was next to a hole in the ice, holding a big fish	90
he had caught. He looked really proud. And there was a young boy	103
in the picture too. It looked like the boy was helping my Grandpa.	116
"Who's that boy in the picture?" I asked. "Hmm, I really don't	128
know, Sophia," my father said. "But maybe we can find out who	140
it is on our visit." Now I was really excited. There's nothing I love	154
more than a good mystery. I might even become a detective one day!	167

Test Preparation

Taking Tests

You will often take tests that help show what you know. Follow these tips to improve your test-taking skills.

Coaching Corner

Answering Test Items for Revising and Editing

- Revising and Editing Tests often ask you to look for corrections and improvements a writer should make.

- Before you read the written selection, preview the questions and answer choices.

- After reading the whole selection, go back and carefully reread the sentence mentioned in the question. Do you notice any mistakes in grammar or punctuation?

- Read each of the answer choices to yourself to see if one of them sounds better than the sentence in the selection. Choose the answer that does the most to improve the whole sentence.

- Remember that sometimes the sentence will not need any corrections or improvements.

Practice

Read the selection. Look for any corrections and improvements that may be needed, then answer the questions.

(1) The city where I live has three interesting museums. (2) They are the Museum of History the Museum of Archaeology, and the Museum of Art. (3) The Museum of History is the largest of the three. (4) I live close to the Museum of History I go there a lot. (5) My mom is a volunteer at some of the events. (6) She says "if you come to our city, try to visit this museum. (7) I agree. (8) There is something for everyone here.

1 What change, if any, should be made in sentence 2?

   A Delete the comma after *Archaeology*

   B Insert a comma after *History*

   C Change *They are* to *They were*

   D Make no change

2 What change, if any, should be made in sentence 4?

   F I go to the museum of History a lot.

   G I go to the close by Museum of History.

   H I live close to the Museum of History, so I go there a lot.

   J No revision is needed.

3 What is the BEST way to revise sentence 6?

   A She says, "if you come to our city." Try to visit this museum

   B She says "If you come to our city try to visit this museum."

   C She says if you come to our city, try to visit this museum."

   D She says, "If you come to our city, try to visit this museum."

Tips

✓ Think about how to combine clauses using connecting words. What's the best way to combine the clauses in sentence 4?

✓ Read each answer choice to yourself. Remember the rules for punctuating quotations.

Handbook

Study Skills and Language Learning

How to Learn Language 383
How to Study 384
How to Build Vocabulary / How to Use a Book 385
How to Use a Dictionary and Thesaurus 386
How to Take Tests 387

Viewing and Representing Information

How to Read Maps and Diagrams 388
How to Read Graphs 389

Grammar Handbook

Parts of Speech
    Nouns and Articles 390
    Pronouns 391
    Verbs 392
    Adjectives and Adverbs 393
    Prepositions 394
    Conjunctions and Interjections 395
Sentences
    Clauses and Sentences 396
    Sentence Types 396
Punctuation 397

Writing Handbook

Modes of Writing 399
The Writing Process 400
Peer Review Checklist 402
Rubric for Writing 404
Writing and Research 405
    Library Reference 405
    Citing Sources 406
    Internet Research 408
    Information Media 410
How to Use Technology in Writing 412

Study Skills and Language Learning

How to Learn Language

Learning a language involves listening, speaking, reading, and writing. You can use these tips to make the most of your language learning.

Listening
1. Listen with a purpose.
2. Listen actively.
3. Take notes.
4. Listen to speakers on the radio, television, and internet.

Speaking
1. Think before you speak.
2. Speak appropriately for your audience.
3. Practice reading aloud to a partner.
4. Practice speaking with friends and family members.
5. Remember, it is okay to make mistakes.

Reading
1. Read every day.
2. Use the visuals to help you figure out what words mean.
3. Reread parts that you do not understand.
4. Read many kinds of literature.
5. Ask for help.

Writing
1. Write something every day.
2. Plan your writing before you begin.
3. Read aloud what you write. Ask yourself whether it makes sense.
4. Check for spelling and grammar mistakes.

Handbook

How to Study

Here are some tips for developing good study habits.

- **Schedule a time for studying.** It is easier to develop good study habits if you set aside the same time every day to study. Once you have a study routine, it will be easier for you to find time to prepare for larger projects or tests.
- **Create a special place for studying.** Find a study area where you are comfortable and where you have everything you need for studying. If possible, choose an area that is away from telephones or television. You can play music if it helps you to concentrate.
- **Read the directions first.** Make sure you understand what you are supposed to do. Ask a partner or your teacher about anything you do not understand.
- **Preview the reading.** Look at the pictures, illustrations, and captions in the reading. They will help you understand the text.
- **Learn unfamiliar words.** Try to figure out what unfamiliar words mean by finding context clues in the reading. If you still can't figure out the meaning, use a dictionary.
- **Take notes.** Keep notes in a notebook or journal of important things you want to remember from the reading.
- **Ask questions.** Write any questions you have from the reading. Discuss them with a partner or your teacher.

How to Build Vocabulary

Use these ideas to help you remember the meanings of new words.

Keep a Vocabulary Notebook Keep a notebook of vocabulary words and their definitions. Test yourself by covering either the word or the definition.

Make Flashcards On the front of an index card, write a word you want to remember. On the back, write the meaning. Use the cards to review the words with a partner or family member.

Say the Words Aloud Use your new words in sentences. Say the sentences to a partner or a family member.

How to Use a Book

The Title Page The title page states the title, the author, and the publisher.

The Table of Contents The table of contents is at the front of a book. The page on which a chapter begins is next to its name.

The Glossary The glossary is a small dictionary at the back of a book. It will tell you the meaning of a word and sometimes how to pronounce it. Use the glossary the same way you would use a dictionary.

The Index The index is at the back of a book. It lists subjects and names that are in the book, along with page numbers where you can find information.

The Bibliography The bibliography at the back of a book or chapter lets you know the books or sources where an author got information.

Handbook

How to Use a Dictionary and Thesaurus

The Dictionary

You can find the **spelling**, **pronunciation**, **part of speech**, and **definitions** of words in the dictionary.

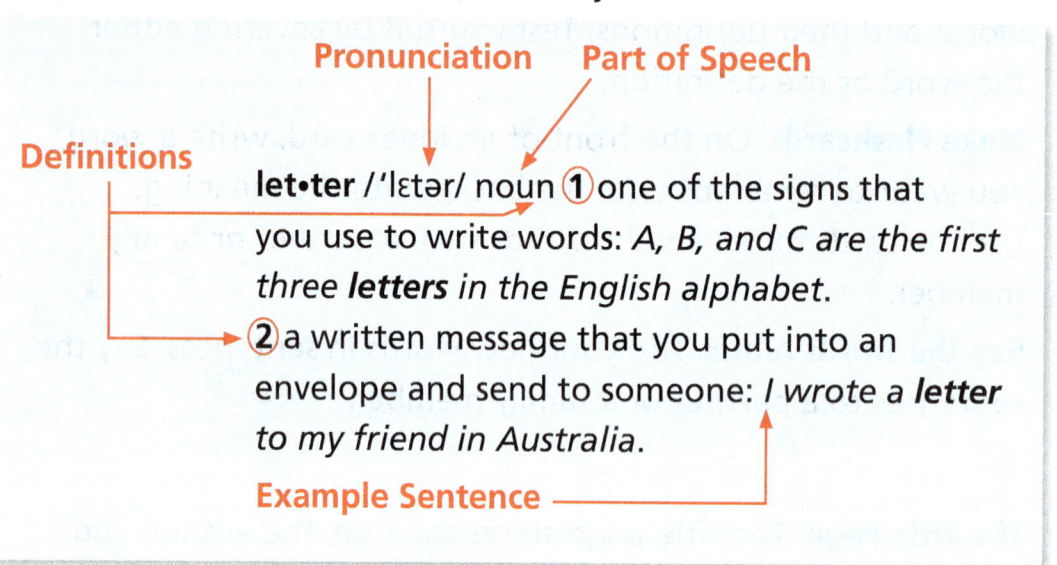

Definitions → **let•ter** /ˈlɛtər/ **noun** ① one of the signs that you use to write words: *A, B, and C are the first three letters in the English alphabet.*
② a written message that you put into an envelope and send to someone: *I wrote a letter to my friend in Australia.*

(Pronunciation, Part of Speech, Example Sentence labeled)

The Thesaurus

A thesaurus is a specialized dictionary that lists **synonyms**, or words with similar meanings, and **antonyms**, or words with opposite meanings. Words in a thesaurus are arranged alphabetically. You can look up the word just as you would look it up in a dictionary.

Main entry: sad
Part of speech: adjective
Definition: unhappy
Synonyms: bitter, depressed, despairing, down, downcast, gloomy, glum, heartbroken, low, melancholy, morose, pessimistic, sorry, troubled, weeping
Antonyms: cheerful, happy

How to Take Tests

Taking tests is part of going to school. Use these tips to help you answer the kinds of questions you often see on tests.

True-False Questions
- If a statement seems true, make sure it is *all* true.
- The word *not* can change the meaning of a statement.
- Pay attention to words such as *all*, *always*, *never*, *no*, *none*, and *only*. They often make a statement false.
- Words such as *generally*, *much*, *many*, *sometimes*, and *usually* often make a statement true.

Multiple Choice Questions
- Try to answer the question before reading the choices. If your answer is one of the choices, choose it.
- Eliminate answers you know are wrong.
- Don't change your answer unless you know it is wrong.

Matching Questions
- Count each group to see whether any items will be left over.
- Read all the items before you start matching.
- Match the items you know first.

Fill-In-the-Blank Questions or Completions
- Read the question or incomplete sentence carefully.
- Look for clues in the question or sentence that might help you figure out the answer.
- If you are given possible answers, cross out each one as you use it.

Short Answers and Essays
- Take a few minutes to organize your thoughts.
- Give only the information that is asked for.
- Answer as clearly as possible.
- Leave time to proofread your response or essay.

Handbook

Viewing and Representing Information

How to Read Maps and Diagrams

Informational texts often use maps, diagrams, graphs, and charts. These tools help illustrate and explain the topic.

Maps

Maps show the location of places such as countries, states, and cities. They can also show where mountains, rivers, lakes, and streets are located. A compass rose on the map shows which way is north. A scale shows how distances are represented on the map.

Diagrams

Diagrams are drawings that explain things or show how things work. Some diagrams show pictures of how objects look on the outside or on the inside. Others show the different steps in a process.

This diagram shows the steps of the Scientific Method. It helps you understand the order and importance of each step.

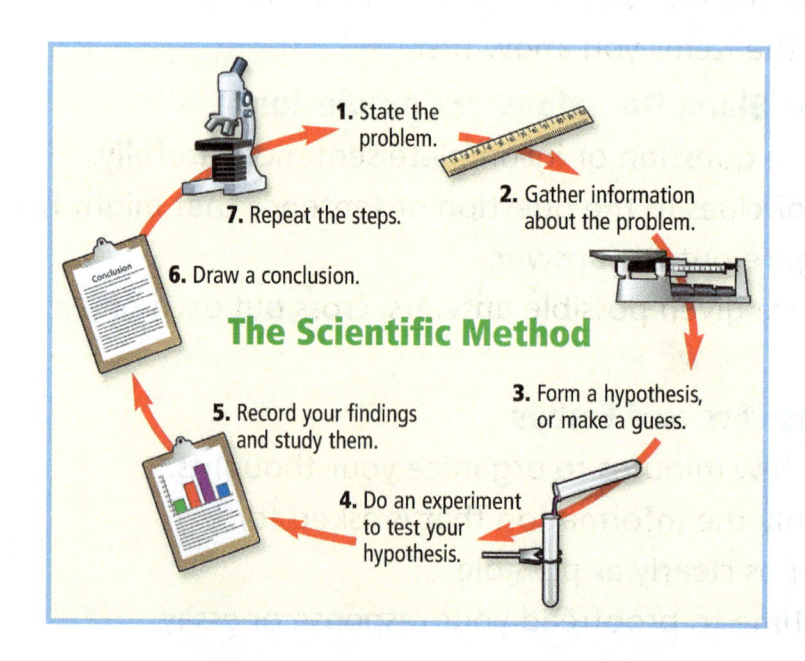

The Scientific Method

1. State the problem.
2. Gather information about the problem.
3. Form a hypothesis, or make a guess.
4. Do an experiment to test your hypothesis.
5. Record your findings and study them.
6. Draw a conclusion.
7. Repeat the steps.

How to Read Graphs

Graphs show how two or more kinds of information are related or alike. Three common kinds of graphs are **line graphs**, **bar graphs**, and **circle graphs**.

Line Graph

A **line graph** shows how information changes over a period of time. This line graph explains how the Native American population of Central Mexico changed over 120 years.

Native American Population of Central Mexico

Bar Graphs

We use **bar graphs** to compare information. For example, this bar graph compares the populations of the 13 states that made up the U.S.A. in 1790.

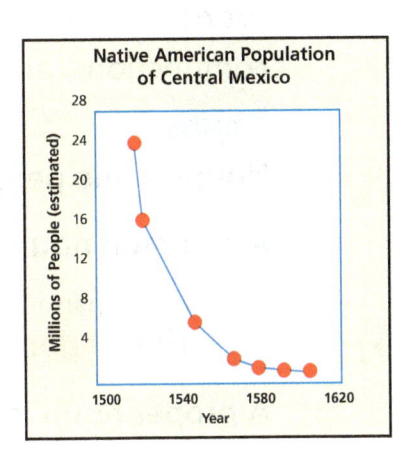

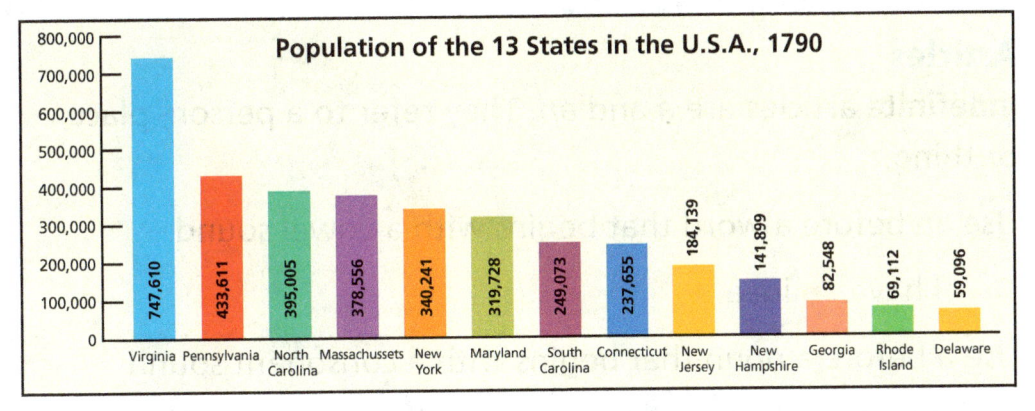

Population of the 13 States in the U.S.A., 1790

State	Population
Virginia	747,610
Pennsylvania	433,611
North Carolina	395,005
Massachussets	378,556
New York	340,241
Maryland	319,728
South Carolina	249,073
Connecticut	237,655
New Jersey	184,139
New Hampshire	141,899
Georgia	82,548
Rhode Island	69,112
Delaware	59,096

Circle Graphs

A **circle graph** is sometimes called a pie chart because it looks like a pie cut into slices. Circle graphs are used to show how different parts of a whole compare to each other.

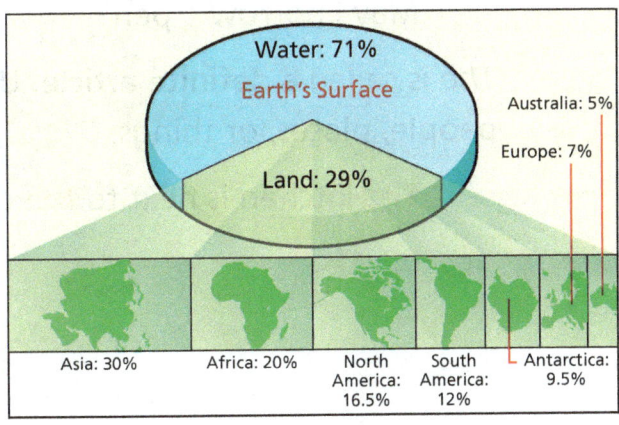

Earth's Surface
- Water: 71%
- Land: 29%
  - Asia: 30%
  - Africa: 20%
  - North America: 16.5%
  - South America: 12%
  - Antarctica: 9.5%
  - Europe: 7%
  - Australia: 5%

389

Grammar Handbook

Parts of Speech

In English there are nine **parts of speech**: nouns, articles, pronouns, verbs, adjectives, adverbs, prepositions, conjunctions, and interjections.

Nouns

Nouns name people, places, or things.

A **common noun** is a general person, place, or thing.

>   person   thing   place
> The **student** brings a **notebook** to **class**.

A **proper noun** is a specific person, place, or thing.

>   person   place   thing
> **Joe** went to **Paris** and saw the **Eiffel Tower**.

Articles

Indefinite articles are *a* and *an*. They refer to a person, place, or thing.

Use *an* before a word that begins with a vowel sound.

> I have **an** idea.

Use *a* before a noun that begins with a consonant sound.

> May I borrow **a** pen?

The is called a **definite article**. Use *the* to talk about specific people, places, or things.

> **The** kitchen is next to **the** dining room.

Pronouns

Pronouns are words that take the place of nouns or proper nouns.

    proper noun   pronoun
Ana is not home. **She** is babysitting.

	Subject Pronouns	Object Pronouns
Singular	I, you, he, she, it	me, you, him, her, it
Plural	we, you, they	us, you, them

A **subject pronoun** replaces the subject of a sentence. A **subject** is who or what a sentence is about.

  subject   subject pronoun (singular)
Dan is a student. **He** goes to school every day.

Object pronouns replace a noun or proper noun that is the object of a verb. An **object** receives the action of a verb.

      object   object pronoun (singular)
Lauren gave **Ed** the notes. Lauren gave **him** the notes.

Possessive pronouns replace nouns or proper nouns. They show who owns something.

	Possessive Pronouns
Singular	mine, yours, hers, his
Plural	ours, yours, theirs

Handbook

Verbs

Verbs express an action or a state of being.

An **action verb** tells what someone or something does or did.

Verbs That Tell Actions You Can See	Verbs That Tell Actions You Cannot See
dance swim	know sense

A **linking verb** shows no action. It links the subject with another word that describes the subject.

Examples of Linking Verbs		
look	smell	sound
be	appear	seem

A helping verb comes before the main verb. It adds to the main verb's meaning.

	Helping Verbs
Forms of the verb *be*	am, is, was, were, being, been
Forms of the verb *do*	do, does, did
Forms of the verb *have*	have, has, had
Other helping verbs	can, must, could, have (to), should, may, will, would

Adjectives

Adjectives describe nouns. An adjective usually comes before the noun it describes.

tall grass   **big** truck

An adjective can come *after* the noun it describes. This often happens when the verb is a linking verb.

The bag is **heavy**. The books smell **new**.

Possessive adjectives describe who or what something belongs to.

possessive adjective
Someone saw **my/your/his/her/its/our/their** eyes.

Adverbs

Adverbs describe the action of verbs. They tell *how* an action happens. Adverbs answer the questions *Where?*, *When?*, *How?*, *How much?*, and *How often?*

Many adverbs end in *-ly*.

easily   slowly

Some adverbs do not end in *-ly*.

seldom   fast   very

In this sentence, the adverb *everywhere* modifies the verb *looked*. It answers the question *Where?*

verb   adverb
Nicole looked **everywhere** for her book.

Handbook

Prepositions

Prepositions show time, place, and direction.

Time	Place	Direction
after	above	across
before	below	down

In this sentence, the preposition *above* shows where the bird flew. It shows place.

                preposition
A bird flew **above** my head.

In this sentence, the preposition *across* shows direction.

                      preposition
The children walked **across** the street.

A **prepositional phrase** starts with a preposition and ends with a noun or pronoun. In this sentence, the preposition is *near* and the noun is *school*.

                ┌─prepositional phrase─┐
The library is **near the new school**.

Conjunctions

A **conjunction** joins words, groups of words, and whole sentences. Common conjunctions include *and*, *but*, and *or*.

The conjunction *and* joins two proper nouns: *Allison and Teresa*.

    proper   proper
    noun   noun
  Allison **and** Teresa are in school.

The conjunction *or* joins two prepositional phrases: *to the movies* and *to the mall*.

              prepositional   prepositional
                 phrase   phrase
  They want to go to the movies **or** to the mall.

The conjunction *but* joins two independent clauses.

      independent clause   independent clause
  Alana baked the cookies, **but** Eric made the lemonade.

Interjections

Interjections are words or phrases that express emotion.

Interjections that express strong emotion are followed by an exclamation point.

  Wow! Did you see that goal?

A comma follows interjections that express mild emotion.

  Gee, I'm sorry that your team lost.

Handbook

Sentences

Clauses

Clauses are groups of words with a subject and a verb.

- An **independent clause** can stand on its own as a complete sentence.
- A **dependent clause** cannot stand alone as a complete sentence.

Sentences

A simple sentence is an independent clause. It has a subject and a verb.

subject   verb
The dog barked.

A **compound sentence** is made up of two or more simple sentences, or independent clauses.

— independent clause —   — independent clause —
The band has a lead singer, **but** it needs a drummer.

Sentence Types

Declarative sentences are statements. They end with a period.

We are going to the beach on Saturday.

Interrogative sentences are questions. They end with a question mark.

Will you come with us?

Imperative sentences are commands. They end with a period or an exclamation point.

Put on your life jacket. Now jump in the water!

Exclamatory sentences express strong feeling. They end with an exclamation point.

I swam all the way from the boat to the shore!

Punctuation

End Marks

End marks come at the end of sentences. There are three kinds of end marks: periods, question marks, and exclamation points.

Periods

- Use a period to end a statement (declarative sentence).
- Use a period to end a command or request (imperative sentence).
- Use a period after a person's initial or abbreviated title.
- Use a period after abbreviations.

Question Marks and Exclamation Points

- Use an exclamation point to express strong feelings.
- Use a question mark at the end of a question.

Commas

Commas separate parts of a sentence or phrase.

- Use a comma to separate two independent clauses linked by a conjunction.
- Use commas to separate the parts in a series. A series is a group of three or more words, phrases, or clauses.
- Use a comma to set off introductory words or phrases.
- Use commas to set off an interrupting word or phrase.
- Use a comma to set off a speaker's quoted words.
- Use commas to set off the name of the person being addressed in a letter or speech.

Handbook

Semicolons and Colons
Semicolons can connect two independent clauses. Use them when the clauses are closely related in meaning or structure.

Colons introduce a list of items or important information. Also use a colon to separate hours and minutes when writing the time.

Quotation Marks
Quotation marks set off direct quotations, dialogue, and some titles.
- Commas and periods always go inside quotation marks.
- If a question mark or exclamation point is not part of the quotation, it goes outside the quotation marks.
- Use quotation marks to set off what people say in a dialogue.
- Use quotation marks around the titles of short works of writing.

Apostrophes
Apostrophes can be used with singular and plural nouns to show ownership or possession. To form the possessive, follow these rules:
- For singular nouns, add an apostrophe and an *s*.
- For singular nouns that end in *s*, add an apostrophe and an *s*.
- For plural nouns that do not end in *s*, add an apostrophe and an *s*.
- For plural nouns that end in *s*, add an apostrophe.
- Apostrophes are also used in contractions to show where a letter or letters have been taken away.

Capitalization
There are five main reasons to use capital letters:
- to begin a sentence
- to write the pronoun *I*
- to write the names of proper nouns
- to write a person's title before his or her name
- to write the title of a work (artwork, written work)

Writing Handbook

Modes of Writing

Narrative Writing is used to tell a story. Here are some types of narrative writing:
- Autobiography is the story of a person's life told by the person.
- Biography is the story of a person's life told by another person.
- A short story is a short, fictional narrative.

Descriptive Writing paints a picture of a person, place, thing, or event.

Expository Writing gives information or explains something. Here are some types of expository writing:
- Compare-and-Contrast writing analyzes the similarities and differences between two or more things.
- Cause-and-Effect writing explains why something happened and what happens as a result.
- Problem-and-Solution writing describes a problem and offers one or more solutions to it.
- How-to writing explains how to do or make something.

Persuasive Writing is writing that tries to convince people to think or act in a certain way.

Functional Writing is writing for real-world uses. Here are some types of functional writing:
- You might fill out a form to sign up for lessons, take a field trip, or apply for a library card.
- You might create an invitation to a holiday party.

Handbook

The Writing Process

The writing process is a series of steps that helps you write clearly.

Step 1: Prewrite

When you prewrite, you explore ideas and choose a topic. You identify your audience, and you choose your purpose for writing.

To choose a topic, try one or more of these strategies:
- **List** many ideas that you might want to write about.
- **Freewrite** about some ideas for five minutes.
- **Brainstorm** a list of ideas with a partner.

To identify your audience, think about who will read your writing. What do they already know? What do you need to explain?

To identify your purpose for writing, ask:
- Do I want to entertain my audience?
- Do I want to inform my audience?
- Do I want to persuade my audience?

Now, decide on the best form for your writing. Gather and organize the details that will support your topic.

Step 2: Draft

You start writing in this step. Put your ideas into sentences. Put your sentences into paragraphs. Begin to put your paragraphs in order. Don't worry too much about grammar and spelling. You will have a chance to correct any errors later.

Step 3: Revise

This is the time to look at your ideas and the organization of your writing. Read your first draft. Ask yourself:
- Are the ideas presented in the best order?
- Is there a clear beginning, middle, and end?
- Does each paragraph have a main idea and supporting details?

Decide what changes you will make. Then revise your draft.

Step 4: Edit/Proofread

This is the time to look at word choice, sentence fluency, and writing conventions. Reread your paper. Proofread for mistakes in spelling, grammar, and punctuation. Correct any mistakes you find.

When you edit and proofread your draft, use the proofreading marks in the chart below to mark the changes.

Editing/Proofreading Marks		
To:	Use This Mark:	Example:
add something	∧	We ate rice, bean, and corn.
delete something	ℓ	We ate rice, beans, and corns.
start a new paragraph	¶	¶ We ate rice, beans, and corn.
add a comma	ˏ	We ate rice, beans and corn.
add a period	⊙	We ate rice, beans, and corn
switch letters or words	∽	We ate rice, baens, and corn.
change to a capital letter	≡	we ate rice, beans, and corn.
change to a lowercase letter	/	WE ate rice, beans, and corn.

Handbook

Peer Review Checklist

Ideas
☐ Is the content interesting and thoughtful?
☐ Is the main idea clearly stated?
☐ Are the main ideas supported by facts and details?
☐ Do the ideas flow from one to the next?

Organization
☐ Are the ideas in an order that makes sense?
☐ Are the ideas connected by transitions and other connecting words?

Voice
☐ Does the writing have energy and personality?

Word Choice
☐ Has the writer chosen precise words?

Sentence Fluency
☐ Do the sentences flow smoothly?
☐ Are the sentences varied in type and length?

Conventions
☐ Do the subjects of sentences agree with the verbs?
☐ Do the pronouns agree with the words they refer to?
☐ Are the verb tenses appropriate and consistent?
☐ Is the possessive case (apostrophe -s) used correctly?
☐ Are negatives and contractions used correctly?
☐ Are the punctuation and capitalization correct?
☐ Is the writing free of spelling errors?

Step 5: Publish

Once you have revised and proofread your paper, share it with others. Look at these publishing ideas:

- Post your paper on the bulletin board.
- Photocopy your paper. Hand it out to your classmates and family members.
- Attach it to an email and send it to friends.
- Send it to a school newspaper or magazine for possible publication.

Once you have shared your work with others, you may want to put it in your portfolio. A portfolio is a folder or envelope in which you keep your writing. If you keep your work in a portfolio, you can look at what you have written over a period of time. This will let you see if your writing is improving. It will help you become a better writer.

Build Your Portfolio

You may want to keep your completed writing in your portfolio. It is a good idea to keep your drafts, too. Keep comments you receive from your teacher or writing partner, as well.

Reflect on Your Writing

Make notes on your writing in a journal. Write how you felt about what you wrote. Use these questions to help you get started:

- What new things did you learn about your topic?
- What helped you organize the details in your writing?
- What helped you revise your writing?
- What did you learn about yourself as you wrote?

Handbook

Rubric for Writing

A rubric is a tool that helps you assess, or evaluate, your work. This rubric shows specific details for you to think about when you write. The scale ranges from 4 to 1, with 4 being the highest score and 1 being the lowest.

4	Writing is clearly focused on the task. Writing is well organized. Ideas follow a logical order. Main idea is fully developed and supported with details. Sentence structure is varied. Writing is free of fragments. There are no errors in writing conventions.
3	Writing is focused, but with some unnecessary information. There is clear organization, but with some ideas out of order. The main idea is supported, but development is uneven. Sentence structure is mostly varied, but with some fragments. Writing conventions are generally followed.
2	Writing is related to the task, but lacks focus. Organization is not clear. Ideas do not fit well together. There is little or no support for the main idea. No variation in sentence structure. Fragments occur often. Frequent errors in writing conventions.
1	The writing is generally unfocused. There is little organization or development. There is no clear main idea. Sentence structure is unvaried. There are many fragments. Many errors in writing conventions and spelling.

Writing and Research

Sometimes when you write, you need to do research to learn more information about your topic. You can do research in the library, on the Internet, and by viewing or listening to information media.

Library Reference

Encyclopedias contain basic facts, background information, and suggestions for additional research.

Biographical references provide brief life histories of famous people in many different fields.

Almanacs contain facts and statistics about many subjects, including government, world history, geography, entertainment, business, and sports.

Periodicals are past editions of magazines. Use a periodical index to find articles on your topic.

Vertical files contain pamphlets on a wide variety of topics.

Electronic databases provide quick access to information on many topics.

Handbook

Citing Sources

When you do research, you read what other people wrote. The material you research is called the source, or reference. When you tell who wrote the material, this is called citing the source. It is important to cite each source you use when you write.

In your paper, note each place in which you use a source. At the end of the paper, provide a list that gives details about all your sources. A bibliography and a works cited list are two types of source lists.

- A **bibliography** provides a listing of all the material you used during your research.
- A **works cited list** shows the sources you have quoted in your paper.

Plagiarism

Plagiarism is presenting someone else's words, ideas, or work as your own. If the idea or words are not yours, be sure to give credit by citing the source in your work. It is a serious offense to plagiarize.

Look at the chart of the Modern Language Association (MLA) on p. 407. Use this format for citing sources. This is the most common format for papers written by middle and high school students, as well as college students.

MLA Style for Listing Sources

Book	Ormiston, Rosalind. *Origins of Modern Art.* London: Flame Tree Publishing, 2015.
Article in a magazine	"He Had a Dream." *Scholastic News* 8 Jan. 2018: 4–5.
Films and DVDs	*Coco.* Dir. Lee Unkrich. Perf. Anthony Gonzalez, Gael García Bernal, Benjamin Bratt, Alanna Ubach, Renée Victor, Ana Ofelia Murguía, and Edward James Olmos. Walt Disney Studios Motion Picture, 2017.
Internet	Green, James. *Beadwork in the Arts of Africa and Beyond.* July 26, 2018. www.metmuseum.org/blogs/collection-insights/2018/beadwork-in-arts-of-africa-and-beyond. Accessed August 21, 2018.
Newspaper	Bowles, Scott. "Ready to Roll at Comic-Con." *USA Today* 22 July 2009: D1 Print.
Personal interview	Smith, Jane. Personal interview. 10 Feb. 2018.

Handbook

🖱 Internet Research

The internet is an international network of computers. The World Wide Web is a part of the internet that lets you find and read information.

To do research on the internet, you need to open a search engine. Type in a keyword on the search engine page. **Keywords** are words or phrases on the topic you want to learn about. For example, if you are looking for information about your favorite musical group, you might use the band's name as a keyword.

To choose a keyword, write a list of all the words you are considering. Then choose a few of the most important words.

Tips

- Spell the keywords correctly.
- Use the most important keyword first, followed by the less important ones.
- Open the pages at the top of the list first. These will usually be the most useful sources.

How to Evaluate Information from the Internet

When you do research on the internet, you need to be sure the information is correct. Use the checklist to decide if you can trust the information on a Web site.

- ✓ Look at the address bar. A URL that ends in "edu" is connected to a school or university. A URL that ends in "gov" means it is a site posted by a state or federal government. These sites should have correct information.
- ✓ Check that the people who write or are quoted on the site are experts, not just people telling their ideas or opinions.
- ✓ Check that the site is free of grammatical and spelling errors. This is often a hint that the site was carefully designed and researched.
- ✓ Check that the site is not trying to sell a product or persuade people.
- ✓ If you are not sure about using a site as a source, ask an adult.

Handbook

Information Media

Media is all the organizations that provide news and information to the public. Media includes television, radio, and newspapers. This chart describes several forms of information media.

Types of Information Media	
Television News Program	• Covers current news events • Gives information objectively
Documentary	• Focuses on one topic of social interest • Sometimes expresses controversial opinions
Television Newsmagazine	• Covers a variety of topics • Entertains and informs
Radio Talk Show	• Covers some current events • Offers a place for people to express opinions
Newspaper Article	• Covers one current event • Gives details and background about the event
Commercial	• Presents products, people, or ideas • Persuades people to buy or take action

How to Evaluate Information from Various Media

Because the media presents large amounts of information, it is important to learn how to analyze this information. Some media sources try to make you think a certain way instead of giving you all the facts. Use these techniques to figure out whether you can trust information from the media.

- ✓ Sort facts from opinions. A fact is a statement that can be proven true. An opinion is how someone feels or thinks about something. Make sure any opinions are supported by facts.

- ✓ Be aware of the kind of media you are watching, reading, or listening to. Is it news or a documentary? Is it a commercial? What is its purpose?

- ✓ Watch out for bias. **Bias** is when the source gives information from only one point of view. Try to gather information from several points of view.

- ✓ Discuss what you learn from different media with your classmates or teachers. This will help you determine if you can trust the information.

- ✓ Read the entire article or watch the whole program before reaching a conclusion. Then develop your own views on the issues, people, and information presented.

Handbook

▶ How To Use Technology in Writing

Writing on a Computer

You can write using a word-processing program. This will help you when you follow the steps in the Writing Process.

- When you write your first draft, save it as a document.
- As you type or revise, you can move words and sentences using the cut, copy, and paste commands.
- When you proofread, you can use the grammar and spell-check functions to help you check your work.

Keeping a Portfolio

Create folders to save your writing in. For example, a folder labeled "Writing Projects—September" can contain all of the writing you do during that month.

Save all the drafts of each paper you write.

Computer Tips

- Rename each of your revised drafts using the SAVE AS function. For example, if your first draft is "Cats," name the second draft "Cats2."
- If you share your computer, create a folder for only your work.
- Always back up your portfolio on a server or a USB flash drive.

Glossary

achieve → celebration

A

achieve succeed in doing something (p. 322)

adapt change to fit a new situation (p. 262)

adopt take a child or animal into your home and take care of it (p. 44)

advice a suggestion about what someone should do (p. 216)

affect produce a change in someone or something (p. 204)

anticipate guess or expect that something will happen (p. 172)

appreciate be grateful for something (p. 154)

appropriate fitting; suitable (p. 92)

architecture shape and style of buildings (p. 260)

ash gray powder that is left after something has been burned (p. 74)

assistance help or support (p. 106)

astronaut someone who travels in space (p. 320)

B

banned officially said that people must not do something or that something is not allowed (p. 44)

bare empty (p. 152)

bartered exchanged one thing for another (p. 356)

bean a seed or seed container of a plant that you eat (p. 202)

benefit something that helps you or gives you an advantage (p. 154)

boasted bragged (p. 170)

bolt white line that appears in the sky (p. 104)

bond special relationship or connection (p. 30)

breath air that you let in and out through your nose and mouth (p. 28)

breeze light wind (p. 104)

C

captured caught (p. 44)

celebration an occasion or party when you do something special because of a particular event (p. 202)

challenge → environment

challenge something that is hard to do (p. 10)

climate the weather that a place usually has (p. 274)

communicates exchanges information with others (p. 8)

communities areas in which people live (p. 230)

community group of people who live in the same area (p. 322)

companion someone you are with, often a friend (p. 28)

concerned worried (p. 230)

considerable large enough to be important (p. 292)

consist of made up of (p. 76)

cooperate work together with someone else (p. 358)

correspond write and receive messages with someone (p. 276)

council group of people who are chosen to make laws and decisions (p. 136)

crater round open top of a volcano (p. 74)

creative making new things and ideas using the imagination (p. 232)

currency money (p. 356)

D

demonstrate show how to do something (p. 92)

display show (p. 172)

duty something you must do because it is right or part of your job (p. 136)

E

efficient working well, quickly, and without waste (p. 260)

electricity kind of energy (p. 90)

eliminate get rid of something completely (p. 204)

emerge appear or come out from somewhere (p. 138)

encounter a meeting (p. 30)

environment world of land, sea, and air that you live in; your surroundings (p. 262)

equipped ➔ infer

equipped provided with things that are needed to do something (p. 340)

erupts explodes and sends out fire and smoke (p. 74)

establish get something started, such as a company, system, or situation, etc. (p. 46)

evaluate judge how good something is (p. 218)

evaporate when a liquid turns into a gas (p. 90)

evidence proof (p. 76)

explorer someone who travels into an unknown area to find out about it (p. 320)

extreme very great (p. 260)

F

feature a part that stands out (p. 92)

fine very nice or of high quality (p. 152)

flatter say nice things to someone because you are trying to please him or her (p. 216)

frisky full of energy, happiness, and fun (p. 28)

G

gardener a person who works in a garden (p. 202)

glowed shined with a steady light (p. 28)

goal something you want to achieve (p. 10)

guzzled drank a lot of something eagerly and quickly (p. 216)

H

harsh very unpleasant, cruel (p. 274)

hiking taking a long walk in the country or in the mountains (p. 338)

hurricane storm with very strong fast winds (p. 104)

I

igloo a house or building made from blocks of hard snow or ice (p. 290)

impact a strong effect (p. 106)

infer form an opinion that something is probably true because of information that you have (p. 152)

initial ➔ **plaque**

initial happening at the beginning (p. 358)

involve include, or be part of (p. 10)

L

labor hard work (p. 292)

lava very hot liquid rock that comes out of the top of a mountain (p. 74)

ledge narrow flat surface of rock that is high above the ground (p. 338)

lightning bright flash of light in the sky that happens during a storm (p. 90)

located be in a particular place (p. 262)

M

machine something mechanical that helps people do work (p. 170)

major big; very important or serious (p. 106)

mighty very strong (p. 170)

mining digging in the ground for coal, iron, gold, etc. (p. 260)

mischief bad behavior, especially by children (p. 136)

mission important job that someone has been given to do (p. 320)

motivated very eager to do or achieve something (p. 340)

N

native growing or living in a particular place (p. 260)

nonsense ideas or behaviors that are not true or seem stupid or annoying (p. 136)

O

objective goal (p. 232)

occur happen or take place (p. 30)

outcome the final result of a meeting, process, etc. (p. 204)

P

plaque piece of flat metal or stone with writing on it (p. 320)

prairie → **secure**

prairie large open area of land that is covered in wheat or long grass (p. 274)

praise words that you say to tell someone that he or she has done something well (p. 216)

previously before (p. 276)

protect prevent someone or something from being harmed or damaged (p. 8)

purpose a reason for doing something; aim (p. 230)

R

rainforest a rainy tropical forest area with trees and plants that are very close together (p. 44)

react say or do something because of something else (p. 138)

record information that is written down so you can look at it later (p. 274)

recover get better to a healthy condition (p. 46)

reindeer a deer with large antlers that lives in cold northern areas (p. 290)

reside live somewhere (p. 276)

resourceful good at finding ways to deal with problems effectively (p. 218)

respond answer (p. 138)

restore repair something to make it seem new again (p. 232)

roots parts of a plant that grow under the ground (p. 202)

route the way from one place to another, especially on a map (p. 340)

rulers people who govern a country, such as presidents or kings (p. 356)

S

satisfied pleased because something has happened in the way that you want (p. 136)

scampered ran with short, quick steps, like a small animal (p. 216)

scenario setting or situation (p. 172)

scheme tricky plan (p. 218)

seal a large sea mammal that eats fish and lives near the coast (p. 290)

secure safe (p. 8)

shelter → unique

shelter a place that protects you from bad weather (p. 290)

shimmer shine with a soft light that seems to shake slightly (p. 28)

signatures people's names, written in their own handwriting (p. 320)

similar almost the same, but not exactly (p. 76)

sled a vehicle without a motor used to slide over snow (p. 290)

sledgehammer an extra large and heavy hammer (p. 170)

sod piece of dirt with grass growing on top (p. 274)

solve find the answer to a problem or mystery (p. 230)

sputter make a coughing noise as if breaking down (p. 170)

stitches small lines of thread sewn onto cloth (p. 152)

strategy a plan used to reach a goal (p. 46)

stroke particular moment in time (p. 152)

surrounded be all around someone or something (p. 320)

T

temperature how hot or cold something is (p. 90)

thrilling exciting and interesting (p. 338)

thrive be very strong and healthy (p. 338)

thunder loud sound that you hear in the sky during a storm (p. 90)

tidbit small piece of food or information (p. 136)

trade exchange one thing for another (p. 356)

tradition something people have done for a long time and continue to (p. 358)

trails paths across open country, or through mountains or woods (p. 338)

U

underground under Earth's surface (p. 260)

undertake take on as a responsibility (p. 292)

unique special, one of a kind (p. 322)

valley ➜ young

V

valley an area of low land between mountains or hills (p. 338)

vine a plant with long stems that climb on other plants, buildings, etc. (p. 202)

volcano mountain with a hole at the top from which come burning rock and fire (p. 74)

volunteers people who do a job to help without being paid (p. 44)

W

warm slightly hot, but not too hot (p. 28)

waste use more of something (time, money, resources) than is sensible (p. 230)

whisk quickly take something or someone somewhere (p. 152)

wink close and open one eye quickly (p. 152)

worth value (p. 356)

Y

young not having lived very long (p. 8)

Index

Genre
  Informational Text
    email, 97
    internet article, 94–95
    literary nonfiction, 78–81
    magazine article, 264–267
    photo essay, 206–209
    poster, 96
    science, 12–19, 48–51
    social studies, 234–237, 294–297, 360–361
  Literature
    fable, 32–37, 220–223
    letters, 278–283
    play, 156–163
    pourquoi tale, 140–145
    short story, 108–113, 324–331, 342–349
    tall tale, 174–177

Grammar
  Parts of Speech
    adjectives, 116–117
      comparatives, 212–213
      superlatives, 226–227
    adverbs of frequency and intensity, 240–241
    nouns
      possessives, 166–167
      proper, 270–271
      singular and plural, 148–149
    prepositions and prepositional phrases, 286–287
    pronouns, possessive, 166–167
    time-order transition words, 100–101
    verbs
      past progressive, 352–353
      present perfect, 300–301
      simple past, *be* verbs, 40–41
      simple past, irregular verbs, 86–87
      simple past, regular verbs, 54–55
      simple present, 24–25
  Punctuation
    capitalizing proper nouns, 270–271
    quotations, 182–183
  Sentences
    complex, 366–367
    compound, 334–335
    imperatives, 100–101

Language Development
  Activities
    research and present about a character, 179
    research and present about a volcano, 83
    research and present about animal babies, 21
  Extensions
    changing the setting of a story, 351
    compare and contrast amusement park rides, 225
    create a setting during a storm, 115
    design a special coin, 365
    develop directions for planting seeds, 211
    draw a picture of a character who wins a contest, 181
    draw or describe a morning at home, 299
    explain how to do a chore, 165
    find evidence about the past, 85
    make a drawing about living underground, 269
    make a poster warning people about danger, 99
    make a visual aid about caring for animals, 53
    play Telephone, 147
    share ideas about solving problems in the community, 239
    write a letter describing where you live, 285
    write a skit about an animal and its baby, 23
    write a skit about a story, 333
  Make Connections
    about adopting a pet, 45
    about being tricked, 217
    about best way to communicate with friends, 275
    about biggest storm, 105
    about caves, 261
    about expressions, 153
    about friends, 29
    about going on a hike, 339
    about helping an animal, 9
    about living as an Inuit, 291
    about trading for something without using money, 357
    about plants and trees, 203
    about plaques saying something about you, 321
    about solving problems, 231
    about special skills, 171
    about sudden events, 75
    about things that use electricity, 91
    about your duties, 137
  Projects
    animal playing cards, 59
    book cover, 187
    character charades, 187
    charades, 305
    comic strip, 245
    flowchart of steps, 245
    graphic organizer, 121
    illustration, 305
    pantomime, 371
    park design, 371
    picture book, 59
    world map, 121

Think It Over
  recall, comprehend, and analyze, 19, 37, 51, 81, 97, 113, 145, 163, 177, 209, 223, 237, 267, 283, 297, 331, 349, 363

Listening and Speaking
  Discussions, 58, 120, 186, 244, 304, 370
  Listening Skills
    be an active listener, 123
    listen for general meaning, 12, 32, 48, 78, 94, 108, 140, 156, 174
    listen for ideas and information not stated directly, 189, 247, 307, 373
    listen for important words and details, 61
    listen for main points and details, 206, 220, 234, 264, 278, 294, 324, 342, 360
    listen for teacher's instructions, 62
    listen for specific facts and observations, 307
    take notes and retell, 324, 342, 360
  Projects
    act it out, 187
    description, 305
    fable, 245
    folktale, 121
    interview, 59, 245, 305
    oral report, 371
    presentation, 59
    tall tale, 371
    20 questions, 187
    vocabulary hunt, 121
  Speaking Skills
    include important details, 61
    use gestures, 9
    use formal language, 61, 123, 247, 373
    use informal language, 61, 189, 307
    use synonyms, 261
    use words you know, 75, 203

View and Respond
    animals, people, and caring, 3
    links to our past, 315
    powerful forces of nature, 69
    problem solvers, 197
    telling tales, 131
    where we live, 255

What About You
    talking about animals, 5, 7
    talking about forces of nature, 71, 73
    talking about homes, 257, 259
    talking about solving problems, 199, 201
    talking about stories and tales, 135
    talking about the past, 317, 319
    talking about things you can read, 133

Workshops
    give a how-to presentation, 122–123
    give a speech, 246–247
    give an oral report, 372–373
    perform a play, 188–189
    play a description guessing game, 60–61
    present a TV talk show, 306–307

Reading
  Apply
    explain, 23
    outline, 115, 333
    retell, 39, 53, 85, 147, 181, 211, 225, 285, 351
    summarize, 165, 269, 299, 365
    take notes, 99, 239, 351

  Before You Go On
    animals, people, and caring, 13, 15, 17, 33, 35, 49
    links to our past, 325, 327, 329, 343, 345, 347, 361
    powerful forces of nature, 79, 95, 109, 111
    problem solvers, 207, 221, 235
    telling tales, 141, 143, 157, 159, 161, 175
    where we live, 265, 279, 281, 295, 361
  Fluency, 65, 127, 193, 251, 311, 379
  Graphic Organizers
    cause and effect chart, 239
    character web, 181
    compare and contrast chart, 285
    details chart, 53
    fact and opinion chart, 269
    infer and predict chart, 165
    KWL chart, 23
    main idea and details chart, 211, 365
    organizational chart, 299
    problem and solution chart, 333
    sequence of events chart, 85, 147, 351
    T-chart, 39, 225
    Venn diagram, 99
    word web, 115
  Kids' Stories from around the World
    animals, people, and caring, 6–7
    forces of nature, 72–73
    links to the past, 318–319
    problem solvers, 200–201
    telling tales, 134–135
    where we live, 258–259
  Link the Readings, 58, 120, 186, 244, 304, 370
    Prepare to Read, 8–11, 28–31, 44–47, 74–77,

421

90–93, 104–107, 136–139, 152–155, 170–173, 202–205, 216–219, 230–233, 260–263, 274–277, 290–293, 320–323, 338–341, 356–359

Skills
  ask for help, 49, 141, 266, 281
  look for patterns, 31, 93, 359
  read definition and use word in a sentence, 15
  read key words, 13
  read picture captions, 16
  sight words, 97, 160
  use pictures, 158

Strategies
  compare and contrast, 220, 223, 224
  identify author's purpose, 278, 283, 284
  identify cause and effect, 234, 237, 238
  identify characters, 174, 177, 180
  identify events in a plot, 140, 145
  identify fact and opinion, 264, 267, 268
  identify fantasy and reality, 32, 37, 38
  identify genre, 94, 97, 98
  identify main idea and details, 206, 209, 210
  identify plot and setting, 342, 349, 350
  identify problem and solution, 324, 331, 332
  identify sequence of events, 84, 146
  make inferences, 156, 163
  make inferences and predictions, 164
  make predictions, 78, 81
  preview, 48, 51, 52
  reread for details, 22
  summarize, 360, 363, 364

use prior knowledge, 12, 19
visualize, 294, 297, 298
visualize setting, 108, 113, 114

Test Preparation, 66–67, 128–129, 194–195, 252–253, 312–313, 380–381

Topics
  Big Question
    animals, people, and caring, 3, 32, 48, 58
    links to our past, 315, 324, 342, 360, 370
    powerful forces of nature, 69, 78, 94, 108, 120
    problem solvers, 197, 206, 220, 234, 244
    telling tales, 131, 140, 156, 174, 186
    where we live, 255, 264, 278, 294, 304
  A Closer Look
    animals and their young, 20–21
    lava flows, 82–83
    tall tale characters, 178–179
  Units
    animals, people, and caring, 2–67
    links to our past, 314–381
    powerful forces of nature, 68–129
    problem solvers, 196–253
    telling tales, 130–195
    where we live, 254–313

Vocabulary
  Academic Words
    achieve, 322
    adapt, 262
    affect, 204
    anticipate, 172
    appreciate, 154
    appropriate, 92
    assistance, 106

benefit, 154
bond, 30
challenge, 10
community, 322
considerable, 292
consist of, 76
cooperate, 358
correspond, 276
creative, 232
demonstrate, 92
display, 172
eliminate, 204
emerge, 138
encounter, 30
environment, 262
equipped, 340
establish, 46
evaluate, 218
evidence, 76
feature, 92
goal, 10
impact, 106
infer, 154
initial, 358
involve, 10
labor, 292
located, 262
major, 106
motivated, 340
objective, 232
occur, 30
outcome, 204
previously, 276
react, 138
recover, 46
reside, 276
resourceful, 218
respond, 138
restore, 232
route, 340
scenario, 172
scheme, 218
similar, 76
strategy, 46
tradition, 358
undertake, 292
unique, 322

422

Activities
  add a page to vocabulary notebook, 45, 105, 171, 217, 261, 339, 357
  create a vocabulary notebook, 29
  draw a picture, 291
  make vocabulary flash cards, 9, 91, 137, 153, 203, 231, 275, 321

Build Unit Vocabulary
  alligator, 4
  apartment, 256
  architect, 199
  blizzard, 71
  board game, 133
  brainstorm, 198
  cave paintings, 316
  cereal box, 132
  cloudy, 70
  computer, 133
  cookbook, 133
  debate, 198
  design, 198
  detective, 199
  directions, 132
  eat dinner, 257
  elephant, 4
  flood, 71
  foggy, 70
  fossils, 316
  giraffe, 4
  grasslands, 5
  houseboat, 256
  hurricane, 71
  inventors, 199
  investigate, 198
  journals, 316
  magazine, 132
  museums, 316
  newspaper, 132
  parrot, 4
  photographs, 133, 316
  play on the swings, 257
  politicians, 199
  prehistoric animals, 317
  prehistoric people, 317
  raccoon, 4
  rainforest, 5
  rainy, 70
  recipe, 132
  research, 198
  retirement home, 256
  ride an elevator, 257
  single-family home, 256
  skunk, 4
  snowy, 70
  sunny, 70
  swamp, 5
  swim in the water, 257
  townhouse, 256
  treehouse, 256
  website, 132
  what people did, 317
  what people wore, 317
  windy, 70
  woodlands, 5

Key Words
  adopt, 44
  advice, 216
  architecture, 260
  ash, 74
  astronaut, 320
  banned, 44
  bare, 152
  bartered, 356
  bean, 202
  boasted, 170
  bolt, 104
  breath, 28
  breeze, 104
  captured, 44
  celebration, 202
  climate, 274
  communicates, 8
  communities, 230
  companion, 28
  concerned, 230
  council, 136
  crater, 74
  currency, 356
  duty, 136
  efficient, 260
  electricity, 90
  erupts, 74
  evaporate, 90
  explorer, 320
  extreme, 260
  fine, 152
  flatter, 216
  frisky, 28
  gardener, 202
  glowed, 28
  guzzled, 216
  harsh, 274
  hiking, 338
  hurricane, 104
  igloo, 290
  lava, 74
  ledge, 338
  lightning, 90
  machine, 170
  mighty, 170
  mining, 260
  mischief, 136
  mission, 320
  native, 260
  nonsense, 136
  plaque, 320
  prairie, 274
  praise, 216
  protect, 8
  purpose, 230
  rainforest, 44
  record, 274
  reindeer, 290
  roots, 202
  rulers, 356
  satisfied, 136
  scampered, 216
  seal, 290
  secure, 8
  shelter, 104, 290
  shimmer, 28
  signatures, 320
  sled, 290
  sledgehammer, 170
  sod, 274
  solve, 230
  sputter, 170
  stitches, 152
  stroke, 152
  surrounded, 320
  temperature, 90

thrilling, 338
thrive, 338
thunder, 90
tidbit, 136
trade, 356
trails, 338
underground, 260
valley, 338
vine, 202
volcano, 74
volunteers, 44
warm, 28
waste, 230
whisk, 152
wink, 152
worth, 356
young, 8

Phonics
digraph *ow*, 233
digraphs *ch, sh, th*, 107
diphthongs *ow, ou*, 323
long vowel pairs, 139
long vowels with silent *e*, 47
r-controlled *ar, or, ore*, 293
short vowels, 11
soft and hard *c*, 205
variant vowel *oo*, 341
vowel pair *ea*, 155
y as a vowel, 277

Word Study
compound words, 93
ending *-ed*, 77
endings *-s, -es, -ed*, 31
Greek and Latin roots, 359
homophones, 263
synonyms and antonyms, 173
thesaurus, 219

Writing
Projects
adventure story, 59
building proposal, 305
character sketch, 187
history article, 371
journal entry, 305
mixed-up tale, 187
news article, 121, 245
safety guidelines, 121
science article, 59
skit, 245
song, 371

Quick Write
animals, people, and caring, 3
links to our past, 315
powerful forces of nature, 69
problem solvers, 197
telling tales, 131
where we live, 255

Types
descriptive writing
 describe a place you visit, 56–57
 describe an animal, 26–27
 describe yourself, 42–43
expository writing
 explain a process, 118–119
 explain how to do something, 102–103
 organize ideas by cause and effect, 88–89
 organize ideas by problem and solution, 288–289
 write to classify, 272–273
 write to compare and contrast, 302–303
narrative writing
 retell a familiar story, 150–151
 write a dialogue between two characters, 184–185
 write a friendly letter, 168–169
persuasive writing
 write a persuasive brochure, 242–243
 write a persuasive business letter, 214–215
 write an advertisement, 228–229
research writing
 paraphrasing a source, 354–355
 plan a research report, 336–337
 quoting sources, 368–369

Workshops
write a descriptive essay, 62–64
write a how-to essay, 124–126
write a magazine/newspaper article, 308–310
write a research report, 374–378
write a review, 248–250
write a story, 190–192

Writing Checklist, 27, 43, 57, 89, 103, 119, 151, 169, 185, 215, 229, 243, 273, 289, 303

Credits

ILLUSTRATOR: L4U6R2 Grandpa's Footsteps Aptara 314, 342–350

COVER: Haye Kesteloo/Shutterstock

FM: ix (T) Stnazkul/123RF; ix (L) Peter French/Perspectives/Getty Images; ix (R) Reggie David/Design Pics/Newscom; vi Joe McDonald/Shutterstock; vii (T) Sylvain Cordier/Biosphoto/Alamy Stock Photo; vii (B) ArCaLu/Shutterstock; viii Dark Moon Pictures/Shutterstock; xiii (T) Wavebreak Media Ltd/123RF; xiii (L) Black Rock Digital/Shutterstock; xiii (R) Danny E Hooks/Shutterstock; xiv (T) Travelscape Images/Alamy Stock Photo; xiv (B) Patti McConville/Alamy Stock Photo; xv (L) Hi-Story/Alamy Stock Photo; xv (R) Interfoto/History/Alamy Stock Photo.

UNIT 1: 002–003 Nate Allred/Shutterstock; 002 (L) Sean Russell/Getty Images; 002 (R) Merazonia Wildlife Rescue and Rehabilitation; 005 (TL) World Foto/Alamy Stock Photo; 005 (TR) Lvalin/Shutterstock; 005 (BL) Troyka/Shutterstock; 005 (BR) Jason Patrick Ross/Shutterstock; 006 (L) Vladimir Wrangel/Shutterstock; 006 (L Inset) Andrii_K/Shutterstock; 006 (R) Colombo Nicola/Shutterstock; 006 (R Inset) MarcinK3333/Shutterstock; 007 (T) Cherry-hai/Shutterstock; 007 (T Inset) Shutterstock; 007 (B) Kikujungboy/Shutterstock; 007 (B Inset) Sanmongkhol/Shutterstock; 008 (T) Grigorita Ko/Shutterstock; 008 (B) Creativa Images/Shutterstock; 009 (L) Andrea Izzotti/Shutterstock; 009 (R) Jiri Haureljuk/Shutterstock; 010 Vladsilver/Shutterstock; 012–013 Lurii Kazakov/Shutterstock; 014 Emilio100/Shutterstock; 015 Sean Russell/Getty Images; 016 Pawel Papis/123RF; 017 Renee fair hurst/Shutterstock; 018 (T) Anurak Pongpatimet/Shutterstock; 018 (TC) XiXinXing/Shutterstock; 018 (B) Joe McDonald/Shutterstock; 018 (B Inset) Andy Dean Photography/Shutterstock; 019 ArCaLu/Shutterstock; 019 (Inset) Roger Clark Arps/Shutterstock; 020 (TL) Nick Pecker/Shutterstock; 020 (TR) Matthieu Gallet/Shutterstock; 020 (B) Olesya Nickolaeva/Shutterstock; 021 (TL) Rocky Grimes/Shutterstock; 021 (TR) Glenda/Shutterstock; 021 (C) JMx Images/Shutterstock; 021 (B) TonyV3112/Shutterstock; 022 Idiz/Shutterstock; 023 Noicherrybeans/Shutterstock; 025 Maggy Meyer/Shutterstock; 027 Pazargic Liviu/123RF; 028 (T) Muzhik/Shutterstock; 028 (C) Alta Oosthuizen/Shutterstock; 028 (B) Suzanne Tucker/Shutterstock; 029 (T) R. L. Webber/Shutterstock; 029 (C) Nagel Photography/Shutterstock; 029 (B) Chabybucko/E+/Getty Images; 030 Lessydoang/Room/Getty Images; 038 Hadynyah/E+/Getty Images; 041 Rohappy/Shutterstock; 043 Brocreative/Shutterstock; 044 (T) Merazonia Wildlife Rescue and Rehabilitation; 044 (B) Auton/123RF; 045 (T) Laura Stone/Shutterstock; 045 (B) Lillian Tveit/Alamy Stock Photo; 046 Robert Wyatt/Alamy Stock Photo; 048 Asharkyu/Shutterstock; 049 Robert Wyatt/Alamy Stock Photo; 050 Merazonia Wildlife Rescue and Rehabilitation; 051 Sylvain Cordier/Biosphoto/Alamy Stock Photo; 052 Stnazkul/123RF; 053 Asharkyu/Shutterstock; 057 Gabriele Maltinti/Shutterstock; 059 Vladsilver/Shutterstock; 061 K.A.Willis/Shutterstock; 064 DigiPub/Moment/Getty Images.

UNIT 2: 068–069 Nicola Bertolini/Shutterstock; 068 (C) Dark Moon Pictures/Shutterstock; 068 (BL) Benny Marty/Shutterstock; 071 (L) Col/Shutterstock; 071 (C) Playalife2006/123RF; 071 (R) Jerry Sharp/Shutterstock; 072 (L) 2317900 Ontario Ltd. Spirer/123RF; 072 (L Inset) Paul Simcock/123RF; 072 (R) Mia2you/Shutterstock; 072 (R Inset) Cathy Yeulet/123RF; 073 (L) Md Zakir Hossain Sohel/Shutterstock; 073 (L Inset) Filipe Frazao/Shutterstock; 073 (R) Hilaka/Shutterstock; 073 (R Inset) Imtmphoto/123RF; 074 Tom Pfeiffer/Alamy Stock photo; 076 Douglas Peebles Photography/Alamy Stock photo;

077 Mat Hayward/Shutterstock; 078–079 Danita Delimont/Gallo Images/Getty Images; 079 Planet Observer/Universal Images Group North America LLC/Alamy Stock photo; 080 (Bkgrd) WaterFrame_mus/Alamy Stock photo; 080 (Inset) Benny Marty/Shutterstock; 081 (T) Reggie David/Design Pics/Newscom; 081 (B) Peter French/Perspectives/Getty Images; 082 (T) Erich Schmidt/Getty Images; 082 (BL) Douglas Peebles Photography/Alamy Stock photo; 082 (BR) Aurora Photos/WorldFoto/Alamy Stock photo; 083 (TL) Claudio Rossol/Shutterstock; 083 (TR) Tose/Shutterstock; 083 (B) Heather Stirratt/EyeEm/Getty Images; 084 WaterFrame_mus/Alamy Stock photo; 085 Vadim Orlov/123RF; 087 Douglas Peebles Photography/Alamy Stock photo; 089 Claudio Rossol/Shutterstock; 090 (T) Mishoo/123RF; 090 (BL) Jose Gil/Shutterstock; 090 (BC) Natalia Merzlyakova/123RF; 090 (BR) Stephen/Shutterstock; 091 (TL) Cheuk-king Lo./Pearson Education Asia Ltd; 091 (TR) Roman Sigaev/Shutterstock; 091 (B) Discpicture/Shutterstock; 092 ESB Professional/Shutterstock; 093 Remember/Alamy Stock photo; 094 Ross Ellet/Shutterstock; 095 (T) Stnazkul/123RF; 095 (B) Alexander Kazarin/Shutterstock; 096 Sergey Nivens/Shutterstock; 101 Saverio Maria Gallotti/Alamy Stock Photo; 104 (T) 123RF; 104 (B) Mike Hill/Alamy Stock Photo; 105 (T) Alison Wright/Danita Delimont, Agent/Alamy Stock Photo; 105 (B) Andrew Cribb/Alamy Stock Photo; 106 Fuse/Getty Images; 107 Dean Clarke/Shutterstock; 117 Hero Images/Getty Images; 119 Butterfly Hunter/Shutterstock; 123 Viktor Goriachuk/123RF; 126 Willoughby Owen/Moment/Getty Images.

UNIT 3: 130–131 Artapartment/Shutterstock; 133 (TL) Lili Graphie/Shutterstock; 133 (TR) Scanrail/123RF; 133 (BL) Jules Selmes/Pearson Education Ltd; 133 (BR) Bilanol/Shutterstock; 134 Ileana_bt/Shuttestock; 134 (L Inset) Darrin Henry/Shutterstock; 134 (R Inset) Tatsiana Yatsevich/Shutterstock; 135 (T) World History Archive/Alamy Stock Photo; 135 (T inset) Albina Glisic/Shutterstock; 135 (B) Irene Abdou/Alamy Stock Photo; 136 (T) Kontrec/iStock/Getty Images; 136 (C) Asada Nami/Shutterstock; 136 (B) Tom Wang/Shutterstock; 137 (T) Lisa Young/123RF; 137 (BL) Tara Moore/Digital Vision/Getty Images; 137 (BR) Julia Metkalova/Shutterstock; 138 D. Kucharski K. Kucharska/Shutterstock; 149 Arts Vector/Shutterstock; 151 K. Jensen/Shutterstock; 152 (T) World History Archive/Alamy Stock Photo; 152 (C) Marek Masik/Shutterstock; 152 (B) David Lee/Shutterstock; 153 (T) Trendywest/Shutterstock; 153 (B) Viachaslau Rutkouski/123RF; 164 W. Scott McGill/Shutterstock; 169 AnetaPics/Shutterstock; 170 (T) Josef Muellek/123RF; 170 (C) Henning Marquardt/Shutterstock; 170 (B) 123RF; 171 (T) Dmitry Naumov/Shutterstock; 171 (B) Vladimir Konstantinov/Shutterstock; 172 Graphicbee/123RF; 173 Golubenko Svetlana/123RF; 189 Adam Taylor/DigitalVision/Getty Images; 190 Robert McGouey/Wildlife/Alamy Stock Photo; 192 Gerald A. DeBoer/Shutterstock.

UNIT 4: 196–197 Hafiez Razali/Shutterstock; 196 (L) Black Rock Digital/Shutterstock; 196 (R) Bloomberg/Getty Images; 199 (TL) Hiroko Tanaka/Alamy Stock Photo; 199 (TR) Stokkete/Shutterstock; 199 (BL) Goodluz/123RF; 199 (BR) Pressmaster/Shutterstock; 200 (L) Africa Studio/Shutterstock; 200 (L Inset) Hero Images/Getty Images; 200 (R) Hero Images/Getty Images; 200 (R Inset) Jose Manuel Gelpi Diaz/123RF; 201 (L) Sorapong Chaipanya/123RF; 201 (L Inset) Lucy Lambriex/Moment/Getty Images; 201 (R) Zerbor/123RF; 201 (R Inset) Nophamon Yanyapong/123RF; 202 (T) Buntoon Rodseng/Shutterstock; 202 (C) Joshua Resnick/Shutterstock; 202 (B) Windmoon/Shutterstock; 203 Olexandr Panchenko/Shutterstock; 204 Shutterstock; 205 XiXinXing/Shutterstock; 206–207 Johnwoodkim/Shutterstock; 207 (Inset) Black Rock Digital/Shutterstock; 208 Danny E Hooks/Shutterstock; 209 (T) Bob Colley

Photography/Alamy Stock Photo; 209 (Inset) Philip Scalia/Alamy Stock Photo; 210 Philip Scalia/Alamy Stock Photo; 211 Bob Colley Photography/Alamy Stock Photo; 216 (T) Image Source/Photdisk/Getty Images; 216 (C) Vadim Guzhva/123RF; 216 (B) MIA Studio/Shutterstock; 217 (L) Pilens/123RF; 217 (R) Anakondasp/Shutterstock; 218 Africa Studio/Shutterstock; 219 Elnavegante/Shutterstock; 224 (L) Petro Guliaiev/123RF; 224 (R) Jit Pin Lim/123RF; 229 Gresei/Shutterstock; 230 (T) VGstockstudio/Shutterstock; 230 (C) Radu Bercan/Shutterstock; 230 (B) Steve Debenport/E+/Getty Images; 231 (T) Mixa/Getty Images; 231 (B) Luigi Bertello/Shutterstock; 232 Simone Van Den Berg/Shutterstock; 234 Wavebreak Media Ltd/123RF; 235 Bloomberg/Getty Images; 236 (T) Michaelpuche/Shutterstock; 236 (B) ZUMA Press Inc/Alamy Stock Photo; 237 Stephen B. Goodwin/Shutterstock; 238 Blend Images - Sollina Images/Brand X Pictures/Getty Images; 241 123RF; 243 Steve Debenport/E+/Getty Images; 247 Wavebreak Media Ltd/123RF; 250 Kali9/E+/Getty Images.

UNIT 5: 254–255 Graeme Williams/Gallo Images/Getty Images; 254 (BC) Everett Historical/Shutterstock; 254 (BL) Travelscape Images/Alamy Stock Photo; 254 (BR) Marteric/Shutterstock; 257 (TL) Darko Vrcan/123RF; 257 (TR) Igor Golovniov/Shutterstock; 257 (BL) Mixa/Getty Images; 257 (BR) Wave break media/Shutterstock; 258 (L) AnjelikaGr/Shutterstock; 258 (L Inset) Veda J Gonzalez/Shutterstock; 258 (R) Creative Nature Media/Shutterstock; 258 (R Inset) Maryna Kulchytska/Shutterstock; 259 (T) Ken Gillham/Robertharding/Alamy Stock Photo; 259 (T Inset) Imtmphoto/Shutterstock; 259 (B) Sergey Uryadnikov/Shutterstock; 259 (B Inset) Filipe Frazao/Shutterstock; 260 (T) Ralph Loesche/Shutterstock; 260 (BL) Richard A. McGuirk/Shutterstock; 260 (BR) Niall Dunne/Shutterstock; 261 (TL) Gary718/Shutterstock; 261 (TR) Robert J. Daveant/Shutterstock; 261 (C) Iurii Kovalenko/123RF; 261 (B) Lisa Payne Photography/Pearson Education, Ltd.; 262 Artens/Shutterstock; 263 Tina Images/Shutterstock; 264–265 Sinelyov/Shutterstock; 265 (T) Travelscape Images/Alamy Stock Photo; 265 (B) David Wall/Alamy Stock Photo; 266 (T) Tina Images/Shutterstock; 266 (B) U&U_Underwood/United Archives GmbH/Alamy Stock Photo; 267 (T) Andrew Watson/Alamy Stock Photo; 267 (B) Rolf Richardson/Alamy Stock Photo; 268 David Wall/Alamy Stock Photo; 273 FLPA/Alamy Stock Photo; 274 (T) Larry Geddis/Alamy Stock Photo; 274 (B) Ingrid Balabanova/Shutterstock; 275 (T) Jim Zuckerman/Alamy Stock Photo; 275 (B) Polkadot_photo/Shutterstock; 276 Michael Jung/123RF; 277 Everett Historical/Shutterstock; 278 Ian Dagnall Computing/Alamy Stock Photo; 278–279 Mistral9/Shutterstock; 279 Max Voran/Shutterstock; 280 Everett Historical/Shutterstock; 280–281 Rsooll/Shutterstock; 281 Bev Ramm/Shutterstock; 282 GHI/UIG/Universal History Archive/Universal Images Group/Universal Images Group Editorial/Getty Images; 282–283 Mistral9/Shutterstock; 283 Patti McConville/Alamy Stock Photo; 284 Everett Historical/Shutterstock; 286 Margo Harrison/Shutterstock; 287 Scott Prokop/Shutterstock; 289 Saaton/Shutterstock; 290 (T) Vladimir Melnikov/Shutterstock; 290 (C) Stone Nature Photography/Alamy Stock Photo; 290 (B) Sophia Granchinho/Shutterstock; 291 (T) Marteric/Shutterstock; 291 (B) Yongyut Kumsri/Shutterstock; 292 ER_09/Shutterstock; 293 Dennis Frates/Alamy Stock Photo; 294–295 Ton Koene/AGE Fotostock; 296 Hi-Story/Alamy Stock Photo; 297 Interfoto/History/Alamy Stock Photo; 298 Ruta Production/Shutterstock; 300 Kesu/Shutterstock; 303 KPG_Payless/Shutterstock; 305 Ton Koene/AGE Fotostock; 307 Antb/Shutterstock; 310 ER productions Ltd/Blend Images/Getty Images.

UNIT 6: 314–315 Nicola Margaret/E+/Getty Image; 314 (BR) Ragnarock/Shutterstock; 317 (TL) George Marks/Retrofile RF/Getty Images; 317 (TR) Gaertner/Alamy Stock Photo; 317 (BL) Nattituu/123RF; 317 (BR) Everett

427

Collection Historical/Alamy Stock Photo; 318 (L) Lubor Zelinka/Shutterstock; 318 (L inset) Shutterstock; 318 (R) Jose Ignacio Soto/Shutterstock; 318 (R inset) BCFC/Shutterstock; 319 (T) Pichugin Dmitry/Shutterstock; 319 (T inset) Shutterstock; 319 (B) DR Travel Photo and Video/Shutterstock; 319 (B inset) Greenaperture/E+/Getty Images; 320 (T) Stockbroker/123RF; 320 (C) Everett Historical/Shutterstock; 320 (B) Andrey Armyagov/Shutterstock; 321 (T) Image of Sport Image of Sport Photos/Newscom; 321 (C) Soft light/Shutterstock; 321 (B) Sean Pavone/Shutterstock; 322 Baranozdemir/E+/Getty Images; 323 Smereka/Shutterstock; 338 (T) Mitand73/Shutterstock; 338 (C) Katarzyna Golembowska/Shutterstock; 338 (B) Piola666/E+/Getty Images; 339 (TL) Joe McBride/Iconica/Getty Images; 339 (TR) Gianluca D'Alessandria/123RF; 339 (B) 123RF; 340 Alexfan32/Shutterstock; 341 Vitaly Bashkatov/123RF; 355 Historic Collection/Alamy Stock Photo; 356 (T) Viorel Sima/Shutterstock; 356 (C) Moonborne/123RF; 356 (B) Baerbel Schmid/Stone/Getty Images; 357 (T) Nito/Shutterstock; 357 (B) Keith Wheatley/Shutterstock; 358 Hijodeponggol/Shutterstock; 359 Phattranit Wk/Shutterstock; 360 Ragnarock/Shutterstock; 361 (T) Shvadchak Vasyl/123RF; 361 (C) CPC Collection/Alamy Stock Photo; 361 (B) Dallas Events Inc/Shutterstock; 362 (T) Jps/shutterstock; 362 (BL) Black Rock Digital/Shutterstock; 362 (BR) Tyler Olson/123RF; 363 (T) Goncharuk/Shutterstock; 363 (BL) Lagui/Shutterstock; 363 (BR) Ae Cherayut/Shutterstock; 364 Steve Debenport/E+/Getty Images; 365 Ragnarock/Shutterstock; 369 Ullstein bild/Getty Images; 370 Tyler Olson/123RF; 373 NASA Archive/Alamy Stock Photo; 378 Leonard Zhukovsky/Shuterstock.